CHINA'S ECONOMIC GLOBALIZATION THROUGH THE WTO

China's Economic Globalization through the WTO

Edited by

DING LU
National University of Singapore

GUANZHONG JAMES WEN
Trinity College

HUIZHONG ZHOU
Western Michigan University

Routledge
Taylor & Francis Group
LONDON AND NEW YORK

First published 2003 by Ashgate Publishing

Reissued 2018 by Routledge
2 Park Square, Milton Park, Abingdon, Oxon OX14 4RN
711 Third Avenue, New York, NY 10017, USA

Routledge is an imprint of the Taylor & Francis Group, an informa business

A Library of Congress record exists under LC control number: 2002190882

ISBN 13: 978-1-138-70777-1 (hbk)
ISBN 13: 978-1-138-70775-7 (pbk)
ISBN 13: 978-1-315-19885-9 (ebk)

Contents

List of Tables

List of Figures

The Editors

Ding Lu obtained his PhD in economics from Northwestern University (USA) and his MA and BA from Fudan University (China). He is currently Associate Professor of Economics at the National University of Singapore. Before he joined the NUS in 1992, Dr. Lu held various teaching or research positions at Fudan University, the Illinois State Government, Northwestern University and the University of Nebraska at Omaha. He has published books and refereed journal articles in the areas of industrial economics, international trade and investment, money and banking and transitional economies. Most of these publications have a focus on the Asia-Pacific region, including the Chinese economy in particular. In 1999–2000, he was director of the Chinese Economists Society. In 2000–2001, he served as Honorary Secretary of the Economic Society of Singapore.

Guanzhong James Wen has taught in Fudan University, Columbia University, Baruch College of the City University of New York and Peking University. He received his MA from Fudan University and his PhD from the University of Chicago. Currently Dr. Wen is Associate Professor of Economics at Trinity College, USA. He served as vice president of the Chinese Economists Society during the period 1995–1996 and as its president during the period 1999–2000. He is also on the editorial boards of the *Chinese Economic Review*, the *China Journal of Economic Review* and *Modern China*. He has published numerous papers in economic journals and edited several books on China's economic reforms and development.

Huizhong Zhou is Professor of Economics at Western Michigan University, a visiting professor at Beijing University and Fudan University in China and a research associate at Rikkyo University in Japan. He received his Ph.D. degree in managerial economics from the Kellogg Graduate School of Management at Northwestern University. He has published dozens of refereed journal papers in areas of industrial organization and regulatory economics. He served as director of the Chinese Economists Society in 1999–2000.

List of Contributors

Eglin, Richard. Director, WTO Secretariat, Geneva.

Holz, Carsten. Assistant Professor, Social Science Division of the Hong Kong University of Science and Technology, China.

Kong, Qingjiang. Associate Professor, Hangzhou University of Commerce, China; Visiting Research Fellow at the East Asian Institute, National University of Singapore, Singapore.

Li, Ling. Assistant Professor of Management, Hong Kong Polytechnic University, China.

Liang, Yanfen. Director, the World Economic and Trade Department of the Institute of the Ministry of Foreign Trade and Economic Co-operation, China.

Pomponio, Xun. Associate Professor, Department of Economics, St. Olaf College, Northfield, Minnesota, USA.

Song, Shunfeng. Professor, Department of Economics, University of Nevada at Reno, USA.

Wen, Guanzhong James. Associate Professor of Economics, Trinity College, USA.

Woo, Wing Thye. Professor, Department of Economics, University of California at Davis, USA.

Yang, Wenyan. Social Affairs Officer, Intergovernmental Policy Branch of the Division for Social Policy and Development, Department of Economic and Social Affairs, United Nations.

Yuen, Peter. Professor in Health Services Management, Department of Management, Hong Kong Polytechnic University, China.

Zhang, Kevin H. Professor, Department of Economics, Illinois State University at Normal, USA.

Zheng, Zhihai. President, the Chinese Academy of International Trade & Economic Co-operation, the Ministry of Foreign Trade & Economic Co-operation (MOFTEC), China.

Zhu, Tian. Assistant Professor in the Division of Social Science at Hong Kong University of Science and Technology, China.

Preface

A few years ago, a book titled *China Can Say No* was published in China. As those who have read it will know, that book was a xenophobic answer to the question, can China say no? The great weakness of such a book, it seems to me, is that it answers an obvious question while ignoring the deeper and more difficult question: to what should China say yes? China's process of economic reform and opening to the outside world, ever since its beginnings in 1978, has had an uneven history and still faces many difficult unresolved issues, but nonetheless represents – it seems to me – a brave attempt to tackle difficult questions and to say yes to constructive changes.

On 11 November 2001, at Qatar, China's accession to the WTO was officially approved. This event marked the end of a long, arduous process of negotiation, and is rightly seen as a major success. It was a resounding 'Yes' to the reform agenda, perhaps as important in its own way as the decisions taken by the nation's top leaders in 1978. At the same time, however, it is clear that China's membership in the WTO is not the culmination of economic reform but merely another step along a lengthy and twisting road. So it is very useful to have further, well-informed discussion of the many consequences of China's WTO membership.

This book is an important contribution to that discussion. It operates at two levels. Some of the chapters deal with high-level systems issues, such as the challenges that state-owned enterprises will face from increased competition, and the costs and benefits of foreign direct investment. Other chapters deal with the details of specific sectoral issues, in banking, health care, agriculture, telecommunications, etc. Taken together, the two groups of chapters provide a detailed, nuanced exploration of the implications of WTO membership from multiple viewpoints. The authors and editors have done a real service by bringing this volume to us.

Ralph W. Huenemann
Professor of International Business
University of Victoria, Canada
1 July 2002

Acknowledgements

Most of the papers in this volume were presented originally at the international conference, *Developing through Globalization: China's Opportunities and Challenges in the New Century*, Shanghai, China, 5–7 July 2000. We would like to thank the many people involved in the organization and execution of this conference. The Chinese Economists Society (USA) and the Chinese Academy of International Trade and Economic Cooperation were the main initiators and organizers of the conference. These two organizations were also responsible in soliciting the few papers included in the volume which were not presented at the conference. Other institutions involved in organizing the conference include Shanghai Academy of Social Sciences, Shanghai Pudong New Area International Exchange Center and Shanghai Pudong Development Institute.

The conference was sponsored by the Ford Foundation, Asian Development Bank, BP AMOCO, the World Bank, China Online, the Yingcai Foundation, the China Bridge International, Spring Light Foundation, Eurasian Educational Foundation, Asian Business Consulting Co. Lt., ABN-AMRO Bank, General Motors and Shanghai Lansheng Group. We are most grateful to these sponsors for their financial support and encouragement.

We wish to thank all the conference participants who contributed to the discussions on these papers and all the referees involved in the paper selection process. We would like to express our appreciation to the editorial board of the *China Economic Review* for granting us permission to reprint a paper published in the journal.

Great appreciation also goes to David F. Gates, our editorial consultant, for his patience and efforts in preparing the camera-ready copy of this volume for publication. Finally, we thank Carolyn Court and other staff at Ashgate Publishing Ltd for their administrative support.

Chapter 1

Introduction

Ding Lu, Guanzhong James Wen and Huizhong Zhou

Introduction

Economic globalization has brought opportunities as well as challenges to China, a country of 1.26 billion people. Over the past two decades, the size of the Chinese economy has sextupled by riding on a hyper growth rate of around nine per cent per annum. This remarkable performance is mainly a result of a market-oriented reform that has progressed in tandem with the opening of the economy to foreign trade and investment. Since the early 1980s, the share of export of goods and services in China's Gross Domestic Product has risen from six per cent to over 20 per cent. Meanwhile, China's exports have increased at a staggering annual rate of 17 per cent, from US$13.7 billion in 1979 to US$250 billion in 2000, making the country the world's seventh largest exporting economy. The rising economic power and market potential also have made China a gigantic magnet for international capital. From 1988 to 2000, actual or utilized foreign direct investment (FDI) in China increased at an annual rate of 23 per cent to reach a cumulative total of US$339 billion. As the largest host to FDI among the developing countries, China has benefited tremendously from globalization by sucking in huge flows of foreign capital that brings in technology and managerial skills.

Globalization also poses challenges to businesses and policy makers in China. As China becomes a member of the World Trade Organization (WTO), it has to further open its domestic market for foreign goods and capital. Its indigenous producers have to compete with foreign firms on a more leveled playing field. Its domestic industrial and regional development policies must not conflict with the internationally accepted practice formulated by the WTO rules. Its market institutions must be revamped to meet international standards.

This volume examines these issues by providing comprehensive and updated accounts of recent policy changes and developments in several important aspects of the Chinese economy. Most of the chapters in this volume are selected from nearly 80 research papers presented at the international conference, *Developing Through Globalization: China's Opportunities and Challenges in the New Century*, held in Shanghai, China on 5–7 July 2000. Other chapters, solicited by the editors, were written by experts in China who have been closely involved in consulting and policy making in their specialized areas. The conference was co-organized by the Chinese Economists Society (CES), a non-profit research organization registered in the United States and the Chinese Academy of International Trade and Economic Cooperation (CAITEC), a research arm of the Ministry of Foreign Trade and Economic Cooperation (MOFTEC) in China.

Authors of the volume are scholars and professionals in renowned institutions in or outside China. Most of them are members of the Chinese Economists Society, including those who were born and grew up in China, maintaining close and functioning ties with their motherland. Their academic qualifications and professional experience provide a unique combination of an outsider's broad perspective and an insider's sensitivities to nuances and details. All this enables the authors to conduct in-depth analyses of recent developments in China and provide balanced assessments of their implications for China and the rest of the world.

The authors of the next two chapters are senior researchers in Chinese government institutions, directly or indirectly involved in policy making towards foreign trade and economic cooperation. Their views provide the readers with a rare channel to understand the rationale behind Beijing's decision to participate in economic globalization through WTO membership. The first paper, 'Economic Globalization and Development of China's Foreign Economic Cooperation and Trade', by Zheng Zhihai, President of CAITEC, presents what he describes as the 'principal train of thoughts' (mainstream thoughts) about the development of China's foreign trade and economic cooperation in response to the challenges from economic globalization. In particular, he highlights several aspects on which China's readjustment should focus, namely, macro management and controls over foreign trade and economic cooperation, laws and regulations governing foreign-related economic activities, trade restructuring, utilization of foreign capital and participation in multilateral and regional economic and trade cooperation. In 'Transformation of Thinking and Adaptation to New Environments', Liang Yanfen, Director of the World Economic and Trade Department of MOFTEC, discusses the impact of China's accession to the WTO on the Chinese economy at the government level and at the enterprise level. Such impact includes both the expected benefits and the obligations the Chinese government and businesses will enjoy and have to bear. An interesting observation made here is the prospect of China as a WTO member 'to win more rights and interests for itself and for most developing countries in the formulation of agendas and trade rules in the future'.

China's accession to the WTO is widely perceived as a boon to the country's market-oriented reform. In 'China's WTO Accession and the State Sector Reform', Carsten Holz and Tian Zhu, of Hong Kong University of Science & Technology, point out that the problems with China's state sector lie in the state monopoly of the financial sector and the state ownership of enterprises. The WTO accession will help solving the problems by facilitating the process of diversifying the state ownership into the hands of high-stake non-state owners and the development of market institutions that are less subject to government interference. Wenyan Yang, an economist at the United Nations, in 'Domestic Banking under Financial Liberalization: Lessons for China as a Member of the WTO', takes a comparative approach to analyze the banking reform and liberalization experiences of Eastern European transition economies and Latin American developing countries. In order to strengthen the banking sector, the author proposes a combination of supervision and regulatory framework and policy measures to first stop the creation of new non-performing loans and calls for the gradual and orderly removal of entry barriers in banking business.

The chapter 'The Joy and Sorrow of Capital Inflow', by Xun Pomponio of St. Olaf College, compares the experiences of capital inflow in China and Mexico to highlight the gains and risks of integration into the world capital market. In this chapter, historical data for Mexico and China respectively are compared in the areas of overall macroeconomic situations, balance of payments, composition of investment portfolios, and capital flight. It warns against capital market opening without a sound economic infrastructure.

Foreign direct investment into China has a significant impact on the country's regional growth. This issue is dealt with in the chapter, 'How Does Inward FDI Interact with Regional Economic Growth in China', authored by Kevin H. Zhang and Shunfeng Song of Illinois State University and University of Nevada. Using city-level data, this chapter investigates the interaction between FDI and regional economic growth through the two-stage estimation approach. According to the results, regional differences in economic development have strong influences on the location decisions of foreign investors, because location advantages in attracting FDI are determined by local labor costs, human capital, infrastructure and cultural-historical links to investors. Meanwhile FDI is shown to be a major factor to enhance local economic growth, through capital formation, technology transfer and industrial upgrading, exports and access to international markets, and human capital development and employment.

In 'Closing the Productivity Gap: the Role of Globalization in Shanghai's Economic Transformation', Kevin H. Zhang looks into the efficiency effect of international trade and investment on productivity growth in Shanghai, China's largest industrial and financial center. The empirical results suggest that FDI has not only benefited Shanghai in terms of capital formation, employment augmentation, export promotion and human capital development, but also facilitated its market-oriented transition, which in turn has enhanced Shanghai's income growth.

Becoming a member of WTO, China has made important commitments to implementing the principle of National Treatment by making its service sector more accessible to foreign investors. Insurance, health care and telecommunications are among those sectors opening for foreign competition. In 'China's Health Care System Reform under Globalization', Ling Li and Peter Yuen of Hong Kong Polytechnic University discuss the issue of China's health care system reform under globalization. They show that openness of China's financial and insurance markets will bring new opportunities and challenges for reforming China's health care system. Based on international experience, the authors suggest that China's health care system should consist of the individual medical savings accounts combining with catastrophic insurance through private insurance companies. The authors observe that such a system is portable, flexible, and manageable and can balance the goals of risk sharing and cost containment.

In the telecommunications sector, China's entry to the WTO will bring in profound changes to the market environment and consumer welfare. An important aspect of these changes is the opening of Internet services to foreign participation. The regulatory framework must be adapted to the changes. In 'Where Will China's Internet Regulation Go After WTO Accession', Qingjiang Kong, a researcher at East Asian Institute of National University of Singapore, examines the regulatory framework of China's Internet service sector in light of the WTO norms and China's entry commitments. A real challenge for the Chinese government, pointed out by the author, is to balance the need to promote Internet development and the regime's efforts to control the information flow.

Agriculture is another sector that will feel the shock of the WTO entry. Guanzhong James Wen of Trinity College looks into the issue in the chapter titled 'Challenges and Opportunities for China's Agriculture after its WTO Accession'. According to Wen's analysis, accession into the WTO implies that this nation will no longer need to feed its largest population on earth almost exclusively by itself. Nor will China need to force most of its laborers to find a living in agriculture. This will allow China to reallocate resources based on its dynamic comparative advantages.

The last chapter, 'Recent Claims of China's Economic Exceptionalism: Reflections Inspired by WTO Accession', by Wing Thye Woo of the University of California at Davis, explores the implications of China's decision to join the WTO from a long-term and strategic perspective. It offers a conjecture that the decision represents an attempt by the reformers to lock economic policies on to a market-oriented course that would be costly to reverse. This opinion is based on a careful discourse on an experimentalist interpretation of China's phenomenal economic success.

We append to this volume a background brief, 'What WTO Accession Means to China', prepared by Richard Eglin, Director of the WTO Secretariat, who gives a succinct description of the principles and organizational structures of the World Trade Organization. With a clear presentation of the members' rights and obligations, the brief serves as an excellent reference source for understanding the implications of WTO membership for China.

Chapter 2

Economic Globalization and Development of China's Foreign Economic Cooperation and Trade

Zhihai Zheng

Trend of Development of Economic Globalization

Economic globalization is becoming a hot issue of concern and study at present. There are several reasons for the development of such a phenomenon, including the great momentum with which it forges ahead and the huge influences it produces. Since the 1990s, in particular, economic globalization has swept into every corner of the world and all fields of economic life of various countries with an irresistible force. With the in-depth development of economic globalization, the economies of all countries in the world have been brought into a unified world economic system, and mutual penetration and interdependence of the economies of various countries have become an important feature of the present time.

The significance of economic globalization as a fundamental feature of the present-day development of the world economy is obvious. Due to the development of a global market, all countries in the world can enjoy an even broader space for development and transcend the limitations of the size of singular national markets and the endowment of resources to optimize disposition of resources in a global arena, thus reaping even bigger economic returns. Since economic globalization is based on an information revolution that has resulted in globalization of information and trade, it is now possible for the rapid disposition and flow of key economic factors across the globe. The development of economic globalization calls for participants not only to follow a market economic system but also to open their markets to the outside world. Under a global economic system, the modes, practices and rules of economic performance will all move toward unification. So far as its development is concerned, economic globalization will grow further in both breadth and depth in the future. The further development of this process will, in turn, produce far-reaching influences upon the economic development of all countries in the world.

Injection of New Stimulus into Development and Globalization of the World Economy through the Advancement of Technology

High-tech development in the world will focus on information technology, biological technology, new materials, new energy, aviation and space technology, environmental protection, and other fields during the 21st century. In the coming 10 years, the greatest influence on the global economy will come from the industrialization and extensive commercial application of information technology. On 26 June 2000 the 'Human Genome Program', known as the 'Moon Landing Plan' of life science, announced to the world that a working map of the human gene had been drawn up successfully. This marked a milestone step forward in the understanding of life by mankind. As mankind deepens its understanding of itself, tremendous energy will be injected into medical science and biological pharmacy in the future and new industries will be created one after another through tapping the potential commercial value. With the constant shortening of the cycle of scientific and technical achievements – technical opening – and commercialization, the role of scientific discovery and technical invention in promoting economic growth will become more and more direct and rapid with each passing day.

Creation of Opportunities for and Placement of Challenges to Developing Countries by International Readjustment of Industrial Structures

With the proliferation and application of high technology across the globe, all countries have been vying with each other in increasing their investment in the high-tech industry with the purpose of gaining a leading edge in a new round of competition. Structural readjustment has taken on, therefore, an increasingly strong tint of globalization. The target of the United States in the new round of structural readjustment is to adapt to the structural changes of a knowledge-based economy and a service economy in a network era; to develop information technology, aviation and space technology, defense technology, and biochemical technology as pillar industries; and snatch an even bigger share of the international market during the process of globalization by taking advantage of its sharp edge of competition in the financial and information industries. The emphasis of readjustment of the European Union, meanwhile, is to advance the market-oriented readjustment of its system, employment, technology and industrial structures by way of market and currency unification. Japan has also set sharpening of its competitive edges as the major goal of its structural readjustment and is devoting its efforts mainly to the readjustment of the management structures of big trans-national corporations and the opening and regrouping of some of its industries such as the banking, real estate, construction and retailing industries that have long been put under protection with the purpose of increasing the degree of their internationalization. In the case of the rising industrial countries, the spearhead of their structural readjustment has been directed to upgrading their high-tech industries. Some have also made certain breakthroughs in this field. As for other developing countries, they are exposed to huge pressures for readjustment of their industrial structures.

Thrust of a Double-bladed Sword into Developing Countries by Economic Globalization

In the years after the conclusion of the Cold War, people have come to feel ever more clearly the multi-layered and profound influences from economic globalization. All countries will have to re-examine the trend of development of economic globalization and try their best to gain advantages and minimize disadvantages. Due to differences in economic strength, industrial structure and competitive abilities, various countries in the world will have different access to opportunities and face different challenges during the process of economic globalization. After hundreds of years of development, developed countries boast comparatively mature economic systems, market economic systems, and mechanisms for market economic operation. They also boast perfect systems for macro regulation and control. For this reason, these countries will be the most important beneficiaries of economic globalization. Developing countries, on the other hand, do not have any compete systems or methods to control globalization. Adding in the various kinds of restrictions and unfavorable conditions, the influence from the development of economic globalization on developing countries will become all the more uncertain. As a result, developing countries can not but accept the status quo under which developed countries tyrannize international systems and rules. Economic globalization is not, however, a choice to be made by developing countries today. Instead, it is a reality. As the situation stands, to work out a development strategy that fits the current drive of economic globalization will be an arduous task lying before most developing countries.

Economic globalization is an inevitability in the development of the world economy and an objective historical trend. Looking into the 21st century, economic globalization will surely make new headway through readjustment. The further development of economic globalization will lead to global readjustment and reform of economic structures, re-disposition of resources on a world basis, invention of new systems by various countries, and unprecedented liveliness of competition and cooperation in the field of international economic affairs and trade. Since the 1990s, however, the international financial sector has suffered one upheaval after another. In view of this situation, how to stabilize the performance of the global economy, minimize risks, and mitigate upheavals and crises will be an important issue raised to the international community by economic globalization. The 21st century should be an era in which all countries in the world unite with each other, adapt themselves to the great trend of acceleration of the momentum of globalization, and excise appropriate and effective macro regulation and control of the global economy.

Influences of Economic Globalization upon the Development of China's Foreign Trade and Economic Cooperation

In the more than 20 years since it initiated the policy of reform and opening-up, China has seen rapid development of its foreign trade and economic cooperation. All kinds of businesses in the foreign trade and economic cooperation sector have grown to a certain scale, and inter-dependence between its national economy and foreign trade and economic cooperation has been reaching new heights with each passing day. In the field of foreign trade and economic cooperation, China's total value of imports and exports was merely US$20.6 billion in 1978. By 1999, however, the figure soared to US$323.9 billion, an increase of more than 15 times. During this period, China saw the fastest development of its foreign trade in the years since 1992, when it established introduction of a socialist market economic system as its goal of economic development. China's volume of foreign trade between 1992 and 1999, for instance, surpassed its total volume of foreign trade in the years from 1949 to 1991, registering an average annual growth of 15 per cent. This was eight percentage points higher than the average annual growth of world trade as a whole during this period. Utilization of overseas investment has become an inseparably important part of China's national economy and social life. Since 1993 China has ranked first among developing countries in terms of utilization of overseas investment for seven years running. Over the 20 years the export-oriented content of the Chinese economy has been increased substantially, with exports making up about 20 per cent of its GDP. The important role of foreign trade and economic cooperation in the development of the country's national economy has now been acknowledged by the whole society.

To look back on its course of development over the past more than 20 years, China has made outstanding achievements in its trade in imports and exports and utilization of overseas investment, promoted the fast growth of its domestic economy, and become one of the biggest beneficiaries among developing countries of economic globalization precisely because it has grasped fairly well the opportunities arising from the international readjustment of industrial structures during its drive for reform and opening-up.

In the early years of the 21st century some fundamental changes will take place in the environments in which China conducts its foreign trade and economic cooperation. In the coming 10 years China will make a strategic readjustment of its economic structure, carry out an in-depth reform of its economic system, further implement the policy of revitalizing the country through reliance upon science and education and accelerate its pace of opening-up on all fronts. With its participation in the World Trade Organization, in particular, China will face a completely new situation in so far as its drive toward opening-up is concerned. China will take part in the process of economic globalization with an even more active attitude and an even greater range.

Participation in the WTO will be conducive to the further improvement of the international environment for China to develop its foreign trade and economic cooperation. China will have, for instance, access to the conveniences of free trade and investment enjoyed by all WTO members under the principle of multilateral, stable and unconditional most favored nation treatment established by the WTO. This will enable China to bring its economy into the world economic system; promote the development of its foreign trade and the utilization of overseas investment; take part in international economic cooperation and adapt itself better to the trend of development of economic globalization. While being granted access to corresponding rights, China will also be subjected to the fulfillment of due obligations after participation in the WTO, of course, and will carry out the promises it has made. This may pose new challenges to and add new pressures on the development of its foreign trade and economic cooperation.

In order to join the WTO, receive in return a comparatively stable external environment and win the right to enter the markets of other countries, the Chinese Government has made a promise on the gradual opening of its market. Moreover, most of the measures in this regard will be put into implementation in the coming five years. The new international and domestic situation lying ahead will create a series of rare opportunities for and pose, at the same time, new and stern challenges for the development of China's foreign trade and economic cooperation. This calls, objectively, for China to readjust its strategy of opening-up. Its new strategy of opening-up should be like this: Development of an export-oriented economy by grasping the opportunity from its participation in the WTO, sharpening its edge in international competition by focusing its efforts on the optimization of its structures and improvement of economic efficiency and bringing into play its comparative superiority and superiority of belated development and taking part in international division of work on all fronts, and establishment of an economic and trade system complying with international norms and standards and a flexible and high-efficiency mechanism for macro regulation and control at the earliest date possible.

Principal Thoughts on the Development of China's Foreign Trade and Economic Cooperation for the Future in Response to the Challenges of Economic Globalization

The new century will be an important historic era for China to perfect its socialist market economic system and take part in international economic cooperation and competition on even greater breadth and depth. We should gain an accurate command of the international and domestic situation on the basis of looking squarely at and seeing clearly the trend of development of economic globalization, march into the outside world with an even more active attitude, develop and perfect an open economic system, tap international markets with resolute efforts, and open the domestic market to the outside world on a gradual basis so as to sharpen our edge in international competition and keep and multiply the achievements we have made so far in the field of reform and opening-up and in economic construction as a whole.

In the early years of the 21st century, the market and system environment for China's conduct of foreign trade and economic cooperation will experience a fundamental change from those in the past. China's range of opening-up, for instance, will be extended from limited areas and fields to all fronts, from policy opening-up of an experimental character to predictable opening-up within a legal framework, and from self-opening of mainly a unilateral character to mutual opening between China and all WTO members. To promote the development of its foreign trade and economic cooperation, China will have to study carefully the major trend of development of economic globalization and think all things over against the overall background of global readjustment of economic structures so as to gain advantages and shun disadvantages in the development of its economy during the process of economic globalization, earn the biggest benefits possible, and prevent and mitigate possible risks. In view of China's status quo and with consideration to the requirements for membership in the WTO, China's focus of readjustment and reform of the development of its foreign trade and economic cooperation should be put mainly on the following aspects:

1 Vigorous reform of the system for the macro management and control of foreign trade and economic cooperation and establishment and perfection of a system for the macro regulation of foreign trade and economic cooperation that

conforms to the opening of the domestic market and the source of market-oriented development of trade activities in line with WTO rules and the requirement for the establishment of a socialist market economic system.

Economic globalization is a double-bladed sword that both serves and cuts. Whether a country will benefit or suffer from it will be determined by its system arrangement. The early years of the 21st century will exactly be a period for China to gradually fulfill its various kinds of promises including the opening of its market under the framework of multilateral agreements, with readjustment of its foreign trade system to gain the spotlight. For this reason, China will grasp the opportunity from its participation in the WTO to focus its work in foreign trade and economic cooperation in the years to come on system preparation and perfection. During the course of its development of a socialist market economy in the future, China will borrow the successful experiences of countries with mature market economies to establish an economic and trade system conforming to international norms and standards by starting from its national conditions and emphasizing standardization. If its economy or trade falls out of line with international norms or standards, China can by no means take part in international division of work or exchange. At the same time, it should be noted that an open economy is even more vulnerable to external impacts and subject to greater risks of economic fluctuations. For this reason, it places even higher demands on the level and mechanisms of macro economic management. In order to gain advantages and shun disadvantages, bring various kinds of risks under control, and guarantee the safety of its economy during the course of developing an open economy, China will have to establish a flexible and highly efficient system for macro economic management.

2 Seizing the time to enrich, readjust and perfect existing laws and regulations governing foreign-related economic activities in line with the requirements for the development of a socialist market economy and the participation in the WTO so as to further strengthen management of foreign economic and trade activities in legal and economic ways.

China should amend and perfect its three basic laws governing overseas investment – the Foreign Trade Law, the Law on Sino-Foreign Contractual Joint Ventures and the Law on Foreign-Funded Enterprises – at the earliest date possible and complete its anti-dumping legislation by upgrading its anti-dumping regulations to a State law. In line with the new situation that will develop after its participation in the WTO, China should actively organize forces to respond to anti-dumping charges and take up other kinds of foreign-related work such as legal disputes. The current focus of its work should be put on the sorting and amendment of existing foreign-related economic laws and regulations and departmental rules that are out of line with WTO rules or unfavorable to its deepening of reform or intensification of opening-up. The pace of enactment of foreign-related economic laws and regulations should be quickened, and laws or regulations on the import and export of commodities, agency service in foreign trade, border trade, processing trade, the import and export of technology, the management of places of origin, cooperation in labor service, overseas investment, foreign aid, e-commerce, anti-dumping, anti-subsidization and protective measures should all be formulated as soon as possible.

3 Starting from the new field of vision of economic globalization to bring out its comparative superiority and superiority of belated development, optimize the line-up of its export commodities, vigorously implement the strategy of revitalization of its foreign trade by relying upon science and technology and take part in international trade on all fronts.

Sharpening the competitive edge of its export commodities will be the key for China to participate in economic globalization and the basis for it to take part in international division of work and competition. For this purpose, it is necessary to launch a drive for structural optimization in all sectors of its foreign trade so as to create a cutting edge for Chinese export commodities by way of an optimized combination of the country's human resources, international technology and the key factor of capital. In order to adapt to the trend of development of international trade in the direction of high added value, high technical content, and in-depth processing and enlarge the share of Chinese products in the international market, it is necessary for China to pay close attention to the issue of sharpening the competitive edge of its export products. To implement the strategy of revitalization of foreign trade by relying on science and technology will be an effective strategy for us to respond to the challenges. Implementation of the strategy means the directing foreign trade onto the track of greater reliance on science and technology, increasing the scientific and technical ability of Chinese products to compete in the international market and turn around the situation of reliance upon price as the chief weapon in competition. Fixing its eye on rational disposition of resources and improvement of economic efficiency and taking the international market as a guide, China will continue its implementation of a series of policies that encourage optimization of the line-up of export commodities, and vigorously reform its mode of management of processing trade in line with international norms and standards to promote the healthy development of this trade. The various kinds of State policies on the encouragement of export of machinery and electrical products should be put into earnest implementation and the system for the export and after-sale service of machinery and electrical products should be perfected. Experiments with establishment of industrial parks specializing in the export of high tech products should be promoted, high and new technology should be used to renovate traditional industries, and key efforts should be devoted to the tackling of issues in industries with large export potential such as the machinery and electrical product sector, the textile sector and the farm goods processing sector.

4 Seizing of the opportunity from the world-wide readjustment of industrial structures and in line with China's practical conditions, to bring in overseas investment to serve the development of the Chinese economy in a better way.

According to the needs of its national economy and the promises it has made to the outside world for its participation in the WTO, China will further enlarge its fields of opening-up. It will gradually advance the opening of its commerce, foreign trade, finance, insurance, telecommunications, tourism and other sectors to the outside world, and allow overseas business people to set up Sino-foreign equity or contractual joint ventures or exclusively foreign-funded enterprises in these sectors in accordance with pertinent Chinese rules and regulations. China will also enlarge the land coverage; quantity and business scope of its opening-up, and encourage overseas business people to invest in its agriculture, infrastructure construction, environmental protection, and high tech industry. At the same time it will encourage its enterprises with due conditions to invest and do businesses abroad so as to enhance economic and trade exchanges and cooperation between the Chinese people and the people of other countries. The various kinds of policy measures announced by the Chinese Government for the support of development of foreign trade and economic cooperation in the central and western parts of the country will be put into earnest implementation. The local governments in these areas will be stimulated to work out and promulgate lists of local industries and projects suitable for overseas investment. Foreign-funded enterprises in the coastal areas of the country will be guided to invest in the central and western parts of the country and the central and western regions will be encouraged to vigorously promote their development of border trade.

5 Further perfection of its pattern of opening-up and active participation in multilateral and regional economic and trade cooperation.

World economic organizations are the products of economic globalization, and provide at the same time a system guarantee to the further promotion of economic globalization. The important role of international economic organizations is brought into play mainly through two channels: exercise of organization and management and formation of regulations and rules. The WTO provides a system guarantee to the development and liberalization of global trade and its potential will be brought into full play in the 21st century. In order to adapt to the new international economic environment developing from economic globalization, we should take an active part in global and regional economic cooperation and in the formulation of new rules on international trade and investment, in particular. During the course of promotion of liberalization of trade and investment by multilateral or regional organizations, China should try to safeguard the interests of developing countries and work hard for the establishment of a fair and rationalized new international economic and trade order based on equalization of rights and obligations.

Chapter 3

Transformation of Thinking and Adaptation to New Environments – A Discussion of the Influences on China from its Participation in the WTO

Yanfen Liang

The World Trade Organization (WTO) is an international organization specializing in the handling of multilateral trade relations on the basis of reciprocity and mutual benefit. All the protocols and agreements of the WTO have been signed by its members on the basis of negotiation. On the one hand these protocols and agreements restrict the policy behavior of the governments of its member countries and on the other hand they standardize the commercial behavior of product manufacturers, service providers, and importers and exporters. For this reason, our analysis of the influences on China from its participation in the WTO will be made at two levels: the government level and the enterprise level.

Winning the Right to Take Part in the Formulation of World Trade Rules as the Government of a WTO Member Country

As the Chinese saying goes, one can not get a square without a rule or a circle without a compass. WTO norms and standards are not only big in number and minute in detail, but also extremely inclusive in coverage. They touch almost all fields of today's world economy and trade ranging from pure cargo trade originally administered by GATT, its predecessor, to service trade being conducted at present, trade-related intellectual property rights and investment measures, and a series of issues that may be raised for discussion in the coming round of multilateral trade negotiations such as trade and environment, policies on competition, trade and labor standards and e-trade. What is undeniable is that all these protocols and agreements have been formulated or advocated basically under the manipulation of major countries well developed in trade and that few agreements that are favorable for developing countries, such as those on textiles and on agriculture, have been put into faithful implementation in the conduction of international trade. If China finally succeeds in getting its membership in the WTO in the capacity of a developing country, it will try to win more rights and interests for itself and for most developing countries in the formulation of agendas and trade rules in the future.

Settlement of Trade Disputes via the WTO

Compared with the mechanism for the settlement of trade disputes under the GATT, the mechanism of the WTO for the settlement of disputes is even more perfect and effective. First of all, there is a clear-cut timetable for ruling, with the time for the settlement of disputes being fixed at no longer than one year in the usual case and the time for the conclusion of lawsuit cases set at 15 months. Secondly, it is stipulated that the losing party shall not interfere in adjudication. According to past GATT procedures, a ruling should be given only under the condition of reaching unanimity through consultation, which meant that opposition from any of the parties to a case could prevent the giving of a ruling. In the third place, all rulings have the effect of automatic execution. The mechanism for the settlement of disputes is responsible for supervising the implementation of all rules and suggestions, and has the right to authorize retaliation against a disobedient country. What is most important is the stipulation of reversed unanimity established under the new mechanism for the settlement of disputes, which means that any resolution under study may be passed so long as it is not opposed unanimously. After becoming a WTO member, China can make full use of its mechanism for the settlement of disputes to handle and settle its economic and trade disputes with other WTO members on an equal footing and prevent the development of economic and trade issues into political ones. Apart from bilateral channels, China will get a multi-pronged channel and method for the settlement of trade disputes and gain much more leeway when it comes to handling its foreign economic and trade relations.

Dovetailing of the Chinese Economy More Closely with the Process of Economic Globalization

Over the recent 20 years, the ratio of reliance of the development of the Chinese economy upon foreign trade has risen from 9.8 per cent to 35 per cent. If the growth rate of China's trade in imports and exports continues to stay above that of its GDP, this ratio will become even bigger. China's volume of trade with WTO members accounts for about 90 per cent of its total volume of trade in imports and exports. In the trend of economic globalization, no country will be able to dissociate itself from the world economic system. In the 1970s, the world trade volume was US$315 billion. By 1999, the figure soared to nearly US$7,000 billion, an increase of more than 22 times. In the international division of trade, the proportion of developing countries has kept growing and the scale of the production and business activities of multinational corporations has kept extending. On the one hand, economic globalization has promoted economic growth and increased the output of the world and on the other hand, it has resulted in increasing interdependence between all countries in economic activity and trade. The prosperity or depression of the economy of one country now produces bigger influences upon the economic development and trade of other countries or regions. After becoming a WTO member, China will be able to benefit from the opening of markets by other countries and regions. The discriminative trade barriers erected by major trading countries against China will also be gradually removed. This will play a big role in China's efforts to increase exports and to develop its industries with a comparatively sharper cutting edge (such as its textile, household electric appliance and light industries). Take its textile products for an example. At present more than US$10 billion worth of China's textile products, or 25 per cent of its total exports of textile products, is subject to quota restrictions imposed by the United States, the European Union and other countries. On the basis of enjoyment of the right and opportunity mentioned above, the Chinese Government and Chinese enterprises will fulfill due obligations.

Firstly, WTO Rules Shall Be Observed in the Handling of All Businesses

The principle of non-discrimination shall be upheld. All WTO members shall be treated equally without any discrimination and inequality shall not be allowed between trade partners. This includes, of course, most favored nation treatment and national treatment. If China grants any special preferential treatment to a WTO member, such as imposition of a lower tariff rate on a certain product exported to China by this member, it shall grant, unconditionally, similar treatment to all other WTO members. When any products from WTO members are exported to it, China shall not impose, directly or indirectly, any more taxes or charges upon these products than those it imposes, directly or indirectly, on similar domestically manufactured products. These foreign products shall also enjoy treatment no poorer than that enjoyed by similar domestically manufactured products in terms of marketing, purchase, transportation or distribution or in legal terms. The treatment granted to domestic enterprises and citizens shall also be accessible by foreign enterprises and citizens.

Policies shall be kept transparent The procedure and time of the formulation of all decrees and regulations on the trade of imports and exports including administrative decisions and trade policies by both the central government and local governments shall be made public. No trade policies that are not published shall be put into implementation.

Quantitative restrictions shall be removed gradually Exercise of quantitative control by way of establishment or maintenance of quotas, import and export licenses, or other measures is a reflection of protectionism, and a practice banned by WTO in usual case. If it is indeed necessary for a member that is a developing country to exercise quantitative control, it shall do so only on the basis of the principle of non-discrimination and most favored nation treatment. First of all, it shall set global quotas under the precondition of transparency. In other words, it shall grant quotas according to the sequence of order of application by importers till all the quotas are used up. Secondly, if it is necessary to fix quotas on a country-by-country basis, the quotas shall be fixed by contracting importers and exporters through consultation. Thirdly, the license system may be introduced if it is impossible to implement a quota system. It is not allowed, however, to stipulate the source of import of any products in licenses.

Secondly, All Members Shall Subject Themselves to Examination and Supervision by the WTO

It is required by the WTO that all its members shall keep their promises and refrain from revising their trade systems or other domestic policies relating to trade at will. To guarantee the smooth implementation of this rule, the WTO has established a mechanism for the examination and study of trade systems. Two methods are usually used for such examination and study. First, routine examination and study. By way of routine and systematic examination and supervision, it tries to learn whether its members have observed and kept the disciplines and promises in multilateral agreements. At the same time, it keeps track of the trade policies and practices of all member countries, and tries to increase the transparency of their trade policies and measures. Second, regular examination and study. The trade systems and policies of developing countries are examined and studied once every six years in usual case.

Thirdly, China Will Further Perfect its Laws and Regulations

The operational mechanism of the WTO is based on a market economy. China's system for economic management will be subject to the restriction of WTO rules to a certain extent. Facing the impacts from a different system, it is unavoidable for China to amend and sort out laws and regulations that run out of line with WTO rules. In order to fulfill its WTO obligations, China can no longer manage its economic activities or trade in the traditional way. Promotion of development of its national drive of reform and opening-up and acceleration of its pace of establishment and perfection of a socialist market calls for changes both in thinking and system. Government departments and enterprise managers should also adapt themselves to the new situation in so far as their work style is concerned. Specifically speaking, government functions should be transformed, management methods should be legalized, and a monitoring system and an agile and transparent planning, statistical and macro management system should be established. The efficiency and transparency of government work should also be increased. In the field of market development, a market system that is unified, open and orderly in competition should be established. To open to the outside world, it is necessary to open domestically first. Trade borders should be removed gradually, and random charging shall be prevented.

As for the influences of China's participation in the WTO upon Chinese enterprises, the key will lie in the degree of the openness of the Chinese market and the competitive edge of the products of these enterprises, although comparatively big changes will take place in the business thinking and concept of the leaders of Chinese enterprises. Generally speaking, the Chinese market will not be put at meticulous protection and the pace of trade liberalization will be quickened after China becomes a WTO member. The improvement of the international environment will provide Chinese enterprises with even more opportunities to enter the international market and an even wider space for trade and economic cooperation. This will facilitate efforts by Chinese enterprises to open the international market, and help them increase exports. China's output and export of labor-intensive products such as textiles and light industrial products as well as shoes and headwear, in particular, will grow. Calculated according to the growth rate of quotas set in WTO agreements, China will see its export of textile products increase by at least US$50 million a year after it enters the WTO. According to other analyses, China's trade volume will hit US$600 billion by the year 2005. New changes are also expected in China's utilization of overseas investment. Due to its slow pace of readjustment of the structure of utilization of overseas investment, China has suffered a drop in the amount of overseas investment in recent years. In 1999, direct overseas investment in China was US$38 billion, 17 per cent less than the US$45.59 billion in 1998. One of the factors leading to the drop is the ebbing of interest from overseas business people in investing in products for cargo trade and the rise of the service sector as a new hot spot for investment. China now has set up a comparatively big number of restrictions in this sector. This situation can hopefully improve after China has opened its market to the outside world.

In the Sino-US and Sino-European agreements, the basic rights of China have been basically guaranteed. The United States has promised to grant China the permanent normal trade relation, to give up general provisions on guarantee, to loosen its control over high-tech exports to China and to give up its 10–year-old quota management of China's textile products. It has also agreed to set a timetable for the cancellation of provisions on special guarantee and anti-dumping provisions against non-market economic countries. China, meanwhile, has promised to cut its tariff rates, lowering the level of its average tariff rates from the current 22.1 per cent to 17 per cent. It has also promised to increase customs quotas by 15 per cent each year and totally lift its quota and quantitative control and cancel all export subsidies within five years. In addition, China has promised to lower the average tariff rate of its industrial products to 9.4 per cent by the year 2005 (China's nominal tariff rate of industrial products is 17 per cent at present. Except for a very few products, the cut in tariff rates will not produce any big influences upon China's industrial sector as a whole). The tariff rates of some labor-intensive products in which China boasts some superiority, such as light industrial, construction and textile products, are still a little bit too high. The influences coming from the non-tariff direction, however, will be fairly big, and will be somewhat difficult to control. About cancellation of non-tariff measures, absolute quota management of farm produce including grain will be changed into tariff quota management. Import quotas for industrial products will be gradually cancelled before the year 2005. China will keep under State management the trading of eight major categories of bulk products that have a bearing on its national economy and the livelihood of its people. These are crude oil, refined products, chemical fertilizer, grain, cotton, vegetable oil, sugar and tobacco. Trading will be handled by designated companies. The major problem haunting China's textile and light industrial sectors is the keeping the anti-dumping provisions and the provisions on special guarantees. The keeping of the anti-dumping provisions indicates that the United States still regards China as a non-market economic country and holds an attitude of discrimination against China. As the situation stands, there may be the possibility of willfulness and irrational use of the product of a third party as the pricing basis in case of investigation of an anti-dumping case. This will be unfavorable for Chinese export products. The inclusion of some raw materials in quota management and the increase of quotas by 15 per cent each year will produce some influences on raw materials from China. The US$6 billion quota for automobiles is far bigger than the record figure of automobile imports ever made by China. In addition, this quota will have to be increased by 15 per cent each year and all the quotas shall be cancelled between 2004 and 2005 to allow free import of automobiles. The pressure lying ahead for China's automobile industry will be, therefore, fairly big.

In the agricultural sector, the average tariff rate will be lowered to 17 per cent before January 2004. That of the priority products of the United States will be lowered to 14.5 per cent. Quotas will be kept for wheat, maize, cotton, barley and rice. Apart from specialized management by State-owned trade companies, privately owned enterprises can also apply for quotas to import these products. Subsidization of farm produce will be stopped. State control over the trading of soybean oil will be gradually lifted. The opening of China's farm produce market to the outside world will not produce any big influence upon its agriculture as a whole. The influences upon different varieties of farm produce, however, will be different. Soybeans, fruits and vegetables, for instance, will suffer comparatively bigger influences.

As for the service industry, most restrictions on foreign shares in all major service sectors will be removed after a rational period of transition. China has also agreed to sign the Global Basic Telecommunications Agreement and the Global Financial Service Trade Agreement. The opening of China's service market to the outside world will produce a positive influence upon China's macro economy and its consumers. It will stimulate, in particular, the development of China's commercial and legal services. It may promote the development of China's service industry as a whole, and turn the industry into a new force behind and hot spot in the country's economic growth. The impacts upon a few industries, such as the banking industry and the telecommunications industry, however, will be apparent.

As for imports and distributive rights, China will provide US companies with trading and distributive rights for the first time. Trading rights will be granted on a gradual basis within a time span of three years, while distributive rights will be put into execution during the process of wholesaling, transportation and maintenance. Restrictions on distributive services for most products will be removed on a gradual basis within a time span of three years. In the field of auxiliary distribution, China has promised to remove its restrictions on leasing, express mail, warehousing and transportation, cargo holding, advertising, technical testing and analysis and packaging service on a gradual basis within a time span of three years. To allow foreign companies to distribute goods will put comparatively big pressure on China's industrial sector because China's system for the distribution of industrial products is not complete and China has not yet attached due importance to this sector. Since half of the profits of industrial goods comes from distribution, the granting of distributive rights to foreign companies will put comparatively big pressure on China's industrial goods.

China has now begun its final sprint toward its membership in the WTO. It is expected to officially become a WTO member within this year. In front of this new environment, we have some issues to study and attend to.

First of all, all of the rights that China will enjoy and all the obligations it will fulfill after it becomes a WTO member will be based on the basic principles of the WTO and on the opening of its market to the outside world. Since the Chinese

Government has made various promises for its membership in the WTO, it will surely fulfill them. It will not, however, accept any discriminative treatment that goes beyond the reach of the WTO or that runs counter to WTO principles. According to the stipulations set forth in the WTO mechanism for the examination and study of trade systems, the trade policies of developing countries will be examined and studied every six years. The WTO has a complete and perfect mechanism for the settlement of disputes. Recently, however, the governments of some countries are planning to set aside part of their budgets to set up a special group to supervise and force China to fulfill its WTO obligations. They also plan to set up a team to specialize in the supervision of China's practices in subsidization so as to make sure that China fulfills its promises. In addition, they plan to introduce a procedure of fast investigation and discourage settlement of disputes via the WTO mechanism. They have decided that within 14 days of receiving a complaint from a company, the special quick reaction group will demand that Chinese officials work out a solution for the issue. If no solution is found for the issue within 90 days, the group will consider taking further action. Whether these practices conform to international practices or they are fair call for our study.

Secondly, the preferential treatment from the WTO to developing countries will be put into best use. In view of the gap between developed and developing countries in economic development, many of the WTO agreements provide certain preferential treatments for developing countries. For instance, these countries boast comparatively more rights, are allowed to be more flexible in their fulfillment of obligations, are treated preferentially in tariffs, and can separate their general obligations from their specific promises when it comes to the access of their service trade markets. They are also granted a comparatively longer period of transition. Developing countries can have, for instance, a transitional period of five years before they outlaw their trade-related investment measures. The time span allowed for most underdeveloped countries is seven years. Similar preferential treatment is also provided in the WTO Agreement on Information Technology. Developed countries are subject to a demand that they open their cargo and service trade markets with preference to developing countries. They are also obliged to provide developing countries with technical assistance and training of human resources and help developing countries in their implementation of the Intellectual Property Right Convention. Since China will join the WTO in the status of a developing country, it must make full use of these policies.

In the third place, active efforts should made to promote the application and implementation of the mechanism guaranteeing the access to service trade markets. It is stipulated in the Agreement on Guarantee Measures of the WTO Agreement on Cargo Trade that when an industry of a WTO member country suffers any damages from a sudden big increase in the import of products, this country can set up temporary import restrictions. Specific measures to be taken for this purpose may include tariff and non-tariff barriers or even a total cut in imports. The United States, for instance, has retained the right to take such a guarantee measure against China's textile products. Among the 155 sectors of service trade, most are weak and lack a cutting edge in competition in developing countries. Even developed countries accept this fact. As the situation stands, it is allowed in the General Agreement on Service Trade that developing countries can separate their general obligations from their specific promises when it comes to the opening of the service trade markets to the outside world and can open these markets on a gradual basis. They are also allowed to subsidize and protect their service industries to a certain extent. In other words, if their service industries suffer any big damages from the massive onslaught of foreign service companies, these countries can take protective measures. No clear-cut stipulations have been worked out yet, however, on the evaluation of the extent of damage to a service market or on the specific contents of the guarantee measures allowed to be taken.

Chapter 4

China's WTO Accession and State Sector Reform

Carsten Holz and Tian Zhu

Introduction[1]

Within the next three to five years, China, as a WTO member, will have to open up many of its industries that have so far been relatively immune to foreign competition. These include telecommunications, banking and finance, insurance, agriculture, movies, tourism, exports and local retail as well as other services and support industries (for example, transportation, distribution and advertising). In addition, China will gradually reduce tariffs and remove import quotas.

The question naturally arises as to whether China's inefficient loss-making state owned enterprises (SOEs) and bad loan ridden state owned banks (SOBs) can ever become internationally competitive. It is often argued that reform must speed up before SOEs and state banks fall victim to foreign competition after the WTO accession. Indeed, the reform of the SOEs and the banking system has become the top priority on the government's agenda. However, we argue that the objective of state sector reform should not be to make SOEs and SOBs more competitive because they can never become truly competitive as SOEs or SOBs. The objective should be to use WTO accession as a great opportunity fundamentally to transform the state ownership of enterprises and to establish an institutional environment conducive to business autonomy and corporate governance.

The losses of China's SOEs and the bad loan problems have been well-documented (Holz, 1998; Lardy, 1998; Zheng, 1998; Zhu, 1999; Holz and Zhu, 2000). At least one third and possibly two thirds of China's SOEs are loss makers. The 3rd Industrial Census (OTNIC, 1997) shows that 33.8 per cent of industrial SOEs lost money in 1995, compared with 15 per cent for township-owned enterprises (see Table 4.1).[2] According to official statistics, the losses of state-owned industrial enterprises increased almost twenty-fold between 1978 and 1997, for an annualized growth rate of 17 per cent. Profits in the same period fell in absolute terms (ZGTJNJ, 1999). Estimates of the extent of 'bad loans' in China usually range from a low of 20 per cent to a high of about 50 per cent (Xia, 1996; Chen and Cong, 1997; Holz, 1998).

Prior to the Asian financial crisis, the increasing losses and worsening inefficiencies of the SOEs attracted much attention from the press as well as academia. But it is the pervasive extent of the bad loans in the banking system that has since received more publicity. However, the bad loan problem and the losses of the SOEs are deeply intertwined. This is because, since the fiscal reforms in the mid-1980s, Chinese enterprises have relied almost exclusively on the state banks for external finance. In the absence of an independent banking system, bank loans have since become the new source of soft budget constraints. China's bad loan problem is directly related to the growth in SOE losses in the past two decades. The state-controlled banking system was always meant to serve the state-owned economy. In 1978, 91.1 per cent of all loans extended by the state banks went to the state-owned sector of the economy. In 1998 the percentage for the SOEs was still 82.8 (Holz, 1998).

Table 4.1 The performance of state-owned versus township-owned industrial enterprises

Enterprise type	Percentage of loss-making enterprises	Ratio of total taxes to pre-tax profits	Ratio of net profits to equity	Ratio of pre-tax profits to equity	Ratio of sum of total wages, pension and pre-tax profits to equity
State-owned	33.8	0.77	0.022	0.177	0.367
Township-owned	15.9	0.54	0.114	0.330	0.612

Source: The Data of the Third National Industrial Census in 1995 (OTNIC, 1997).

In this chapter, we argue that the problems with China's state sector lie in the state monopoly of the financial sector and the state ownership of enterprises. Reforms of the state sector are constrained by the slow process of diversifying the state ownership into the hands of high stake non-state owners and the slow development of rule-based market institutions, which make it difficult to establish effective corporate governance in the restructured enterprises. We then show why WTO accession provides the best chance for the restructuring of the state sector by helping to solve these problems more quickly and effectively.

Bank Loans as a Soft Budget Constraint

At first sight the inefficiency of the SOEs appears to have caused the bad loan problem (Wang, 1998). However, this conclusion is misleading. If the banks had autonomy and incentives to make sound lending decisions, they would not have lent so much money to the loss-making SOEs. And if SOEs could not get easy loans, they would either have had to strive for efficiency in order to survive or simply go bankrupt. Thus, the causality could equally well be the reverse, that is, state control and the resulting inefficiency of the banking system leads to a soft budget constraint for the SOEs and consequently, the inefficiencies in the real sector.

Since the beginning of economic reforms in 1978, the Chinese government has gradually abandoned its tight control over the real economy. But it has not relaxed its hold on the monetary sphere. To the contrary, the credit planning system has become a central policy instrument. The degree of government involvement varies, ranging from solely government decisions to guidelines on what sectors or types of enterprises to support. But all policy loans have in common that the bank is not making independent lending decisions.[3] Various types of policy loans are extended in the knowledge that repayment is highly unlikely. Local government departments frequently try to influence bank-lending decisions in favor of the SOEs that are under local jurisdiction. Pressure is exerted on banks to lend for investment to increase production and thus to accelerate economic growth, as well as for regular production and, if the enterprise is unprofitable, for social security measures and even enterprise tax payments (Xia, 1996; Holz, 1998). Econometric studies by Wei and Wang (1997), using a city-level data set for 1989 through 1991 provide clear evidence that China's bank loans do favor SOEs.

In the case of an enterprise bankruptcy, banks are frequently prevented by local governments from exercising the few rights they formally enjoy and courts tend to do the bidding of their local government (Chen et al., 1997). China's bankruptcy law, enacted in 1986, is long outdated and the company law of 1993 is ambiguous about the rights of debt-holders. There are no specific rules regarding the rights of debt-holders in the case of enterprise default, while government departments enjoy far-reaching powers. The company law stipulates that liquidation teams be composed of 'relevant' shareholders, government departments and professionals. Debt-holders are not given any control rights in liquidation. In practice, it is often government bodies that decide whether to close an enterprise or not. Because of these flaws, many enterprises have tried to evade repaying debts by declaring bankruptcy. According to a nationwide survey of 145 of the 1520 enterprises which were declared bankrupt between 1993 and 1995, the average loan repayment rate among the 101 enterprises which by the survey date had completed the bankruptcy procedures was only 9.2 per cent (ZGJRNJ 1997, p.285).

In such an environment, enterprise managers have strong incentives to seek as much bank lending as they can and few incentives to repay bank loans. With the incentive structure of the enterprise management tilted towards tax payment, investment and enterprise-internal social welfare projects, there is continuous reliance on banks to fund production. The state commercial banks then are nothing but a new source of a soft budget constraint.

The difficult position of the state commercial banks originates from their lack of autonomy and is then exacerbated by a lack of adequate incentives. The lack of autonomy implies that banks cannot be held accountable for bad loans. But if banks cannot be held accountable for the accumulation of bad loans, they have few incentives to monitor continuously the quality of their loans and to take proper measures to prevent loans from turning bad. This lack of embedded incentives for efficient operation is not counterbalanced by any government-imposed incentive structure that would induce bank managers to act as if they were responsible for the accumulation of bad loans. To the contrary, incentives are such that banks prefer to roll over bad loans rather than enforce repayment. Lack of autonomy and poor governance are crucial characteristics and weaknesses of China's banking system.

Inefficiency of State Ownership

In addition to soft budget constraints, state ownership of enterprises also contributes to the increasing inefficiency of the state sector. The losses of Chinese SOEs have often been attributed to their labor redundancy and excessive welfare burdens (Hu, 1996; Lardy, 1998; Lin et al., 1998; Zheng et al., 1998). SOEs are required to create employment for urban residents even if many workers hired by SOEs are not needed for operations. SOEs also have a much higher percentage of retired workers on their payrolls than other types of enterprises, which typically have a shorter history and thus younger workers (Hu, 1996). SOEs until today provide most of their employees with various fringe benefits and service facilities such as free or almost-free housing. Finally, SOEs have shouldered more than their fair share (given their value-added) of the tax burden.[4]

It would thus appear that SOEs are strongly disadvantaged in comparison to other enterprises, such as the township-owned enterprises. This could explain why in the 1995 industrial census the average ratio of net profits to equity was only 0.022 for industrial SOEs as compared to 0.114 for industrial township-owned enterprises (see Table 4.1). However, the ratio of industrial SOEs' *pre-tax* profits to equity was 0.177 as compared to 0.330 for industrial township-owned enterprises. The heavier tax burden thus cannot fully account for the lower profitability of the SOEs.

In order to further consider the state sector's labor redundancy and pension burden, we calculate for each type of enterprise the sum of total wages, pensions and pre-tax profits, which roughly measures a firm's value-added minus interest and miscellaneous fee payments, and divide it by the amount of equity. The difference in performance still remains in that the ratio is 0.367 for SOEs and 0.612 for township-owned enterprises.

Some authors have also attributed SOE losses to their heavy debt burden (Chi et al., 1996; Lin et al., 1998). Since the 1983/85 fiscal reform, Chinese firms have relied almost exclusively on the state banks for external financing. This over-reliance on bank funds makes them excessively leveraged. Official statistics show that China's SOEs have a debt-asset ratio of about 66 per cent (see Table 3.2). But if assets are overvalued, this official ratio is lower than the actual one. Some authors estimate that the SOE debt-asset ratio is between 75 per cent and 80 per cent, compared to a ratio of about 40 per cent in the U.S. and about 60 per cent in Japan and Germany (Chi et al., 1996).

However, as shown in Table 4.2, township-owned enterprises are even more highly leveraged. In 1995, the state-owned industrial enterprises had a debt-equity ratio of 1.92, while the figure for township-owned industrial enterprises was 2.33. Township-owned enterprises thus should face a higher interest bill per equity and therefore have lower profits per equity. In addition, the average interest rate on loans to township run enterprises is higher than on loans to SOEs. Thus a high rate of leverage per se need not be the cause of the poor performance of the SOEs. It is relevant not so much because it implies high interest costs but because it implies that the state ownership of enterprises is a result of the leverage effect rather than of the government's equity ownership. When a firm's asset value is well below its debt level and its equity thus negative, it is still said to be state-owned. Such firms should already be in the hands of the debt-holders; but the debt-holders (depositors) are represented by the state. It does not matter whether the state provides capital to the SOEs directly in the form of a 'free' equity contribution or indirectly, as the 'owner' of state banks, in the form of debt. Debt thus does not come with external control and monitoring. The final investors, that is, the depositors, would have incentives to care about the use of their money if it were invested at their own risk. But because the state has insisted on maintaining its rights of ultimate control over enterprises and therefore has limited the development of alternative investment channels, the final investors are left with few choices other than bank deposits. In this context they may very well rationally choose to put their money into banks as long as they are paid a good risk-free interest rate that may not have been justified by the overall rate of return on assets.

Table 4.2 The leverage status of state-owned versus township-owned industrial enterprises

Enterprise type	Total assets (billion yuan)	Total debt (billion yuan)	Total equity (billion yuan)	Debt-equity ratio	Debt-asset ratio
State-owned	4,747.2	3,124.2	1,623.0	1.92	66%
Township-owned	703.2	492.3	210.9	2.33	70%

Source: The Data of the Third National Industrial Census (OTNIC, 1997).

Thus, overall, SOEs are inefficient, or less efficient than township-owned enterprises, not just because they have too many redundant workers, too high a welfare burden, or too much debt. The argument put forward by some economists (for example, Lin et al., 1998) that SOEs can become competitive once they are relieved of these financial burdens, does not hold. A more fundamental reason for the loss making of the SOEs is the agency or incentive problem associated with state ownership (Zhu, 1999).

The agency problem in the case of SOEs is two-tiered. Government bureaucrats, as agents, act on behalf of the government (or the people) and enterprise managers, as agents, act on behalf of the government bureaucrats. Although bureaucrats are supposed to act as owners, they are not legally entitled to the residual income rights that owners of private enterprises would normally have. Their behavior all too often exhibits private or departmental rent seeking. Corruption, red tape and soft budget constraints are all manifestations of the agency problem on the part of the bureaucrats.

On the second tier, an effective governance structure to provide adequate incentives and impose discipline on managers is lacking. SOE managers often take advantage of their scope for maneuvering to pursue reckless operations or engage in rent-seeking activities, thereby causing their SOEs to incur losses (Qian, 1996). Managerial misbehavior includes dining and wining on the company, buying luxury cars, traveling for pleasure at the company's expense, using company funds to speculate in the property and stock markets and asset stripping such as diverting state assets to set up financially suspicious subsidiary companies.

Reforms of the State Sector: Progress and Constraints

Many recent reform measures China has taken to stabilize its financial institutions and to reform the SOEs in the wake of the Asian financial crisis have been largely re-distributive rather than efficiency-enhancing (Holz and Zhu, 2000; Zhu, 1999). Specifically, China's financial reform has focused on resolving the problem of accumulated past bad loans primarily through an increase in government debt, rather than through creating mechanisms and incentives for state banks to adopt a more market-oriented lending behavior. SOE reform has focused on the socialization of SOEs' welfare, employment and debt burdens, rather than on changing incentives for bureaucrat owners and managers to take market-oriented production and investment decisions. Fundamentally, reforms should not be aimed at shifting the financial losses between different agents of the economy but at transforming the ownership and governance structure of both the state-owned banks and enterprises.

To be sure, some substantive changes have taken place in the past few years. In the banking sector, for example, the supervisory role of the central bank was supposedly strengthened in late 1998 by merging provincial branches into a dozen supra-provincial regional branches which are expected to operate independently of provincial governments. The independence of commercial banks has at least in principle been acknowledged. There have also been improvements in bank management such as the gradual granting of lending autonomy and the introduction of risk-based loan classifications. But progress appears to be slow. These piece-meal measures may no longer be enough to improve substantially the efficiency of the allocation of financial resources. Given that SOEs' production patterns are still distorted by management and government bureaucrats unchecked particular objectives, the government will have to continue to interfere in banking operations in order to stave off a systemic collapse in the state-owned production sector (see Holz, 1998).

The speed of the restructuring of the SOEs has also accelerated in the past few years. Since 1993, the Chinese government has embarked on a major effort to shift the focus of SOE reform from delegation of decision-making authority to enterprises, which was the predominant strategy in the preceding decade, to corporatization. The corporatization strategy aims to turn SOEs into shareholding companies that are independent in decision-making, diverse in ownership without serious erosion of dominant public ownership and fully guided by the market. It is intended to separate the government from enterprises by establishing a modern corporate governance structure. The separation is deemed necessary both for enterprises to achieve full autonomy in both structural and operational decisions and for the government to limit its liabilities to the enterprises and hence to harden the budget constraint (Wang and Chen, 1997).

Reform is to be implemented in the entire state sector. However, based on a national survey dataset, Lin and Zhu (2001) find that so far corporatization has been carried out in a relatively small number of SOEs, that the state has retained a majority ownership stake in over half of the restructured enterprises and that there are widespread inconsistencies between the blue-print for reform and the actual organizational features of restructured enterprises. A number of Chinese economists have also pointed out many problems with reform such as too much concentration of state ownership in corporatized enterprises, irregularities in corporate governance, insider control, lack of liquidity in state and legal person shares, lack of substantive changes in ownership and management and asset stripping during the process of reform (Wu et al., 1998; Shen and Liu, 1998; Xia, 1999; Zhang, 1999).

On the other hand, the corporatization reform has brought about some substantive changes, such as an increase in decision-making autonomy, diversification of ownership structure and adoption of managerial and employee stake holding (Lin and Zhu, 2001). It remains to be seen to what extent these new arrangements can improve the performance of corporatized enterprises.

China's corporatization scheme is apparently modeled on the Western-style corporate organization. But what has been overlooked and poorly understood is the fact that in the West the emergence of public corporations, characterized by the separation of ownership and control, is a result of an endogenous, evolutionary process based on voluntary exchanges of private property rights in pursuit of gains from specialization (Fama and Jensen, 1983). In the process various corporate governance mechanisms have been developed to safeguard the interests of the owners from managerial infringement (see Hart, 1995; Shleifer and Vishny, 1997). Moreover, in even the largest corporations, there are normally shareholders who hold significant ownership stakes. Large shareholders have both the ability and the incentive to exercise effective control rights and monitor management. More importantly, effective corporate governance needs the support of a well functioning, rule-based market-oriented business and especially legal institutions (Zhu, 1999). Without these institutional underpinnings, corporatization by itself cannot solve the two-tiered incentive problem we described above.

China's market reform in the past two decades has been exclusively on the economic front. The more difficult task of establishing the rule of law has been largely ignored or deliberately avoided. The country's legal and institutional framework has become increasingly incompatible with a modern market economy. Despite the passage of numerous commercial laws, their enforcement is still lacking. The judiciary system is insufficiently independent of the party and the government. There is also a shortage of properly trained lawyers and judges. It is the rule of law that will provide the most effective protection to business organizations and their owners from arbitrary interventions and the abuse of power by government officials. Only when the rule of law is established can the government truly be separated from enterprises. China's company law, however, lacks specific rules governing corporatization of SOEs, the transfer of state assets and particularly, rules clarifying the autonomous rights of companies, which would prevent arbitrary administrative interventions (Zhu, 1999).

WTO Accession and the Restructuring of the State Sector

Any serious attempt to resolve the twin problems of losses and bad loans in China's state sector requires substantive restructuring of the state's real as well as financial engagements. The inefficiency of China's state-owned banks and enterprises stems from the same sources, namely, the lack of sufficient autonomy on the one hand and the lack of proper incentives and control structures on the other. Successful reform requires changes in ownership and governance structures across the state sector as a whole. A well-implemented reform of the banking sector is particularly important because rigorous banking practices will automatically exert pressure on the SOEs and their bureaucratic owners to reform. SOE reform by itself would have few compelling implications for banking reform and thus the efficient allocation of funds and ultimately again SOE efficiency.

At the present stage of economic reform, improvements in bank management, such as the gradual granting of lending autonomy, may no longer be enough to yield continuous improvements in system-wide efficiency. Within five years of China's WTO membership, foreign banks will be allowed full access to the domestic banking sector.[5] China's domestic securities industry will be liberalized with foreigners allowed to own 33 per cent of Chinese securities brokerages and fund management companies, rising to 49 per cent three years after China's WTO accession (Yu and Zheng, 2000). But can China's banks reform rapidly enough that they are ready for the potential onslaught by foreign banks in five years time? The current reform measures as well as the changes achieved since the passing of the Commercial Bank Law in 1995 raise severe doubts. Time is running out. A wholehearted banking reform that creates a competitive financial sector with free entry and exit may be unavoidable.

Bank and enterprise autonomy, as well as proper incentive structures, can be achieved through diversification of state ownership. But given the size of China's state-owned financial institutions and large SOEs, it is virtually impossible to sell the state ownership to private individuals or institutions without causing too dispersed an ownership structure and as a result poor governance on self-interested behavior of business managers. Viewed from this perspective, it is not surprising that SOEs turned corporations tend to have their majority shares owned by state agencies or state-owned institutions (Lin and Zhu, 2001). A midway approach is to diversify ownership of the SOEs and predominantly state-owned companies by selling or giving shares to several minority shareholders (Li and Zhu, 1998; Zhu, 1999). These shareholders could be wholly or partly state-owned institutions. Such a diversified ownership has an important advantage over concentrated state ownership. That is, no individual shareholder has dominant control power and hence is in a position to abuse his power to reap private gains. But each shareholder has a stake that is significant enough to have both incentives and the ability to monitor the firm's performance.[6]

In the long run, however, major shareholding by non-state owners could be essential for the success of the ownership reform as state-owned entities always carry the danger of continued indirect government meddling and bureaucratic rent seeking. Relying on domestic non-state firms to acquire significant stakes in large SOEs may take too much time. Institutions capable of an independent take-over of large SOEs are still few in number and may never be forthcoming under the present focus on state ownership of all major economic entities. Opening up China's state sector to foreign ownership thus may well be one of the most reliable choices. WTO accession provides a golden opportunity for such a strategy. Even if this were only a small part of an overall package to change the current ownership patterns, it could set the pace and standards of openness and competition.

In the aftermath of the Asian financial crisis, China's leaders have become more cautious about opening up the country's financial sector. It is true that a closed financial sector has helped China to avoid financial crises. But the lack of free entry and exit and the continuation of state control is also the cause of the sector's inefficiencies and its bad debts. Foreign shareholders in China's banks would bring in the market-oriented banking expertise that Chinese banks currently lack.

An even further step would be to give foreign banks unrestricted access to China's financial market. Introducing outside competition would impose strong pressures on the existing banks to improve their efficiency. But competition alone does not guarantee efficiency. In the absence of fundamental changes in incentives and governance structures, state banks could lose much of their business. As the extent of the bad loans becomes exposed, the government would have to step in as the implicit guarantor of at least household deposits, a formidable task. Hence, a better strategy may well be to sell off major stakes in at least some of the state commercial banks at a time when their branch networks and physical assets are of some value to more capable owners, that is, when independent entry to China's financial sector is not yet an option.

Given the large amount of non-performing loans, state banks may have difficulty finding buyers. It may thus be necessary to write off their bad assets before putting them on sale. The banking sector's hidden bad assets would turn into an explicit financing requirement. When the proceeds from a bank's sale are insufficient to make up the shortfall, the government could choose to issue long-term public debt or to offer subsidies over several years. Postponing the (at least majority) sale of the state commercial banks on account of the large extent of bad loans is a poor choice as banks operating under the current conditions have proven to be poor collectors of debts. Time is not on the government's side.

Financial opening would lead to a reallocation of financial resources from loss-making SOEs to more efficient SOEs as well as to non-state firms. Consequently, inefficient SOEs could face difficulties borrowing money. Making life difficult for SOEs, however, is precisely the point. Entry into the WTO will threaten the survival of the SOEs anyway, not only because they will no longer be shielded from foreign competition but also because WTO rules require SOEs to operate solely on commercial terms and prohibit governments from channeling subsidies and easy loans to SOEs. Financial opening strengthens this important commitment and will exert further pressure to force many inefficient SOEs either to go out of existence or to restructure themselves to become competitive in a leveled playing field.

International investors bring in not only much-needed technology and management expertise but also self-motivated owners and time-proven incentive structures that are crucial for increasing efficiency. More importantly, because of their higher degree of political independence from the Chinese government and because of the lobbying power they may enjoy through international organizations and their own governments, foreign-invested firms could have more leverage than domestic firms to push for institutional changes and, in particular, for the creation of a rule-based regulatory and legal institutions, which China lacks, but is important to business autonomy and sound corporate governance. Government agencies would be under great pressure to treat all firms equally thereby improving operating conditions, even for solely domestic-owned entities.

The strategy of selling off major stakes in state-owned banks and enterprises on the one hand solves the dual problem of a lack of autonomy and poor incentive structures and on the other hand, may also provide badly needed revenues for the government. If state-owned assets are sold in a fair and open-bid fashion, foreign competition for these assets can only increase the price they will fetch. The proceeds from the sales could go towards cleaning up the accumulated bad loans in the banking sector, or help with SOE reform, such as through the establishment of a viable social security system.

China's WTO accession will eventually force many, if not most, of China's financial institutions and SOEs either to restructure, exit, or go on sale. The question then is hardly any longer whether China should reform the ownership and governance structure of its state-owned banks and enterprises or whether it should open up its state sector to foreign buyers. The question rather is how the government can create an environment and establish implementation mechanisms that will improve efficiency economy-wide as quickly as possible and that will allow the government to sell state assets at as high a price as possible.[7]

Conclusion

In this chapter we have attempted to show that soft budget constraints due to state-control of the banking system and inadequate incentive and governance due to state ownership are the fundamental causes of the bad loan problem in the banking system and the losses of the SOEs. A fundamental transformation of state ownership of both the financial and the real sector must be the future direction of reform. The development of rule-based market-oriented regulatory and legal institutions is also essential. It is in these two crucial areas that the reform process has been slow. We have also argued that WTO accession provides a great opportunity as well as the pressure for China to expedite the ownership reform of the state sector by introducing self-motivated large stakeholders in the state-owned banks and enterprises. It will also help to solve the soft budget constraint problem by tying the interfering hands of the government and improving the independence and governance of the banking system. More importantly, WTO accession will help China to commit to and develop a rule-based institutional framework that is crucial for business autonomy and effective corporate governance.

Despite its radical appearance, opening up the financial sector and consequently SOEs to diversified ownership forms, in particular to foreign ownership, is perfectly consistent with Deng Xiaoping's reform approach that invoked an open-door policy to promote the domestic reform agenda. Similarly, WTO accession today should provide Chinese leaders with a powerful instrument to overcome formidable economic and political obstacles and the best opportunities to achieve the final success in reforming the country's inefficient financial and corporate systems.

Notes

1 An earlier version of the chapter was presented at the *Pudong Conference on Developing through Globalization: China's Opportunities and Challenges in the New Century*, 4–7 July 2000, Shanghai, China. We thank Wen Hai, Shan Li, Yimin Lin and Shangjin Wei for helpful discussions and comments. Financial support from the Research Grants Council of Hong Kong (HKUST6053/98H) is gratefully acknowledged.

2 These numbers are likely to be an underestimate as SOEs use various means of creative accounting to cover up losses. According to another source (UPI News, 2 March 1997), in 1996 some 70 per cent of SOEs lost money and 45 per cent recorded chronic losses.

3 On the extent of policy loans in 1991, see Xiao (1997, p. 374). According to his calculations, formal policy loans accounted for 58.0 per cent of CBC lending, 51.2 per cent of ABC lending, 66.6 per cent of BoC lending and 17.9 per cent of ICBC lending.

4 According to the 1995 industrial census, the average ratio of total taxes to pre-tax profits was 0.77 for state-owned industrial enterprises, while the figures for township-owned enterprises and wholly foreign-owned enterprises were 0.54 and 0.35, respectively (OTNIC, 1997).

5 Currently only two dozen foreign banks are allowed to conduct lending business in domestic currency; but their scale of operation is still very small and they face severe restrictions.

6 A recent study (Xu and Wang, 1999) provides some empirical support for the diversification of state ownership. Xu and Wang's empirical analysis of China's listed stock companies shows that a firm's profitability is positively correlated with the fraction of legal person (institutional) shares; but it is either negatively correlated or uncorrelated with the fraction of state and household shares. Labor productivity is also shown to decline as the proportion of state shares increases.

7 Numerous measures, however, may need to be implemented first to pave the way for the sales. These include writing off the bad debt and reducing the inflated work force. If state-owned assets are sold in a fair and open-bid fashion, foreign competition for these assets can only increase the price they will fetch. The proceeds from the sales could help pay for a viable social security system.

References

Chen, Yimin et al. (1997), 'Pochan zhidu de bu wanshan yingxiang gaige de jincheng' ('The Imperfections of the Bankruptcy System Hinders the Progress of Reform'), *Jinrong Yanjiu Baogao*, No. 17 (June 17).

Chen, Yuansheng and Ming, Cong (1997), 'Guanyu Fangfan He Huajie Jingrong Fengxian de Fenxi' ('An Analysis on Preventing and Resolving Financial Risk'), *Jingji Yanjiu Cankao*, No. 101, pp. 2–6 (1 November).

Chi, Fulin et al. (1996), *Zhaiwu Yu Guoyou Qiye Gaige* (*Debt and the SOE Reform*), Minzhu yu Jianshe, Beijing.

Fama, Eugene and Jensen, Michael (1983), 'Separation of Ownership and Control', *Journal of Law and Economics*, Vol. 26, pp. 301–25.

Hart, Oliver (1995), 'Corporate Governance: Some Theory and Implications', *Economic Journal*, Vol. 105, pp. 678–89.

Holz, Carsten (1998), 'China's Bad Loan Problem', Working Papers in the Social Sciences, No. 44, Hong Kong University of Science and Technology, Hong Kong.

Holz, Carsten and Zhu, Tian (2000), 'Banking and Enterprise Reforms in the People's Republic of China after the Asian Financial Crisis: An Appraisal', *Asian Development Review*, Vol. 18, pp. 73–93.

Hu, Xiaoyi (1996), 'Reducing SOEs' Social Burdens and Establishing a Social Insurance System', in Harry Broadman (ed.), *Policy Options for Reform of Chinese SOEs*, World Bank Discussion Paper No. 335, Washington, DC, pp. 125–48.

Jensen, Michael and Meckling, William (1976), 'Theory of the Firm: Managerial Behavior, Agent Costs, and Capital Structure', *Journal of Financial Economics*, Vol. 3, pp. 305–60.

Lardy, Nicholas R. (1998), *China's Unfinished Economic Revolution*, Brookings Institution, Washington, D.C.

Li, Shan and Zhu, Tian (1998), 'China, Too, Faces Financial Perils', *Wall Street Journal*, 28 October.

Lin, Justin Y. et al. (1998), 'Competition, Policy Burdens, and State-Owned Enterprise Reform', *American Economic Review Papers and Proceedings*, Vol. 88, pp. 422–27.

Lin, Yi-min and Zhu, Tian (2001), 'Ownership Restructuring in Chinese State Industry: An Analysis of Evidence on Initial Organizational Changes', *China Quarterly*, Vol. 166, pp. 305–41.

OTNIC (Office for the Third National Industrial Census) (1997), *The Data of the Third National Industrial Census of the People's Republic of China of 1995*, China Statistical Press, Beijing.

Qian, Yingyi (1996), 'Enterprise Reform in China: Agency Problems and Political Control', *Economics of Transition*, Vol. 4, pp. 422–47.

Shleifer, Andrei and Vishny, Robert (1997), 'A Survey of Corporate Governance', *Journal of Finance*, Vol. 52, pp. 737–83.

Wang, Huaqing (1998), 'Lessons from the Southeast Asian Financial Crisis', *Jingrong Shibao* (*Financial Times*), 16 January.

Wang, Luolin and Chen, Jiagui (1997), *Xiandai qiye zhidu de lilun yu shijian* (*Theories and Practices of Modern Enterprise System*), Economic Management Press, Beijing.

Wei, Shangjin and Wang, Tao (1997), 'The Siamese Twins: Do State-Owned Banks Favor State-Owned Enterprises in China?' *China Economic Review*, Vol. 8, pp. 19–30.

Wu Jinglian et al. (1998), *Guoyou jingji de zhanluexin gaizu (Strategic restructuring of the state-owned economy)*, China Development Press, Beijing.

Xia, Deren (1996), 'Guanyu zhongguo jingji zhuangui shiqi guoyou yinhang buliang zhaiquan wenti de yanjiu' ('A Study of the Unhealthy Loan Problem of State Banks during China's Economic Transition'), *Guanli Shijie* (*The World of Management*), November, pp. 40–7.

Xia, Xunge (1999), 'Zhongguo de gongsi zhili jiegou gaige' ('The Reform of Corporate Governance Structure in China'), *Jingji yanjiu ziliao* (*Economic Research Materials*), No. 2, pp. 9–14.

Xiao, Geng (1997), *Chanquan yu zhongguo de jingji gaige* (*Property Rights and China's Economic Reforms*), China Social Science Press, Beijing.

Xu, Xiaonian and Wang, Yan (1999), 'Ownership Structure and Corporate Governance in Chinese Stock Companies', *China Economic Review*, Vol. 10, pp. 75–98.

Yu, Yongding and Zhang, Bingwen (2000), *Zhongguo rushi yanjiu baogao: jinru WTO de zhongguo chanyan* (*The Research Report on China's Entry into WTO: The Analysis of the China's Industries*), Social Science Literature Publishing House, Beijing.

ZGJRNJ (1997), *Zhongguo jinrong nianjian* (*Almanac of China's Finance and Banking*), China Statistical Press, Beijing.

ZGTJNJ (1999), *Zhongguo tongji nianjian* (*China Statistical Yearbook*), China Statistical Press, Beijing.

Zhang, Xiaowen (1999), 'Xiandai qiye zhidu shidian qiye de xianzhuang diaocha yu fenxi' ('A Survey and Analysis of the Current Status of the Pilot Enterprises that Experimented with the Modern Enterprise System'), *Jingji yanjiu cankao* (*Economic Research References*), No. 22, pp. 2–14.

Zheng, Haihang et al. (1998), *Guoyou qiye kuisun yanjiu* (*A Study of Loss-Making by SOEs*), Economic Management Press, Beijing.

Zhu, Tian (1999), 'China's Corporatization Drive: An Evaluation and Policy Implications', *Contemporary Economic Policy*, Vol. 17, pp. 530–9.

Chapter 5

Domestic Banking under Financial Liberalization: Lessons for China as a Member of the WTO

Wenyan Yang*

Introduction

China has recently become a member of the World Trade Organization (WTO). The terms of its accession include liberalization of the financial services sector to allow foreign entry. The banking sector is one such area where foreign participation is envisaged.

China's banking system is already suffering under the burden of the legacy of central planning, with outdated technology and bad loans accounting for over 20 per cent of the total outstanding loan portfolio.[1] Once financial liberalization is implemented, the weaknesses of China's banks could threaten to subject the country to potential financial crises and contagion. In the least it is unlikely that these banks in their current state could survive under intense competition from better-managed, more experienced foreign banks once barriers to entry are removed. On the other hand, as a matter of national policy, governments typically do not wish to relinquish the control over their countries' banking system, which is a critical component of their macroeconomic policy system, to foreign commercial interests. Therefore, to avoid being involved in future financial crises and to maintain a degree of national control over the banking system requires a strong domestic banking sector as a country opens itself up to the great benefits as well as the perils of globalization. In the case of China, this implies greater urgency for banking reform as she joins the WTO.

It will be argued that the need to push forward fundamental reforms in banking has, indeed, become paramount as China assumes the responsibilities of membership in the WTO. The argument will be supported by a comparative analysis of transition and developing country experiences in financial liberalization and financial crises. The chapter will first summarize the current state of banking reform and the banking system in China. Then, the WTO terms and their implications for the banking sector will be analyzed before the experiences of transition and developing countries in banking liberalization are presented. Finally, policy conclusions will be attempted, with a view to incorporate lessons for China from other countries' experiences.

The Current State of Banks and Banking Reform in China

China weathered the Asian crisis relatively unscathed except for a deceleration in economic growth as export growth suffered. There were two factors behind China's ability to avoid the fate of its neighbors. First, at the time the crisis was hitting one Asian economy after another, China was sitting comfortably on top of about US$140 billion in foreign exchange reserves. Secondly, perhaps more importantly, China's currency was not (and still is not) freely convertible. Being slow in its liberalization effort, China had relaxed its non-convertibility rule to allow free conversion for current account transactions only since December 1996. There was also very limited foreign presence in China's banking sector and their operations were confined to a narrow range of business transactions servicing foreign-funded companies. Restrictions such as these prevented money managers from building up positions again the Chinese currency in the foreign exchange market, although quasi-speculation contracts were conjured up in anticipation of a possible devaluation.

Although China avoided the contagion of the Asian crisis, its economic weaknesses came into light. As the causes of the crisis were being analyzed, comparisons between crisis countries and China were also made. Since weak, poorly-supervised domestic banks played a crucial role in triggering and spreading financial crises during the 1990s, the state of China's banking system attracted due attention.[2]

Institutional Development in China's Banking Sector

The Government of China has implemented banking sector reforms aimed at replacing central government directed credit planning with a system wherein lending is based on commercial banking principles. These included institutional restructuring that separated central banking from commercial banking in 1984. Parallel to the emergence of a central bank, the metamorphosis of the mono-bank system was accomplished through transforming existing specialized banks and establishing new state banks to take over the commercial banking functions formerly conducted by the People's Bank of China (now the central bank). Beginning in the mid-1980s the government also instituted regulations to allow the establishment of joint stock banks and non-bank financial institutions such as urban credit co-operatives, trust and investment companies, and finance companies affiliated with state-owned conglomerates.

Despite of the above institutional changes, banking is still under tight state control via the dominance of state-owned commercial banks since entry by non-state banks, both foreign and domestic, is extremely difficult and restrictions on the scope of their business are also severe.[3] Even among state-owned banks, concentration is high. The four state-owned commercial banks dominate the landscape of China's banking sector, accounting for over 60 per cent of total financial assets and about 70 per cent of total domestic credits.

The Asian Crisis and Banking Reform in China

Banking crises in other transition economies in Eastern Europe and the former USSR (see later section) illustrated the need for continued banking reforms in establishing a viable banking system. The outbreak and the contagion effect of the Asian financial crisis further highlighted the need for strengthening a country's banking system in order to withstand external shocks. Given the above outlined weaknesses in the banking system in China, banking reform, which the Government has been pursuing, became an even more urgent task.

In 1998, the Chinese Government implemented loan-to-asset guidelines to replace national credit plans, thus furthering the transition to market-based banking. The immediate impact of this reform measure was a slow-down in bank lending, with indications that banks were paying more attention to the quality of loans and to the assessment of credit risk in their decision-making. To encourage bank lending as the national economy showed signs of excessive slowing and to bolster the capital base of the four largest commercial banks, the Government issued RMB270 billion (about $34 billion) in special bonds ear-marked for the recapitalization of state-owned commercial banks. These actions all helped to strengthen China's banking system somewhat, although the overall health of the banking sector remains questionable.

The Chinese Government also stepped up efforts at reining in the trust and investment companies that had served a useful purpose in the development of the country's financial sector but often operated outside the reach of the regulators. Consolidation through mergers and closures reduced the number of these companies from over 1000 at the peak in 1992 to about one-fourth that number at present. The onset of the Asian crisis and its subsequent impact on the real economies of Asia exposed weaknesses in many of the internationally oriented trust and investment companies (collectively known as the ITICs).

As many of these ITICs came under financial pressure, the Chinese Government adopted a policy stance of not bailing them out. On 10 January 1999 China's second largest trust and investment company, the Guangdong International Trust and Investment Corporation (GITIC), announced its bankruptcy and Chinese bankruptcy law would not grant priority in debt payment to foreign creditors whose loans were not approved by the central authority. This announcement dispelled the often-held assumption that the Chinese government was explicitly or implicitly guaranteeing the foreign borrowing of Chinese enterprises. Combined with later revelations of missed debt payments by more trust and investment companies (ITICs), this development caused serious concerns over the possibility of defaults by many more Chinese borrowers and furthermore, over the precarious state of China's financial system. To alleviate investor anxiety, the governor of China's central bank announced on 27 January 1999 that the country's ITICs would be able to convert local currency to meet payments on their foreign debts registered with (thus, approved by) central authorities. At the same time, the Government also urged debt restructuring, signaling that the central government would not assume the role of a guarantor to these companies. Although the announcement caused foreign investors to reassess the risk of lending to Chinese enterprises and thus, may have lead to reduced capital flows to the country in the short-term, it would tend to help in strengthening China's financial sector in the longer term.

The Government has also taken some initial steps to solve the bad loan problem plaguing the banking system. Since 1999 four asset management companies (AMCs), each with 10 billion *renminbi* ($1.2 billion) capital, have been set up to unload the non-performing loans (overdue by two years or more) of the four state-owned commercial banks.[4] These AMCs were the spun-off trust and investment subsidiaries of the four State commercial banks, taking over bad loans in accordance with bad loan resolution plans outlined by the Governor of the central bank. Meanwhile, the securities business of these subsidiaries would be merged into a new entity under the State Development Bank. This move gives some indication as to how the Government would deal with bad loans burdening the banking sector while also consolidating the country's faltering trust and investment companies though restructuring. Debt-equity swaps, albeit on a limited scale, have been arranged. A broader financial restructuring plan, however, remains elusive.

The Government has indicated that it would no longer act as the implicit guarantor of last resort to banks once the bad loan workout is completed. This would push banks to base decisions on risk assessment and other commercial principles, that is, to operate like commercial banks in a market economy. Nonetheless, when it felt it was necessary, the government still ordered banks to increase lending, as had been the case in the last few years of the 1990s. This continuation of a central planning mentality on the part of the Government undermines its own effort at strengthening the banking system.

At this juncture work plans to strengthen the banking system are still sketchy and a considerable amount of detail needs to be fleshed out. One lesson the Chinese government has drawn from the Asian crisis is the need for further reforms. Government announcements indicating an intent to consolidate financial institutions and to recapitalize banks, albeit without much detail, are in line with such a plan. On 19 July 2000, the governor of the central bank announced plans to first free rates on foreign currency deposit and lending and then rates on rural credits. The final step will be the decontrol of the bank deposit rate after the band for the lending rate has been expanded. This plan will be implemented in the next three years. This reform plan is viewed as an important step in banking liberalization as it grants greater autonomy to domestic banks, while further enforcing the market orientation of the banking sector. However, the close link between the dominating banks and the SOE sector underscores the importance of pursuing enterprise reform in conjunction with financial reforms. Unless their main clients are in better financial health, recapitalization of commercial banks will be temporary and will not result in improved performance of banks in the long-term.

Issues to be Addressed by Further Reform

The transition process is not yet complete, as would be expected, since establishing a viable banking system is not an easy task by any means. Managers and employees alike need to be trained in the ways of banking in a market environment. Prudential regulation and oversight also require skilled personnel and corresponding institutions. Furthermore, during this transition period, elements of central planning co-exist with market forces, thus presenting a unique set of problems to be addressed by further reforms.

Among the issues that have to be resolved, the most pressing is the stock of non-performing loans banks carry on their books while at the same time, new ones have been accumulating. The initial stock of such bad loans resulted from government directed lending to inefficient state-owned enterprises before economic reforms were put on the agenda. However, continued government control over credit allocation (through the national credit plan before 1997) during the reform period led to a ballooning of the problem. Even as the credit plan was being replaced with loan-to-asset ratio guidelines, government interference in lending continued. Loans made under such circumstances are much more likely to turn into non-performing ones, since otherwise the interference would not have been necessary in the first place. As a result, bad loans amount to an alarming proportion of total loans. Official estimates put the ratio of non-performing loans to total loans outstanding at 20 per cent. Given the weakness in loan classification, the non-performing loan ratio is widely believed to be higher than the official estimate if internationally accepted standards are applied. Private estimates are as high as 40 per cent. In any case, even the more conservative of these estimates is high enough to be alarming. In comparison, the non-performing loan ratio in the Southeast Asian crisis countries ranged from 16 per cent in the Philippines to 40 per cent in Indonesia and Thailand in 1998.[5]

As a result of the continuation of directed lending during the reform period, the banking system is quite weak. In addition to a high bad loan ratio, another indicator is the paid-in capital to loan ratio, which actually declined in China's four largest commercial banks from 12.1 per cent in 1985 to only 2.2 per cent by 1996. This is based on official data.[6] If international standards were applied, some of China's banks would have had negative capital (Lardy, 1998).

Other than the absence of political intervention in bank lending decisions, adequate prudential supervision and regulation, internationally accepted accounting rules are also important factors determining the financial health of a banking sector. In China, such capacity is being built up, but at present, the institutions are rudimentary and trained personnel are scarce. This results in lax enforcement of existing regulations, which is another area of weakness. For instance, Chinese banks set up trust and investment subsidiaries and security companies partly to skirt prudential regulations in order to engage in risky business activities. Therefore, capacity building in the areas of supervision and enforcement will complement other efforts at strengthening the banking sector.

Although institution building in the areas of bank supervision, risk management and regulation are all vitally important in strengthening the banking system, the health of the financial system is linked directly to the performance of the SOEs. While better banking regulation and supervision are needed in many developing countries and even in more developed capitalist economies, the problem created by the SOE sector for banking in China is unique to transition economies.

Most lending by state-owned commercial banks is to SOEs. For example, at the end of 1995, over 80 per cent of total bank loans outstanding in China were owed by SOEs. At the end of 1999, the share may have fallen somewhat, but total short-term loans to non-State entities (approximated by agriculture, township enterprises, private enterprises and individuals and foreign-invested enterprises) still accounted for less than 25 per cent of all short-term loans.[7] Bank lending for fixed investment was even more concentrated in SOEs. Given this high concentration of loans in the SOE sector, the financial health of the banking system is inevitably tied to that of the state enterprises. The SOEs are notorious for incurring losses in their business activities, which makes them risky borrowers. Unless the financial performance of their main clients is improved, banks will have little hope of improving loan quality. In a market economy, banks could refuse to lend to some firms while charging higher interest rates on loans to some others, if they were deemed to be high-risk borrowers. In a transition economy like China, however, banks do not have such discretion in making their lending decisions in dealing with SOEs. Moreover, even as banks are being officially instructed to operate on a commercial basis, interest on loans are still not yet liberalized. This circular linkage underscores the need for banking reform to go hand in hand with enterprise reform in transition countries such as China.

Official interference in commercial lending manifests itself in the form of 'policy lending', that is, loans made by commercial banks in support of certain sectors favored by government industrial policy or even to finance pet projects of local officials. Consequently, banks make these loans not as a result of risk/return evaluations, but to comply with administrative directions from central or local governments. This practice lowers the quality of the loans. In the case of China, however, such policy lending by commercial banks started to decline beginning in 1997, three years after three 'policy banks', namely the Development Bank, Import-Export Bank and Agricultural Development Bank, were set up to relieve commercial banks of this responsibility. This was one of the measures the Chinese Government took to improve loan quality and thereby strengthen state-owned commercial banks.

This strategy has problems of its own. The original plan for these policy banks was to have existing policy loans of the commercial banks transferred to them while they assumed the responsibility for future ones, thus enabling the commercialization of other banks. The largest of the three, the State Development Bank would be in charge of financing for long-term infrastructure investment and for supporting strategic or 'pillar' industries. The Agricultural Development Bank would provide short-term loans to State agencies for procurement of agricultural products and would fund projects to assist the rural poor and general agricultural development projects. The Import-Export Bank's primary responsibility would be to provide export sellers credit to promote China's exports while also issuing guarantees of export buyers credit and export credit insurance. The majority of the funding for these banks was to come from existing financial institutions such as the former specialized banks, State budgetary allocation, bond placement to other financial institutions by the central bank on obligatory basis, loans from international organizations, and foreign governments and central bank loans. As so envisaged, the solvency of these policy banks would be unsustainable unless the State were to inject new resources on a regular basis. Indeed, the central bank continued to inject large amounts of money in the form of loans to these banks. In 1994 and 1995, 95 per cent of all central bank loans were loans to the three policy banks. The increasing amount of bonds the central bank placed involuntarily with other financial institutions also met resistance. In the implementation phase, however, most of the existing loans were not transferred and the commercialization of all banks is not yet complete.

Even if the sustainability of these 'policy banks' is ensured, a change in government practice is required for commercial banks to gain operational independence. For example, in recent past years the government's macroeconomic policy objective was to halt the deceleration in economic growth. Banks have been ordered to boost lending to SOEs in an effort to stimulate investment and growth despite the apparent conflict with another official call, that is, for banks to base their lending on risk evaluation. Total lending grew by 12.5 per cent during 1999, with most of the increased credits granted to SOEs creating more non-performing loans. This practice risks keeping open the flow of bad loans.

Another important issue that needs to be addressed is the lack of competition in commercial banking in China. In a market economy, competition is an effective mechanism through which inefficient institutions are weeded out. A prerequisite for such competition is free entry. This, however, is not at all the case in China's banking sector, where technically insolvent state banks are kept alive by protection resulting from artificial barriers to entry.

It is true that the country's commercial banking system is still in its infancy, if it is put into historical context. It is also a fact that the change from passive deposit taking, government-directed credit-granting agencies to profit-motivated commercial entities and the associated acquisition of technical competence including risk assessment, oversight and regulation, take time. Thus, the Chinese Government is perhaps right to be cautious regarding foreign entry into the banking industry. Competition from foreign banks with long established histories and better technology as well as expertise in commercial banking in a market environment could be detrimental to fledgling domestic banks. To protect them, the government maintains restrictions on the scope of business in which foreign bank representative offices can engage, limiting it to foreign currency transactions and permitting local currency business only in the economic development zone of Pudong in Shanghai and only in transactions involving foreign-invested companies. With China joining the WTO, only one foreign bank has thus far obtained official permission to conduct foreign currency transactions for local individual residents in Shanghai.[8]

Similarly, entry by new domestic banks is also restricted. Given that state-owned commercial banks are still burdened by problem loans to SOEs and their primary borrowers remain SOEs, the entry of new banks with a clean slate and no obligation to support inefficient SOEs would put the existing banks at a disadvantage in a competitive environment. Indeed, new state-owned banks operating without the burden of inherited non-performing loans are more competitive than existing ones. For example, the Bank of Communication, established in 1987, has bucked the trend of declining capital-to-loan ratios and low profitability among large Chinese state-owned banks. In principle, these new banks could use their operating profits to improve services or to offer higher deposit rates in order to attract savers. Thus, interest liberalization would also likely benefit new banks more than existing state banks. Therefore, restrictions on bank entry in China protect state banks from collapsing under the weight of their bad loans for the time being. Nonetheless, many joint stock banks have been licensed, although only one private joint stock bank has been established so far, that in 1995.[9]

Notwithstanding the rationale for protecting the infant banking industry, liberalization is necessary to improve services and profitability of banks through competition in commercial lending. This, in turn, would strengthen the financial sector in general. Liberalizing entry to banking needs to be accompanied by appropriate procedures and requirements. Otherwise, free entry could lead to the proliferation of undercapitalized new banks and undermine public confidence in the banking system, as will be demonstrated in a later section on the experience of some of the Eastern European transition economies.

In spite of continuing restrictions on entry and a controlled interest rate policy, some degree of competition in the banking sector has been introduced as a result of reforms. As the strict separation of business scope among the specialized banks which specialize in different economic sectors, as their names indicate, gradually disappeared, when new banks and non-bank financial institutions were introduced, competition among these institutions increased. However, further promotion of competition in banking is needed in order to improve services and efficiency. China's entry into the World Trade Organization can be the catalyst since it will bring the external pressure of eventual competition from foreign banks.

China's WTO Membership and its Implication for Domestic Banks

In the terms it reached with the United States, China would open its domestic market in order to gain the support of the US for its membership in the World Trade Organization (WTO).[10] One of the most important concessions China made was to further liberalize its financial sector to allow greater foreign participation. More specifically, in the banking industry, foreign banks will be allowed to engage in all foreign currency transactions immediately upon China's entry into the WTO. In addition foreign banks will be permitted to service enterprises in local currency transactions two years after China joins the WTO. They will be able to enter local currency retail banking five years after China's accession. In all these activities, they will gain national treatment, enjoying the same protection as national institutions while being subject to the same set of regulations.

Now that China is a member of the WTO, compliance with these terms implies serious competition for China's domestic banks. Given that China's state-owned commercial banks are in rather poor financial health, it is highly unlikely that they could withstand such competition if the market opening measures were to take place now. First of all, foreign banks, with their accumulated expertise, strong capital base and effective management, will be able to compete for the best and most profitable customers given the poor performance of Chinese banks in customer service. They are also likely to win in the competition for the most competent employees given their capacity to pay higher salaries, thus undercutting Chinese State banks in human resources. Moreover, Chinese banks are still saddled with a large amount of non-performing loans and they are severely under capitalized. The current stability of China's banking system hinges on the willingness of Chinese citizens to entrust their savings to the commercial banks. In the worst-case scenario, where individual depositors were to leave these banks, which would become more likely when multinational banks are allowed to enter retail banking, Chinese banks would be severely undermined and their very survival would be in question. Even if foreign banks focus their competitive efforts only on the few profit centers such as Shanghai and Beijing, rather than on establishing a nationwide network, the health of China's banking system would still be undermined. This is because most branch banks of state-owned commercial banks outside the few profit centers rarely contribute to total profit.

In a large country like China, the prospect of ceding control of the banking system to foreign commercial interests is not a welcome one. From this perspective, strengthening the domestic banking system through deepening market-oriented reforms becomes more urgent and gains vital importance as China readies to fulfill its WTO membership obligations.

Furthermore, when this and the various bilateral agreements come into force, China will no longer possess the same degree of control over its financial system. Liberalization in international trade and finance will tie its economic fate ever so closer to the global economy. Through inter-affiliate lending, multinational banks can move funds in and out of the country even with restrictions on capital movement in place and thus, could be a source of instability. The lessons of the two recent crises also underscore the significance of having stronger banks in an emerging market economy.

The entry of foreign banks could, in principle, improve efficiency and performance of the banking industry through competition and thus result in better and cheaper service to consumers. When domestic resources are not sufficient, foreign investment also helps to fortify the capital base of ailing banks. This is the intention of policy makers when they decide to attract foreign investment into domestic banking in order to inject foreign capital and expertise into the local banking industry. They also hope for improvement in banking discipline through increased competition. Recent developments in Latin American banking sector show that the positive impact of foreign participation in the banking sector is not merely a theoretical possibility.

The experience of transition economies in Central and Eastern Europe, however, highlights the possibility of unintended outcomes if the timing and sequencing of financial liberalization are not carefully thought through. Not only could premature liberalization result in foreign domination of a country's banking system, it could also sow the seeds of financial crisis, as some people would argue was the case in Eastern Europe and even in Latin America and Southeast Asia.

In view of the poor health of its banks and the examples of other countries that have liberalized their financial sector, China needs to strengthen its banking system before the floodgate is opened under WTO terms. If engaged thoughtfully, gradual liberalization of China's banking sector could prepare domestic banks for the shock of intense competition. The different outcomes of liberalization in two regions of the world, which is the subject of the next section, could provide some useful lessons for China.

What Happened after Liberalization – Tales and Lessons from Transition and Developing Countries

Financial liberalization typically involves allowing free entry to banking and the capital market and removing non-market based restrictions and regulations that hinder the development of the financial sector with banking being a building block. The experience of the Eastern European transition economies is highly relevant for China and thus, we will examine banking liberalization in some of these countries first.

Financial liberalization and banking crisis in Eastern European transition economies Due to historical circumstances, the banking sectors in these countries were typically monopolized by the state and their banks were poorly capitalized with large amounts of bad loans on their books at the beginning of the transition process. These countries also lacked a regulatory framework. Governments needed to carry out reforms that would establish new institutions and new rules. One of the things many governments considered to be high priority was to introduce competition in banking while adopting international accounting standards in all enterprises. However, the sequencing of reforms proved to be very important, as banking crises in these countries during their early years of transition demonstrated.

In Hungary, the coming into force in early 1992 of the bankruptcy law, new banking law and the new accounting standards forced the bad loan problem in state-owned banks into the open. As a result, several large state banks faced bankruptcy. By the end of that year, the government agreed to help large state-owned banks clean up their balance sheets to make them into more attractive privatization candidates and also to avoid the economic and social consequences of systemic bank failure.

The rescue focused on consolidation of loans, which was carried out through debt-for-government-bond swaps. Banks were allowed to swap their non-performing loans worth 104 billion *forints* (or $1.3 billion) for special government 'consolidation bonds' totaling 80 billion *forints* ($975 million). This increased the capital base of the banks, removing the short-term threat of systemic bank failure due to capital inadequacy. However, no performance requirement was imposed on banks due to the lack of a carefully formulated strategy. In fact, banks slacked off in their efforts to recover assets once the program was instituted. More importantly, the bailout program created a moral hazard situation since no provision was made to improve the quality of future loans. Bank managers did not suffer consequences resulting from their loan decisions and an expectation was formed that the government would bail out large banks.

By 1993 Hungarian banks were again in dire need of recapitalization, as the flow of bad loans was not dealt with in the first round. This time, the government agreed to recapitalize all large state-owned banks to a zero risk-adjusted capital position. In exchange for a capital injection of 150 billion *forints* ($1.6 billion) in government bonds, the Ministry of Finance would gain a controlling share in nine partly or entirely state-owned banks. Once again, the flow problem was not addressed in the program. One analysis of the situation is that the 1993 recapitalization was primarily motivated by election politics, not the genuine desire to solve the root problems in the banking sector. Some scholars also argue that only the privatization of the banks could change the behavior of the banks so as to prevent future episodes of government rescue.

Estonia's experience with banking liberalization illustrates another issue that needs to be addressed in transition economies, namely, the supervision and regulation of banks. Even before its political independence from the Soviet Union in August 1991, Estonia had started to open its banking sector to new commercial banks. By mid-1991, there were already 12 commercial banks in operation, although only two were of decent size. The minimum capital requirement was only five million *roubles*. Rampant inflation further reduced the requirement in real terms to less than US$40,000 in mid-1992. Economic and financial turmoil in the wake of the collapse of the Soviet Union created a chaotic financial environment where banking was a very profitable business. Banks derived their profits not from financial intermediation since very few savers trusted untested banks in a hyperinflation economy, but from trading foreign exchange and arbitraging among different prices for cash and non-cash *roubles*. Furthermore, there were few restrictions on these activities due to the absence of bank supervision or regulation. On the credit demand side, enterprises were very eager to borrow since inflation had made loans from the central bank cheap in real terms. At the end of 1992, there were 47 registered commercial banks in Estonia, a country of 1.4 million people.

To curb run away inflation, the government decided to leave the *rouble* zone and adopt a monetary board-type scheme to stabilize its currency. While this measure succeeded in fighting inflation, it brought on a liquidity crisis in the banking system by eliminating huge profits from foreign currency trading and other arbitrage activities and also barring the central bank from financing ailing banks by printing money. On 17 November 1992 the central bank announced a moratorium on the country's three largest commercial banks that held deposits accounting for 40 per cent of M2. This signaled the onset of a banking crisis in Estonia.

The government was determined to push through a reform program that would fundamentally change the behavior of banks and their customers alike. Instead of bailing out the ailing banks, the central bank implemented a rescue program that injected capital only under strict terms. Bank management was replaced, depositors saw their savings with troubled banks losing part of its value and shareholders of banks lost most of their capital when the banks were merged and nationalized. Debtors had their assets frozen until a restructuring plan was worked out. The no-bail-out plan led to the bankruptcy of many large and small banks, reducing the number of banks to 23 by early 1993. This program was politically unpopular and the government was booted out of office in 1993. But the credibility of central bank policy and market discipline were firmly established. The public became more vigilant in choosing which bank to use for their savings and bank managers learned the importance of credit risk analysis. As a result of this change in behavior, albeit accomplished at a high economic and political price, the flow of bad loans was stopped and the banking system in Estonia is now considered to be one of the strongest among the Eastern European transition countries.

Foreign Competition and Domestic Banking Reform – Different Outcomes Across Countries

Another aspect of banking liberalization is the introduction of foreign competition. When countries open their banking industry to allow foreign participation, multinational banks (MNBs) may come in to take advantage of their multinational presence to expand into new markets.[11] Like foreign investment in general, foreign participation in a country's banking sector could create competitive pressure for local banks to improve service and efficiency and become stronger as a result. Moreover, MNBs could also bring market discipline, advanced managerial expertise and capital to the host country, helping domestic banks to modernize, and thus, stabilizing the banking system. Nonetheless, it could also happen that foreign banks dominate a country's banking system and abuse their monopoly power after they beat out local banks in competition. They could also undermine the host country's banking system by siphoning off low-risk customers and forcing local banks into riskier lending for the sake of maintaining market share and thus, raising the overall risk level. What happens in practice depends on many factors, including the timing and implementation of liberalization and the strategy of the MNBs.

Data compiled by the Bank for International Settlements show that the activity of MNBs in developing countries and transition economies expanded considerably in the past 15 years. The growth was most rapid in the Eastern European transition economies in the early 1990s and in Latin America in the second half of the 1990s. In terms of market share, these are also the two regions where MNBs have accounted for about 15 per cent of total loans. Although growth had picked up in Asia after the regional financial crisis, MNBs market share is still far smaller than in the other two regions. (See Table 5.1 below.)

Table 5.1 Summary statistics of multinational banks presence – developing and transition economies, by region (US$ million)

	Total MNB credit at year-end, converted at market exchange rate				
	Africa	Asia	Eastern Europe	Latin America	Middle East
1985	3499	15130	77	9773	2608
1986	3397	14454	275	12728	2960
1987	3696	17308	367	14308	3152
1988	4478	17454	365	14358	3345
1989	3852	23332	379	13420	1582
1990	4525	27472	420	15312	1908
1991	3953	30461	708	16668	1932
1992	4054	36395	518	21385	2246
1993	4732	45417	1358	24908	4368
1994	6575	51836	7818	30357	4852
1995	8180	56517	8295	44276	5393
1996	6862	64949	15849	64089	5615
1997	6988	73260	24499	123040	6836
1997 MNB market share	9.13	4.63	14.27	16.93	.41

Sources: from Weller (2000) Table 1, based on BIS and IMF statistics.

So far, Eastern Europe and Latin America have had somewhat different experiences with foreign entry into the domestic banking sector. An analysis of the situation in the two regions where MNBs expanded to capture a significant market share helps to illustrate the conditions under which different outcomes could result from foreign participation in the banking sector.

Hungary and Poland did not allow foreign investment in their banking sector before economic and political liberalization. The two Eastern European countries introduced foreign competition during their economic transition, hoping to speed up the transformation of their former centrally planned mono-bank system. Foreign interest in buying shares in domestic banks was very limited when those countries started their privatization program. The very poor financial health of banks was one deterrent, but more importantly, how to value assets in formerly socialist countries was unclear to all parties involved. Only later into the transition process did foreign banks become interested in entering into these countries.

The entry of foreign banks into these countries has had a positive impact in terms of improved services to consumers due to foreign competition. However, evidence also points to 'cherry-picking' by foreign banks.[12] Data on total credit in these countries also show that the availability of credits shrank, instead of expanding, with financial liberalization (Weller, 2000). This outcome partly resulted from the more traditional mode of operation of MNBs in these countries.

Traditionally, MNBs enter a country and provide services to multinational corporations who may already be customers in other countries. Their advantage lies in services local banks cannot provide or are not familiar with, such as loans in foreign currency, financial services related to international trade and internationally syndicated loans. Due to this advantage, large domestic companies often become MNB clients. Wealthy individuals are also likely customers of MNBs for services such as brokerage, savings products, credit cards and consumer loans. This traditional focus of MNBs partly results from the high costs of obtaining country-specific information. This is particularly the case in transition economies such as Hungary and Poland where necessary information did not even exist in the central planning system. Faced with such informational costs, they typically pick the best corporate and private customers with higher credit worthiness and greater assets. Domestic banks, on the other hand, were left with clients of higher risk and less wealth. When this happened, the domestic banking sector was weakened due to the lowering of the quality of lending by domestic banks. Furthermore, medium to small-sized enterprises might face reduced access to credit compared with the pre-liberalization past.

This happened in Eastern European countries partly because the timing of liberalization was too sudden and domestic banks were not sufficiently prepared. The entry of better-managed foreign competitors with strong capitalization reduced profit margins for banks, decreasing investment through retained earnings. Thus, for local banks that started off with inadequate capitalization and could not add capital, the loss of low-risk customers to MNBs led them to riskier lending since their capital position was already inadequate and such lending imposed little additional risk. Moreover, banking reform in these countries was still incomplete and the domestic banks were still operating with old central planning mentality and ill prepared to assess risk. This raised the overall risk level of the domestic banking system. Banking crises erupted in these countries as a result. Even if domestic banks started with adequate capitalization and were operating on market principles, intensified competition and the loss of low-risk clients caused them to be more cautious and curtail lending in order not to increase the risk level. However, this led to credit contraction.

In Latin America, on the other hand, the effect of the recent liberalization in the banking sector seems to be more positive. To begin with Latin American banks, even if they were state-owned, were never reduced to being cashiers for their governments, as was the case under central planning. Moreover, there is a long history of foreign bank presence in the region. For instance, Citibank has had branches in the region for over 80 years. Historically in Latin America, multinational banks such as Citibank played the role described earlier, namely servicing multinational corporations, blue-chip domestic companies and wealthy individuals. However, a change seems to be taking place in the latest round of banking reforms in Latin America in the post debt crisis era.

As part of the structural adjustment program these countries implemented in the wake of the debt crisis, Latin American countries liberalized their financial sector, opening the doors wider for foreign banks. At the same time, privatization of state-owned enterprises, some of which are banks, also gained momentum. The 1994 Mexican crisis and its 'Tequila Effect' weakened regional financial institutions and many banks were in dire need of capital injection. Financial authorities in the region, in the new policy environment, saw foreign entry into the banking sector in a different light. It is viewed as a means to strengthen the capital base of domestic banks through mergers and acquisitions with foreign partners, to promote competition and to improve the performance of local banks by importing management expertise and practice.

Privatization and the new policy stance encouraged foreign banks to enter the Latin American banking market as direct investors, rather than through the traditional route of setting up branch banks. The resolution of the debt crisis and the eventual stabilization of macroeconomic situation in the region also improved the overall regional economic prospect. Beginning in 1995, direct foreign investment in Latin American banks picked up and has increased rapidly. Banks from Spain, Canada, Italy, the Netherlands and the UK have been actively buying stakes in local banks, hoping to profit from serving the financial needs of the region's increasingly prosperous middle-class. Banks from Chile are also expanding their regional reach in the process. On average, these investor banks control about 65 per cent of the institutions they invested in. But the degree of foreign penetration differs from country to country. In Peru, foreign banks were estimated to control over 60 per cent of total loans. In Argentina, where the penetration rate is also relatively high in terms of loan share, foreign banks control close to 20 per cent of total banking assets. Mexico, on the other hand, had restricted foreign ownership in the country's three largest banks. Consequently, foreign banks controlled a much smaller share of total loans, about one-third. As Mexico had removed the restriction at the end of 1998, foreign penetration has increased.

The impact of the flurry of foreign investment in Latin American banks has been largely positive so far. Besides injecting much needed capital into the region's ailing banks, one of the most significant results has been the improvement in the public's confidence in the banking system. During the debt crisis and in the years of structural adjustment and hyperinflation, public confidence in the banking system was seriously eroded. Foreign banks are perceived by the public as stronger institutions with experience and sound management, thus, less risky financial institutions. Their presence and alliance with local banks improved public perception of the banking system. In a region that had gone through a period of hyperinflation and many episodes of domestic liquidity crises, this change in public perception is very important. This means small depositors and investors who had ceased to be bank customers started to use banks again. The banking system's financial inter-mediation role was strengthened.

Moreover, foreign participation seems to have exerted competitive pressure on domestic banks to improve services, to speed up the adoption of new technology and to improve efficiency. Competition has also reduced the net interest margin in many Latin American countries, although small and medium-sized enterprises and the average households have not benefited much since they are considered to be more risky than large corporations.

These positive outcomes notwithstanding, increasing foreign control over a country's banking system has also caused nationalistic concerns. But the political economy of banking reform in Latin America has so far favored foreign participation in the regional banking system.

Strengthening Domestic Banks in Preparation for Liberalization – some Policy Conclusions

Policy implications can be drawn from the experience of developing and transition economies with banking liberalization. First of all, when countries become integrated in the international economy, certain barriers that may have insulated them from the harmful effects of globalization disappear. To withstand the impact of external shocks, national economic systems have to be strong. A banking system that is adequately capitalized and well supervised is one of the building blocks in fortifying a nation's economy in the globalizing world. Secondly, liberalizing the banking sector and inviting foreign participation could help to strengthen weak banking systems. The form of foreign participation, however, matters in realizing the potential benefit of financial liberalization. Last, but definitely not least, China needs to seize the window of opportunity offered by the phasing in of banking liberalization under its WTO accession terms to deepen economic reform in the sector.

To strengthen its banking system, China first needs to resolve the bad loan problem plaguing state-owned commercial banks. To tackle the stock problem, injection of funds is required. The asset management companies the government of China has created are one possible approach. But it requires the support of clearly defined bankruptcy procedures and adequate capitalization for these companies, which is still not the case. More importantly, the flow has to be stopped. No amount of recapitalization can clear the slate for banks that continue to make loans without getting repaid, as illustrated by the case of Hungary. As pointed out earlier, the problem is caused partly by the historical background of commercial banking in former socialist countries such as China and thus requires a solution that is realistic given the institutional complexity of transition economies. In China it is intimately linked to the reform of the SOE sector, which itself is a very delicate matter. Liberalizing ownership structure and granting non-state enterprises equal legal rights, equal access to finance would be a start. Only a growing economy can generate additional employment opportunities that can absorb redundant workers from the faltering SOEs, making the implementation of much-needed reforms in this area less destabilizing. Furthermore, the government has to refrain from resorting to political interference in commercial bank operations when it sees this as necessary for macroeconomic policy purposes.

If and when the bad loan problem is resolved, Chinese banks still need to bring their capital adequacy and prudential management up to international standards to withstand the shock of new competition and fallout from future international financial crises. The banking crisis in Estonia illustrates this point very clearly.

As the experience of some Latin American countries demonstrated, one source of finance for bank recapitalization is foreign investment. Moreover, foreign participation in domestic banking also brings other long-term benefits associated with international competition. Foreign participation can also be a stabilizing factor in times of financial crisis due to their diversified portfolio and solid reputation. Although the Eastern European experience highlights the short-term adjustment costs of such competition, such costs can be minimized by preparing domestic banks for the eventual intensification of foreign competition. Another way to reduce adjustment costs is to use policy and regulations to encourage joint ventures and strategic partnership with foreign institutions.

In fact, competition could be promoted by first removing entry barriers for domestic entities, while improving prudential supervision and regulation and enforcement of rules. Without competition, state-owned commercial banks do not have sufficient incentives to improve themselves. History shows that protected infant industries rarely grow up if they are not subject to strict performance standards and competition. Besides, if China has to allow foreign banks to compete with domestic state-owned banks in all areas of business five years after its WTO accession, not permitting non-state domestic banks to form would be discriminating against national firms in the banking sector. Allowing non-state banks to enter would deepen banking reform, while creating necessary competition to state-owned banks and prompting them to improve efficiency.

With WTO membership, financial liberalization is inevitable for China. If China desires to keep its banking system under some degree of national control, it is vital that the domestic banking sector improve its financial health and strengthen the regulatory framework before hand. This adds urgency to deepening financial reform now. Removing entry barriers to domestic enterprises would be an important first step.

* The views expressed in this paper are those of the author and not necessarily of the United Nations.

Notes

1 This is an official estimate, while estimates by private sector economists run as high as 40 per cent.
2 For analysis of the emerging market financial crises, see for example Dooley and Walsh (2000), Tornell (1999) and the United Nations (1999).
3 At the present, there is only one private bank, namely the Minsheng Bank, in China.
4 This was announced by the Governor of China's central bank in January 1999.
5 *Oxford Analytica Brief*, 24 February 1999.
6 The Basle Committee guideline calls for a core capital (or tier-one capital, paid-in) to asset (risk-adjusted) ratio of 4 per cent at the minimum.
7 Calculations based on *China Statistical Yearbook* 2000, p. 640.
8 This announcement was accompanied by concerns over the prospect that domestic savers with foreign currency accounts in State-owned banks would rush to take their deposits to the foreign bank expressed by some banking officials.
9 Central and local governments and their agencies and SOEs are typically shareholders of the new joint stock banks. Only one such bank, the Shenzhen Development Bank, was listed on a stock exchange with two-thirds of its shares owned by individual investors, as of end of 1997 (Lardy, 1998).
10 Under WTO equal treatment rule, the most favorable bilateral terms would have to be applied to all parties.
11 Multinational banks are different from international banks. The latter operate across national boarders without establishing physical presence in other countries, which multinational banks do.
12 In banking parlance, the siphoning of high quality customers from competitors is referred to as 'cherry-picking'.

Selected References

Clarke, G., Cull, R., D'Amato, L. and Molinari, A. (1999), 'The Effect of Foreign Entry on Argentina's Domestic Banking Sector', *World Bank Policy Research Working Papers*, No. 2158, The World Bank, Washington, DC.

Dooley, M. and Walsh, C. (2000), 'Capital Controls and Crises: Theory and Experience', paper presented at American Economic Association Meetings, 8 January 2000, New Orleans, Furman, J. and Stiglitz, J. (1998), 'Economic Crises: Evidence and Insights from East Asia', *Brookings Papers on Economic Activity*, No. 2, pp. 1-135. Gros, D. and Steinitsr, A. (1995), *Winds of Change: Economic Transition in Central and Eastern Europe*, Longman, London and New York.

Kahler, M. (1998) (ed.), *Capital Flows and Financial Crises*, A Council on Foreign Relations Book, Cornell University Press, Ithaca, New York.

Lardy, N. (1998), *China's Unfinished Economic Revolution*, Brookings Institution Press, Washington, DC.

Mizsei, K. (1995), 'Lessons from Bad Loan Management in the East Central European Economic Transition for the Second Wave Reform Countries', in Rostowski, J. (ed.), *Banking Reform in Central Europe and the Former Soviet Union*, Central European University Press, Budapest.

Sabi, M. (1996), 'Comparative Analysis of Foreign and Domestic Bank Operations in Hungary', *Journal of Comparative Economics*, Vol. 22 (2).

Tornell, A. (1999), 'Common Fundamentals in the Tequila and Asian Crises', *NBER Working Paper*, 7139.

The United Nations (1999), *World Economic and Social Survey, 1999*, New York.

The United Nations (Itsman, B., Supervising Editor) (1999), *Global Financial Turmoil and Reform — a United Nations Perspective*, The United Nations University Press, Tokyo, New York, Paris.

Weller, C. (2000), 'Multinational Banks in Developing and Transition Economies', Department *of Economic and Social Affairs Discussion Paper*, The United Nations, New York.

Chapter 6

The Joy and Sorrow of Capital Inflow: Are the Lessons of Mexico Relevant to China?

Xun Pomponio

Introduction[1]

China's coming accession to the World Trade Organization has signaled its desire to embark on a new stage of economic reform, namely, full integration with world markets, not only in goods and services markets, but also, in finance. On the eve of the US Congress granting China permanent normal trade (PNTR) status, the *Wall Street Journal* reported that, 'The [Chinese] government pledged to ease open its bond and stock markets to foreign investors, signaling its intention to liberalize the restricted financial markets', (Leggett, 2000). The day after the passing of PNTR, the same journal reported, 'The yuan rose to its strongest level against the dollar in five years' (Leggett, 2000). Additionally, China is showing signs of loosening currency controls and quietly liberalizing its capital markets.[2]

Capital market liberalization in an emerging market has been the center of debate in recent years among both academicians and policymakers. The idea of liberalizing capital markets for long term development in developing economies is not challenged. Rather it is the degree and speed of liberalization or the level of capital control that poses the controversy. How much liberalization can take place and how fast? The main arguments from the literature and variations can be summarized briefly as follows.

Opponents of capital control argue that economic performance suffers unacceptable negative consequences because of control. Not only does control prevent risk spreading through global diversification of portfolios and efficient global allocation of capital; it also prevents the market from exercising discipline over government policies. Bad policies will send capital out of a country and vice versa. Capital control also prevents capital flows from smoothing out current account volatility and finally, encourages corruption at home[3] (Cooper, 1999).

On the other hand, the proponents of capital control argue that free capital flow, under a fixed exchange rate, limits monetary policy autonomy. However, with capital control, monetary policy is more effective. Capitol control prevents the financial instability consequent to capital flight. Besides, it also helps to steer the capital to favored domestic sectors and finally, can help to monitor real exchange rate movements. Since real exchange movements determine the direction of exports and exports are a determinant of economic growth, logically, capital control can also foster export-driven economic growth (Cooper, 1999).

The recent Asian financial crisis magnifies the economic consequences of free capital flow. Professor Rodrik argues that capital control for an emerging market may be the 'second-best' policy (Rodrik, 1998). For emerging economies, without sound financial institutions, open capital markets may prove to be detrimental to economic development. He suggests the use of capital controls on short-term borrowing as a strategy to subdue panic runs, since short-term borrowing forms a major component of capital flight.

Besides 'limiting' short-term borrowing, leading economist Martin Feldstein proposes a self-help list of conditions that would protect emerging economies from financial crisis. Maintaining the following is recommended: a flexible exchange regime, a sustainable current account balance, a substantial foreign exchange reserve, a ready source of foreign borrowing, a well functioning domestic banking system and finally, a sound overall economic situation, one which could resist any regional contagion (Feldstein, 1999).

As apparent in the above, how much liberalization can take place and how fast pose the true questions.

In an effort to find answers to these questions, this chapter examines and compares two large developing economies, China and Mexico, during the period preceding the onset of a financial crisis. The Mexican Peso crisis occurred at the end of 1994 and it took Mexico several years to overcome the trauma. The East Asian financial crisis threatened China in 1997, however, it did not strike. China remained stable, at least on the surface, with a stable currency and a stable macroeconomic situation. Notably, Mexico had a freely convertible capital account or liberalized capital markets, while China had a non-convertible capital account or controlled capital markets. Yet both countries had pegged exchange rate systems and relatively under-developed financial institutions.[4]

So what can we learn about capital flows from these two countries? Can this comparative study lend support for the argument in favor of capital control in a developing country with weak financial institutions? Does China's experience satisfy all the conditions that Professor Feldstein proposed to avoid a tumultuous financial crisis? To answer these and other questions, this chapter compares the two cases, using historical data from these two countries and draws some lessons for developing economies about integrating themselves into global capital markets.

The chapter is divided into five parts. The first part includes an analysis of capital flow and its relationship to GDP growth rates and external factors. The second part gives the composition of capital inflow. The third part compares macroeconomic analyses of capital flow. The fourth part includes the estimated capital flight and the related causes and consequences in the economies of China and Mexico. The fifth part draws some lessons and makes suggestions for China and its ongoing capital market liberalization.

Capital Flow and Growth Rates

After a debt crisis in 1982, Mexico's economy began to make a slow but steady recovery, over the next half dozen years. The pace began to pick up considerably in 1988 when Mexico joined the GATT and started negotiating the North American

Free Trade Agreement (NAFTA) with the United States and Canada. At the same time, Mexico's state banking and enterprise sectors also underwent large-scale privatization and its fiscal deficit and inflation numbers fell markedly.

Thus, in the following analysis, the time period from 1982 to 1987 will be identified as the pre-liberalization period (PRL) and the time period from 1988 to 1994, will be identified as the post-liberalization period (POL).

In the PRL period (1982–1987), Mexico had a near zero (0.2 per cent) average GDP growth rate and a negative (-0.02 per cent) average net capital flow (See Figure 6.1). However, in the POL period (1988–1994) Mexico's creditworthiness with international lenders increased a great deal. As a result, ever larger amounts of foreign capital began to flow into Mexico, especially as the world's industrial economies recovered in the late 1980s and the early 1990s. Mexico's net capital inflow as a percentage of GDP averaged nearly six percent. Its average GDP growth rates increased from near zero per cent to four per cent, corresponding closely to the pattern of capital flow.[5]

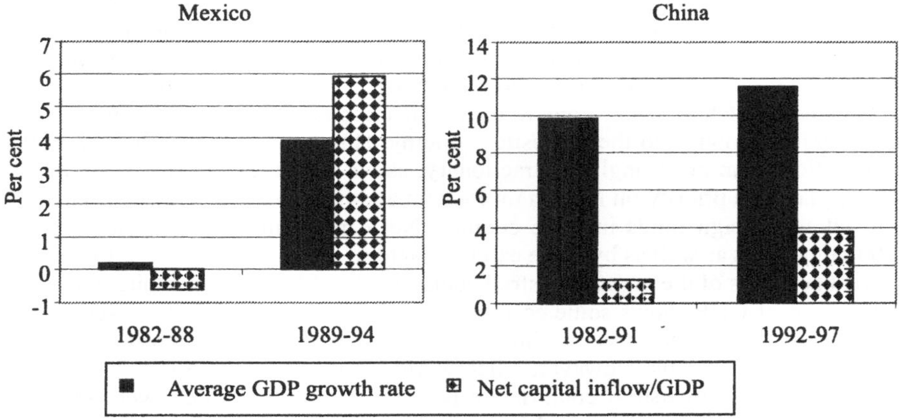

Figure 6.1 GDP growth and net capital flow

The correspondence between the average GDP growth rate and net capital inflow is of course non-causal, since both growth and capital flows depend largely upon similar aspects of the policy and non-policy economic environment. And the causality that does exist runs in more than one direction, since international investors tend to search for regions in which rapid growth can be expected. The correlation can still show that foreign capital flow may play an important role in financing economic growth. Of course, domestic savings are also important sources of financing. However, if a nation has rather low domestic savings, as did Mexico, then the foreign capital inflow can play an essential role in stimulating economic growth.

Like Mexico, China has also experienced two distinguishable periods of economic structuring since the institution of economic reform in 1978. These are from 1982 to 1991 and from 1992 to 1997. The break down of the periods corresponds to Deng's visit to southern China in 1992 and the subsequent changes in policy liberalization toward outside sources, such as a more liberal trade policy and priority treatment to foreign investment as well as an increasingly rapid pace of overall economic reform. Especially in 1994 China made a series of additional financial and macroeconomic readjustments, including currency convergence, financial and enterprise reform and fiscal and tax reform, all of which increased China's attractiveness to world investors. So again the period before 1992 will be identified as pre-liberalization (PRL) and the period after as post-liberalization (POL).

Unlike Mexico, China enjoyed a higher average growth rate both in the PRL and POL. However, its net capital inflow remained low during the PRL period (see Figure 6.1). Not until 1992 did China's net capital inflow increase markedly and then from just more than one per cent of GDP to near four per cent of GDP.[6]

Therefore, China's data show that its net capital flow does closely correspond to its liberalization policies, but not to its persistent growth rates, as with Mexico. This indicates that China's high economic growth during the PRL period had mainly been financed by domestic savings. In the POL period, as China opened more to foreign investors, more external funds flowed in seeking higher returns. In turn, these capital inflows have also fostered a persistent high growth. Both experiences of Mexico and China lead to one to expect that capital flows can provide a strong expansionary impulse to the domestic economy. However, a sharp reduction in the capital flows can be strongly contractionary, as we see in the Mexico case. And a policy placing a priority on foreign investment and healthy growth rates or potential will attract foreign funds into the country. Net capital inflows are influenced by internal policies as well as by some external factors, such as, world interest rates and current accounts of the major industrial countries. The Mexican net capital inflow as percentage of GDP shows some correlation with these external factors (see Figure 6.2). Mexico had a negative net inflow of capital when world interest rates were high in the early 1980s. However, when world interest rates were low in the early 1990s and major industrial countries, especially the United States, were showing signs of recovery from recession, Mexico and its high return rates attracted investors from all parts of the world.[7] The current accounts of the seven industrial countries play a role similar to world interest rates (See Figure 6.2).[8] Funds did not begin to flow freely into Mexico until current accounts of the G-7 countries improved in the 1990s. Overall then, Mexico's capital movement reflects some sensitivity to the external factors as well as to its domestic policies and economic situations.

By comparison, during both the PRL and POL, China's net capital inflow showed some correlation from the movements of world interest rates and G-7 current account balances (See Figure 6.3).[9] However, this may be attributed to the coincidence in the time of China's priority policy to capital inflows and the increase of the world interest rate. Moreover, China has no large and free capital market for short-term investment. Thus, 'hot money' and interest sensitive type money, characterized by investors seeking short-term high yield, made up little of China's capital flow. Rather, long term investment made up its bulk, largely attracted by China's favorable internal policies to foreign investment, especially the steady increase in the inflow after 1992. Also, more importantly, most of the inflow funds came from overseas Chinese (Asian) investors, not from G-7 country investors (Pomponio, 1998).[10] In contrast to Mexico's case, China's capital movement reflects more long term stability, if not a commitment, and less dependence on external factor effects.

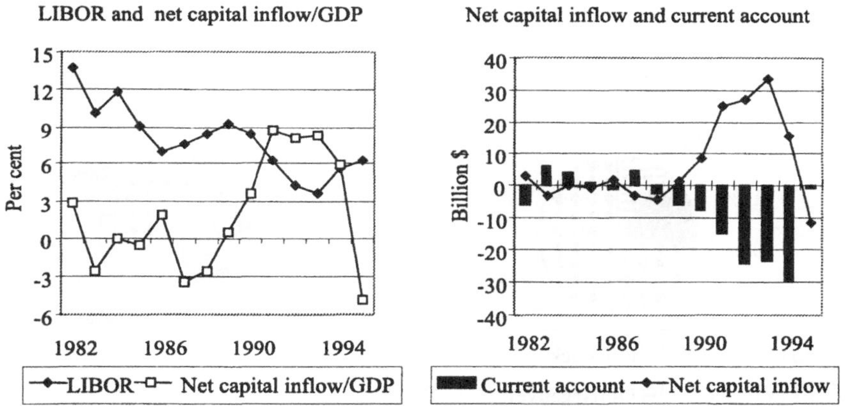

Figure 6.2 Factors affecting net capital inflow in Mexico

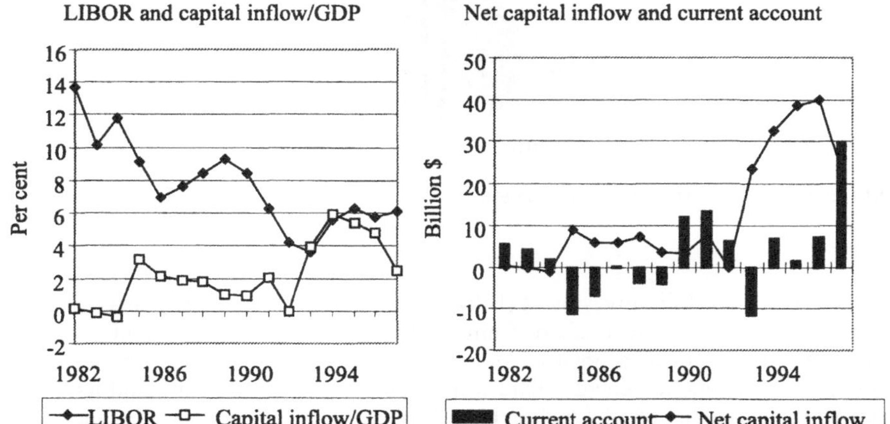

Figure 6.3 Factors affecting net capital inflow in China

Composition of Capital Inflow

Mexico's capital inflow showed a change of composition in its total profile in the two periods, from 1982–1988 to 1989–1994. The first period is pre-liberalization (PRL) and second is post-liberalization (POL). Figure 6.4 shows that the composition of capital inflow in Mexico marked three changes. One change is in foreign portfolio investment; the second change is in foreign direct investment; and the third change is in the other investment.

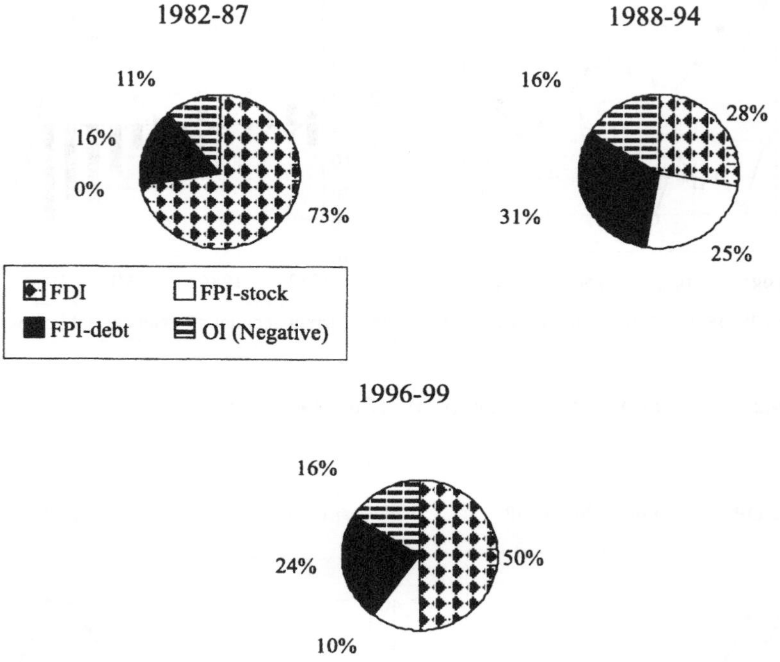

Figure 6.4 Capital flow into Mexico

The foreign portfolio investment (FPI), which includes both equity securities and debt securities, increased its share from 16 per cent to 56 per cent, and its value, from a negative sum to a positive sum from PRL to POL. The equity securities (stock) increased its percentage share form 0 per cent to 25 per cent, and its value, from $0 to an average of $4.1 billion (See Table 6.1). And debt securities increased its percentage share from 16 per cent to 31 per cent, and its value, from an average of $-4 billion to $4.7 billion, a more than eleven–fold increase. These changes marked an opening up of the stock market in 1989 and showed that more foreign investors were resuming their confidence in Mexico and investing in both equity and debt securities during the POL period during which investment environment in Mexico was drastically improved.

Table 6.1 Capital inflows

Capital Inflow Average (Billion $)				
Year	FDI	FPI-stock	FPI-debt	OI
1982–1987	1.80	0.0	–0.4	0.3
1988–1994	4.55	4.1	5.1	2.7
1996–1999	11.2	2.3	5.4	–3.7
Capital Inflows (Million $)				
Year	FDI	FPI-stock	FPI-debt	OI
1982	1901	0	645	1203
1983	2192	0	–515	–1263
1984	1542	0	–435	874
1985	1984	0	–595	–623
1986	2036	0	–517	–50
1987	1184	0	–1001	1549
1988	2011	0	1001	–5753
1989	2785	494	–140	–859
1990	2549	1995	1374	11222
1991	4742	6331	6410	8654
1992	4393	4783	13258	-947
1993	4389	10716	18203	4054
1994	10972	4084	4099	2302
1995	6963	519	–10234	–2645
1996	9180	2081	10616	–10130
1997	12830	3215	1823	–5330
1998	11310	-665	1959	6301
1999	11.57	3769	7021	–5.58

The second change in the composition of capital flow is in foreign direct investment (FDI) which decreased in total share from 73 per cent to 28 per cent from PRL to POL. However, the value of FDI increased from an average of $1.8 billion to

$4.5 billion, almost a two and a half–fold increase. The increases came after Mexico started negotiating NAFTA. The FDI doubled in 1991 and again, in 1994.

The third change in the composition of capital flow is in Other Investment (OI). Other Investment includes both public and private banks' borrowing from foreign banks. The data show that bank loans increased in share and average value, the former, from 11 per cent to 16 per cent, and later, from an average of $.28 billion to $2.7 billion, almost a ten fold increase in absolute value. The increase again indicates that foreign banks were resuming their loans to Mexico in the POL period.

The change in composition above showed two characteristics: firstly, a faster increase in the share of debt financing, such as bond and money market debt instruments, coupled with a slower increase in the share of banking loans. The banking loans included largely loans from foreign governments and banks. This change shifted risks from government and banks to individual investors. Secondly an increase in short term investment, such as stocks and money market debt instruments,[11] coupled with a decrease in share in the long-term investment, such as direct foreign investment and long-term bonds. This change shifted equity financing from long term to short term. Both changes contributed to an increase in the volatility and vulnerability to the sudden withdraw of the existing capital flow.

China's capital inflow also showed a change in the composition of its profile between its PRL and POL periods: the former, 1982–1991, and the later, 1992–1997. Figure 6.5 shows that foreign direct investment had an even greater increase in its share of total investment portfolio compared to Mexico from PRL to POL (42 per cent to 87 per cent) period. And its value increased from an average of $2.8 billion to $32.1 billion (see Table 6.2), more than an eleven-fold increase. This increase, whatever its reasons, indicated that the new composition of capital inflow strengthened its stability and reduced its volatility.

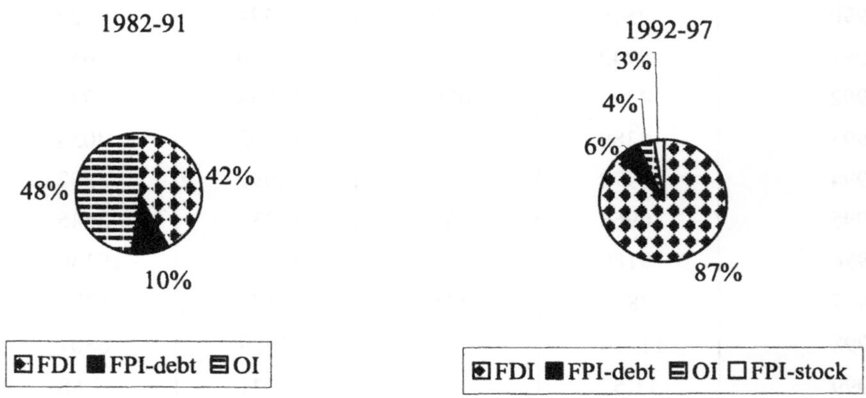

Figure 6.5 Composition of capital inflow into China

China's portfolio investment (PFI) decreased its share in the total profile, but increased in its absolute value from an average value of $.56 billion to $3.13 billion, more than a five fold increase, largely in debt securities. The stock market started only in 1997 for very limited trading. Other Investment (OI) in China also decreased both in its share and its value, with the former, from 48 per cent to four per cent, and later, from an average of $2.6 billion to $1.5 billion. These changes, again, reinforcing the former FDI change, have shifted China away from bank loans into long term equity (FDI) and debt borrowing.

Table 6.2 Capital inflows into China

Capital flow average (Billion $)			
Year	FDI	FPI-debt	OI
82–91	2.8	5.6	2.6
92–97	32.1	31	1.45
Capital flow composition (Million $)			
Year	FDI	FPI-stock	FPI-debt
1982	430	n/a	41
1983	636	n/a	20
1984	1258	n/a	83
1985	1659	n/a	764
1986	1875	n/a	1608
1987	2314	n/a	1191
1988	3194	n/a	1216
1989	3393	n/a	140
1990	3487	n/a	565
1991	4366	n/a	n/a
1992	11156	n/a	393
1993	27515	n/a	3646
1994	33787	n/a	3923
1995	35849	n/a	710
1996	40180	n/a	2372
1997	44236	5657	2046

The investment composition changes in Mexico, shifting risks from government and banks to individuals, and shifting investment from long term to short term, both contributed to volatility and later the sudden reversal of the capital inflow in Mexico as it faced internal and external problems at the end of 1994. Even though Mexico's FDI increased in value, the magnitude of the increase was far less than that of its counterpart, the former with a three-fold increase; and the latter, an 11 fold increase. While China had an opposite shift in its investment composition, shifting its entire portfolio into a more long-term investment, which locked lenders into a commitment in China for better for worse. This prevented a sudden withdraw of funds from China when the Asian financial crisis hit the rest of the Asian countries.[12]

In addition to the historical data, Mexico's post-crisis period, from 1996 to 1999, capital inflow data is added for analysis. In 1996 Mexico entered the WTO as one of the founding members. With two years into NAFTA and out of the financial crisis, the capital composition data shows (see Figure 6.3) that the share of portfolio investment (FPI) decreased from 56 per cent to 34 per cent from POL to Post-crisis period; with stock securities, from 25 per cent to 10 per cent, and debt securities, from 31 per cent to 24 per cent. The absolute value of stock securities decreased to $2.3 billion and debt securities increased to $5.4 billion. FDI increased both in its shares and in its values, with former, from 28 per cent to 50 per cent and the latter, from an average of $4.6 billion to an average of $11.22 billion. Other Investment (OI) decreased in absolute value, from an average of $2.7 billion to an average of $-3.69 billion. The negative sum indicated that foreign bank loans were decreasing.

Post-crisis Mexico, as a founding member of WTO, has learned its lessons from its past. Capital inflow has been composed more of long term equity and debt, less of short-term equity, debt and bank loans. This has been achieved by the Mexican government implementing serious structural reform programs that have strengthened the country's fundamentals and increased its ability to cope with external shocks.[13] At the same time, a freely floating exchange rate regime has helped the balance of capital flow and reduced the vulnerability to financial crises.[14] For China to deal with the shocks of entry into membership in the WTO, post-crisis Mexico's experience may serve as a good example of how to achieve a liberalized capital market with a minimum amount of vulnerability.

Macroeconomic Analysis of Capital Flow

In 1989 Mexico had almost 95 per cent of its foreign exchange reserve to its net capital inflow (see Figure 6.6). The percentage quickly decreased over the next four years. This indicated that the amount of foreign exchange reserve was depleting with respect to net capital inflow. Usually the greater the reserve in a central bank, the greater its ability to defend its currency from sliding downward. By the end of 1994 Mexico foreign exchange reserve had declined into a negative number. This indicated that Mexico central bank could no longer defend its currency. This triggered a panic run on foreign exchange, a sharp drop in the value of the peso and the consequent financial crisis.

Reserve depletion was the result of deeper problems than a run on foreign exchange. Mexico was having domestic political and economic problems at the time. Politically, a peasant uprising was not well resolved and the President was suspected of ordering the murder of a political opponent. This almost triggered a civil war in Mexico. Economically, its macroeconomic situation was out of balance. All of these factors together shook the confidence of world investors and exacerbated Mexico's financial situation.

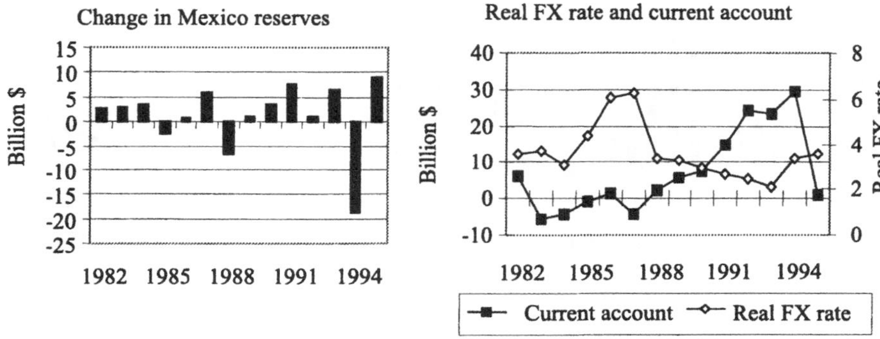

Figure 6.6 Change in Mexico reserves, real FX rate and current account

Mexico suffered a severe current account deficit in the early 1990s (see Figure 6.6). By 1994, the deficit had reached nearly $30 billion dollars. A current account deficit can be caused by either a change in the real exchange rate or by an internal macroeconomic imbalance. In the case of Mexico, both factors affected the current account. Mexico had a crawling peg exchange regime in 1989. Because the asset price was rising very fast with inflation, yet its nominal exchange rate was depreciating in a much slower pace, its real exchange rate appreciated after 1989 (see Figure 6.6). This certainly contributed to the deterioration of its current account deficit after 1989. Furthermore, its internal macroeconomic imbalance contributed to the current account deficit.

According to macroeconomic theory, the following equation is an equilibrium identity: $S - I + T - G = X - M$. According to this identity, internal balances must equal the trade balance. This equation gives rise to the following question: Which of the left hand side elements contributed to the current account deficit? Is it either because saving (S) was too low compared to private investment (I), or was it because the government was spending beyond its means and running a fiscal deficit?

The data showed that the government of Mexico actually balanced its budget deficit in 1992 (see Figure 6.7), the year in which it was running a surplus. Therefore, the problem must have come from its saving and investment. In figure 6.7 it also shows that Mexico's private saving was steadily decreasing, but its investment was increasing slightly after 1982. By 1993, its saving was only 17 per cent of GDP, yet investment was near 21 per cent of GDP. Apparently Mexico spent more than it produced and saved during the POL period. Therefore foreign borrowing must have financed excess investment over domestic savings and excess consumption of foreign goods.

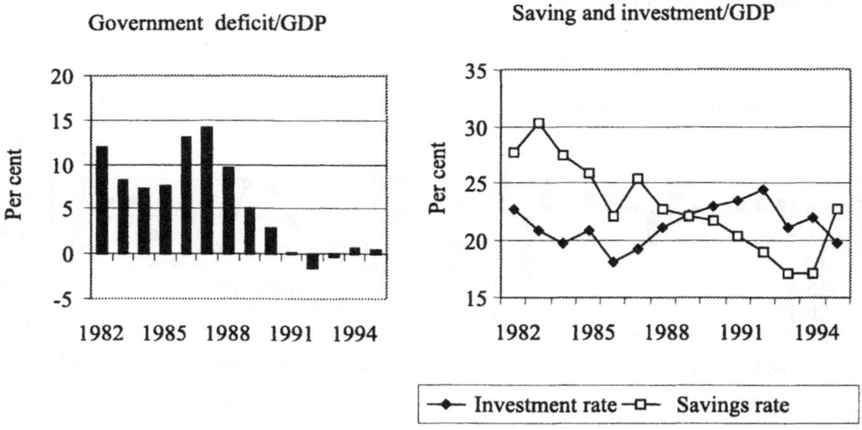

Figure 6.7 Mexico government deficit, savings and investment

In contrast to Mexico, China's real exchange rate has shown some mild correlation with its current account deficit (see Figure 6.8). The real exchange rate depreciated from 1993 to 1994 before its currency convergence reform. It then appreciated in the next two years and stayed the same in 1996 and 1997. While Mexico's exchange rate movement affected its current account deficit, China's real exchange rate has not moved much and thus has not played a determinant role in generating current account movements.

Examining China's macroeconomic identity, we see that China has had a current account surplus by virtue of its large accumulation of foreign reserves (see Figure 6.8). Since the current account surplus must equal the sum of T – G and S – I. Figure 6.8 shows that the government budget is nearly balanced.[15] In addition, its private saving and investment rates run as high as 40 per cent of GDP in POL period, with the saving side even higher (see Figure 6.9). So domestic savings are fully financing domestic investment, with plenty of savings left in reserve. Therefore, China is running surplus both in its domestic private savings net of investment and in its trade, the later contributing to large accumulation of foreign reserves.

Overall, China's macroeconomic situation is almost the complete opposite of Mexico's macroeconomic situation. China was running a current account surplus and accumulated a large amount of foreign exchange reserve. In contrast, Mexico was running a severe trade deficit with foreign exchange reserve depleted to negative. Internally, China's domestic investment is financed by its domestic savings with plenty of excess. In contrast, Mexico's domestic savings declined below its domestic investment, and its consumption of foreign good was in excess, so that its domestic investment and consumption had to be financed by foreign borrowing. Finally, China was stable politically, while Mexico was on the brink of a civil war. So from both macroeconomic and political perspectives, China is in a much stronger position to handle an approaching financial crisis than Mexico.

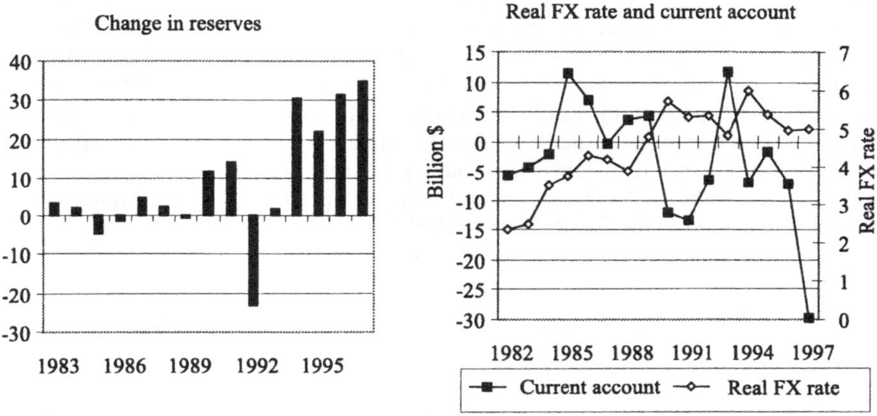

Figure 6.8 China reserves, real FX rate and current account

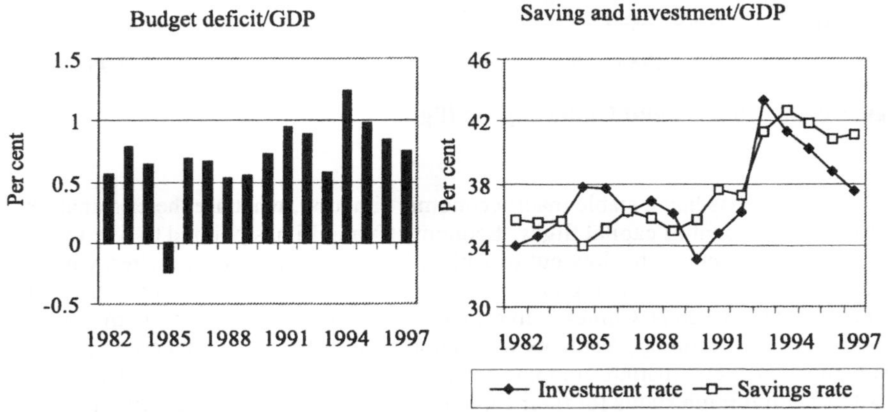

Figure 6.9 China budget, savings and investment

Capital Flight

Mexico had a negative net average capital inflow during the PRL period. Correspondingly, its capital flight was positive in the same period.[16] However, in the POL period, it experienced a continuous net inflow of capital until the end of 1994, when its economic problems began to multiply as its domestic spending exceeded its income, its current account ran a severe deficit, its foreign reserves ran down, and its currency devalued sharply. At the same time capital fled the country. Mexico suffered more than $30 billion dollars in capital flight in 1995 alone, according to the author's estimate (see Figure 6.10). As the Asian financial crisis approached, China was also experiencing a mild recession. Furthermore, its enterprises and bank reform had come to a halt since any radical move could trigger a financial crisis. Capital in China started to leave the country in large amounts. As much as $50 billion[17] 'took flight' in 1997, according to the author's estimate (see Figure 6.10), and over $40 billion in the first half of 1998.[18]

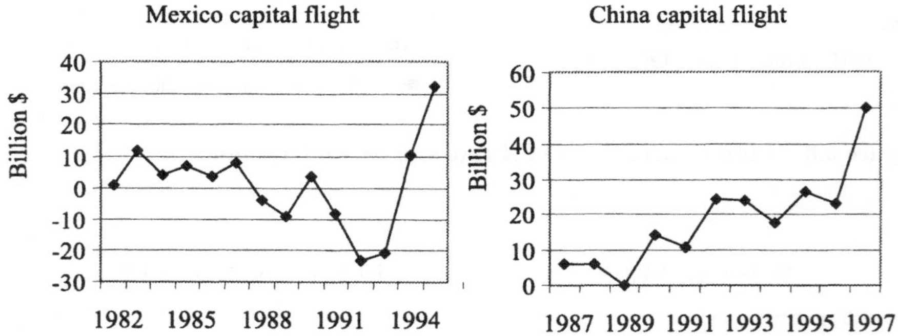

Figure 6.10 Mexico and China capital flight

Since China has had a stable macroeconomic situation, what are the explanations for this large amount of capital flight? Economist Yang Li has pointed to five factors that have caused money to flow out of China. Firstly, as mentioned earlier, China's capital market is severely regulated by the government, even kept artificially depressed, which sends Chinese investors in search of higher return in foreign capital markets. Secondly, residents with some kind of foreign status enjoy priority treatment in financial matters compared to the domestic residents. So residents often seek to obtain foreign status for their capital and then move the money out of China. Thirdly, even though China's RMB currency has not lost much face value over the years, the country's serious bad debt situation and lack of bank depositor insurance has eroded consumer confidence in its financial industry and national currency. Fourthly, China's domestic capital market offers few instruments, which could prevent currency risks, compared to foreign capital markets. For this reason, risk averse Chinese investors will seek to invest in more developed markets. In the fifth place, even though policy encourages getting rich first, China's legal system has not developed laws that adequately protect private property. Thus, in order to protect their property, these get-rich-first people, given connections and conditions, move their wealth abroad, especially those people who have made fortunes in public enterprises or functions related to their official positions.

How badly is this capital outflow hurting the Chinese economy? Less than normal and for the following reasons. Since 1992 China's economic reform has quickened its pace and expanded under more liberalized policies, especially in 1994, when reforms were initiated across the board in all areas of capital control, currency, fiscal policy, tax revenue, finance, and macroeconomics. These measures went a long way toward nullifying the negative force of capital outflow.

Moreover, China's persistently high savings rate, 40 per cent on average since 1990, and high investment yield has kept its foreign investment inflow at a high level, as well as its GDP growth rate. Finally, unlike other developing countries that receive investment funds in a wide variety of forms, China has received its funds mainly in one form, that is, foreign direct investment (FDI), which carries no interest payments. This form of equity finance has additionally provided China with excess capacity to pay other loans.

Lessons and Conclusion

What do we learn from this two-country case? Mexican capital flow up to 1994, the time of the peso crisis, has shown a very different pattern from that of Chinese capital flow up to 1997 and the Asian crisis. The differences arise for the following reasons. Firstly, Mexico had a freely convertible capital account and open, growing capital markets. China, had a freely convertible current account, but did not have a freely convertible capital account and only had a nascent but firmly controlled capital market. Secondly, during the peso crisis, the composition of capital flow in Mexico shifted from longer term to shorter-term duration and from mostly public risk sharing to individual risk sharing. Both changes contributed to the volatility of Mexico's capital movements. In contrast, China's capital inflow increasingly took the form of long term, foreign direct investment, thereby, markedly reducing its potential for volatility.

Thirdly, in Mexico both the internal and external macroeconomic situations were out of balance with overly low saving rates and overly high consumption rates, together with a severe trade deficit, high inflation and a zero level of foreign exchange reserves. In contrast, all macroeconomic indicators in China showed healthy signs, coupled with plenty of foreign exchange reserves. Finally, Mexico suffered political instability in the years immediately preceding the peso crisis, whereas, in contrast, China maintained a stable political situation preceding and throughout the Asian financial crisis.

With so many positive signs for China, is the country today safe from possible financial crisis? Few would agree it is out of danger. Discussion turns inevitably to China's inherent, long standing, internal financial and enterprise structure. If China does not radically restructure those two sectors, and quickly, bad debts carry the potential to eat up its excess domestic savings and foreign reserves and thus trigger a financial crisis, either before or soon after it begins to liberalize its capital markets.

What can China learn from what has happened to Mexico since 1996 and the end of its peso crisis? Mexico has in fact survived yet another financial crisis in the past four years, the Asian one, and finds itself in rather healthy economic condition. Mexico has taken the following steps in order to strengthen its fundamentals and increase its ability to cope with external shocks (Finance and Development, 2000).

- It has adopted a flexible exchange rate regime, which gives the monetary authority more autonomous power on control of monetary policy. It also efficiently regulates the balance of short-term verses long-term capital flows.
- It is continuously liberalizing its trade with the rest of the world, especially now with member countries of the Asian-Pacific Economic Cooperation (APEC) and also with six Central and South American countries.
- It has completely liberalized its capital markets to a point of full integration with world financial markets. Its government has reduced its role in the economy, for the most part limiting itself to providing public services and an adequate legal framework.
- It has taken measures to reform its tax system, in particular, making its collection regime more efficient, transparent, and progressive, thereby markedly reducing its dependency on oil proceeds.
- It has strengthened its banking system by creating new institutions for the protection of savings and by managing a new deposit insurance scheme. Mexico also has allowed foreign investors to hold majority shares in any Mexican commercial bank, regardless of size, and made impressive strides toward strengthening the regulatory and supervisory framework of the financial system. In addition, a new Commission for the Protection of Users of Financial Services was created to help provide more solid and extensive financial culture. Finally, Mexico's supervisory authorities have taken strong measures toward promoting the disclosure of financial information (both public and private), making it all the more transparent, timely, and accessible.
- Mexico currently does not have a government yield curve for fixed-rate securities with maturities of more than one year. Now Mexico has begun issuing a new fixed-rate, three-year government bond. Furthermore, a future and options market was established to provide market participants with better risk management mechanisms while fostering greater depth liquidity in the financial markets.

What lessons does this study offer other developing countries that wish to enter the global capital market, such as China? As long as capital flows freely, nations will be vulnerable to speculative attacks. China's experience may lend some support for a full capital control in the early stage of development in liberalization of domestic markets for countries with weak financial institutions. However, as reform deepens, the lifting of capital control becomes inevitable, then how fast and to what degree a country should lift controls come into question.[19] In China's case, the Mexico experience can lend some lessons for China in transiting into freely convertible capital account and opening up its capital market.

China must first proceed with its internal structural reform, while not forgetting to keep a strong macroeconomic balance, which includes low inflation, healthy domestic demand, and healthy public finance. Second, China can start finance service trade, even not full-fledged liberalization, and let foreign financial institutions enter financial markets in China. This will promote the use of a broad spectrum of financial instruments and allow the less distorted and less volatile capital flows, and promote financial sector stability and help to make the domestic financial institutions in becoming more competitive and efficient.[20] Third, China must have a sound-banking sector. Presently, China is engaging in the reform. Again, Mexico's experience can provide lessons for China. Fourth, China must build a regulatory and supervisory framework for the evolving financial markets. With a sound framework, financial markets can function smoothly. The supervisory functions can serve as information dissemination bodies that will disclose financial information to investors. Only by having transparent, complete, timely, and accessible information, can investors make less emotional more sensible decisions, thus enabling capital flow to be more healthy and less volatile. Fifth, China also needs to perfect its tax system, which can be used to regulating the types of capital flows. Finally, China must pick an appropriate exchange rate regime. China may consider a basket pegging system before transiting into a flexible system, since a flexible system will automatically correct any imbalances in trade flow and capital flow. However, the fluctuation may prove more painful without any hedging markets. Until it enters into a more mature stage China should eventually adopt a flexible exchange regime.

Surely, a developing country aims ultimately to achieve an open and free flowing capital market; this market will facilitate the allocation of capital and trade in a more efficient way. However, if the goal is not supported by a sound economic infrastructure, a financial crisis and the potential damage inherent in such a crisis may erode any efficiency, destroy any benefits, cancel any advantages, commensurate with, achieved through the opening and freeing of the capital market. In a developing or transition economy, a gradualist approach, with error on the side of caution, should be taken in building an open and free capital market.

Notes

1 The author thanks Michael Johnston and Shaomei Zheng for their comments on an earlier draft. The author also thanks Bill Carlson for his help in running some empirical tests and Pat Hall for her tireless editing.

2 Capital markets liberalization excludes currency control. A country can have fixed exchange regime with liberal capital markets.

3 Bai and Wei (1999) found the reverse may also be true. In a more corrupt country, the government would be more likely to adopt capital control since it could not effectively collect revenue through the tax system.

4 China had a nominally pegged-adjustable exchange rate at the time.

5 The correlation coefficient of capital inflow and GDP growth in Mexico is .556 with a p statistic of 0.035. This shows a significant positive correlation between the two variables.

6 The correlation coefficient of capital inflow and GDP growth in China is .164 and the p statistic is .554. This indicates an insignificant correlation between the two variables.

7 However, the correlation of capital inflow and the world interest (LIBOR) rate in Mexico is – .455 with a p statistic of 0.102. This shows an insignificant relationship. A larger sample study may show a more significant correlation (See Hausmann and Rojas-Suarez, 1996).
8 Correlation coefficient shows an insignificant relationship. However, a larger sample study may show a more significant correlation (See Hausmann and Rojas-Suarez, 1996).
9 There is a significant inverse correlation between the capital inflow and the world interest rate (LIBOR). The coefficient value is -.682, and the p statistic is .004. However, the correlation of capital inflow and G-7 current account (CA) is not significant.
10 This may explain why there is no significant correlation between the capital inflow and G-7 CA.
11 In 1994, Mexico stock market was dominated by money market instruments, such as 64.2 per cent of the trading (See Hausmann and Rojas-Suarez, 1996).
12 Furthermore, empirical study shows that foreign direct investments highly benefit domestic investment, while portfolio investments have no discernable impact on domestic investment (Boworth and Collins, 1999).
13 Finance and Development, IMF, March, 2000.
14 Mexico switched to a flexible exchange regime after the 1994 peso crisis.
15 The largest deficit in 1994 was only 1.2 per cent of GDP.
16 Capital flight here is estimated according to the World Bank method: Capital flight equals current account balance plus net direct foreign investment plus change of total external debt minus change of foreign exchange reserves.
17 Part of the $50 billion of 1997 actually left the country. For example, as money that was 'over-invoiced' by importers or 'under-invoiced' by exporters or money that was channeled by simple transfer to foreign branches. The rest of the money went into the vaults of domestic banks, as payment to cover the bad debts and dud debts of China's state owned enterprises.
18 This estimate is based on the statistics published by Cai Jing, 1998.
19 Premature removal of the capital control mandated by outside institutions could reduce rather than enhance economic efficiency (Bai and Wei, 1999).
20 Kono and Schuknecht, 1998.

References

Bai, Chong-En and Wei, Shang-Jin Wei (2000), 'Quality of Bureaucracy and Open-Economy Macro Policies', working paper.

China Statistics Yearbook, 1997, China Statistical Publishing House, Beijing, China.

Cooper, Richard N. (1999), 'Should Capital Controls Be Banished?' Brooking Papers on Economic Activities, Vol. 1.

The Economist, 'Will China be next?', 24 October 1998.

Edwards, Sebastian (1998), 'Capital Flows, Real Exchange Rates and Capital Controls: Some Latin American Experiences,' NBER Working paper 6800.

Edwards, Sebastian (2000), 'Controls on Capital Inflows: Do They Work?', NBER Working paper.

Feldstein, Martin (1999), 'A Self-help Guide for Emerging Markets,' *Foreign Affairs*, March-April.

Finance and Development, March 2000, Vol. 37 (1).

Huang, Yiping and Yang, Yongzheng (1998),'China's Financial Fragility and Policy Responses', *Asian-Pacific Economic Literature*, Vol. 12 (2), November.

International Monetary Fund (1997, 1998), *International Financial Statistics*, International Monetary Fund, Washington, DC.

Konoand, Masamichi and Schuknecht, Ludger (1998), 'Financial Services Trade, Capital Flow, and Financial Stability', Staff Working Paper, ERAD-98–12, WTO.

Leggett, Karby (2000a), 'China Promises Foreign Investors To Open Markets', *Wall Street Journal*, May 22.

Leggett, Karby (2000b), 'China is Showing Signs of Loosening Currency Controls', *Wall Street Journal*, May 25.

Li, Yang (1998), 'China's Capital Movements In the Opening of Economic Process Toward Outside', *Jing Ji Yan Jiu*, #2.

Li, Xingdan and Wei, Zhong (1998), 'Theory and Empirical Analysis of International Capital Flight in China', *Comparative Economic System*, #2.

Macroeconomic Research Group of China Social Science Academy, Economic Research Department (1998), 'General Situation, Financial Risks and External Shock', *Jing Ji Yan Jiu*, #3.

Macroeconomic Research Group of CCER (1998), '1998 Monetary Policy in Retrospect and 1999 in Prospect', Working Paper, October.

Pomponio, Xun (1997), 'Capital Flow in Mexico' in Zhang Chun, Zheng Decheng and Wang Yijiang (eds.), *Strategies for Bank Reform and Development of Regional Financial Center*, China Economic Publishing House, Beijing.

Pomponio, Xun (1998), 'Taiwan's Direct Investment in China: Its Impact on Mainland Manufacturing Trade, in Xinghai Fang and Shunfeng Song (eds.), *Raising International Competitiveness*, China Economic Publishing House, Beijing.

Rodrik, Dani (1999), 'Who Needs Capital-Account Convertibility?' Essay in International Finance Section, Department of Economics, Princeton, May.

Rodrik, Dani and Velasco, Andres (1999), 'Short-term Flows', The World Bank Annual Bank Conference on Development Economics.

Wei, Shangjin (2000), 'Risk and Reward of Embracing Globalization: The Governance Factor,' Paper prepared for the Plenary Session of the AERC Meeting. 21. Wei, Shangjin (1997), 'How Taxing is Corruption on International Investors?' NBER Working Paper 6030, forthcoming *Review and Financial Statistics*. World Table, World Bank, 1995.

Yi, Gang and Zhao Xiao (1998), 'Seeking For Effective Policy Combination under Multi Economic Targets', CCER Working Paper, No. c1998002, March.

Yu, Qiao (1998), 'Asian Financial Crisis and Our Country's Exchange Rate Policy', Working Paper, Singapore National University, Singapore.

Chapter 7

How Does Inward FDI Interact with Regional Economic Growth in China?

Kevin H. Zhang and Shunfeng Song[1]

Introduction

China's economic reform and its opening to the outside world since the late 1970s have been characterized by rapid income growth and huge inward FDI flows. Real gross domestic product (GDP) grew annually at nearly ten per cent during the period 1979–99. After two decades of opening up to the world in 1979, China had tripled its gross domestic product (GDP) twice by 1999. However, Chinese economic growth has been uneven as is evident from disparate growth rates especially between the eastern (coastal) and the western (far inland) regions of the country. The imbalance in economic growth between the two regions has been exacerbated since China further opened the coastal region in 1984. For instance, the economic growth rate of the eastern region was 11.4 per cent on average from 1984 to 1993, while it was 8.9 per cent for the western region, leading to an increased economic gap between the two regions. In 1993, the GDP per capita of the eastern region was 2.3 times as much as that of the western region (SSB, 1999).

The regional disparity can be attributed to many economic, political, and historical factors that are in favor of the eastern region. Among the main factors is inward flow of foreign direct investment (FDI). FDI flows into China rose dramatically with China's open-door policy such that China has become the largest FDI recipient among developing countries and the second globally since 1993 (UNCTAD, 1999). The FDI distribution within China, however, has been quite uneven, with majority in the coastal and large cities but very little in inland and rural areas. Using the city-level data, this paper examines the interaction between inward FDI and regional economic growth. On the one hand, regional disparities in China have significant influences on the location decisions of foreign investors because location advantages that attract FDI are determined by local labor cost and productivity, human capital, infrastructure and cultural-historical links to investors. On the other hand, FDI has been seen as one of the major factors to enhance local economic growth through capital formation, technology transfer and industrial upgrading, exports and access to international markets and human capital development and employment. Guangdong Province, for example, attracted 24 per cent of total FDI in China during 1985–95 due to its strong connection with Hong Kong and superior outward transportation capabilities. As a consequence, its GDP grew at an average rate of 16 per cent in the same period, greater than the national rate of 10 per cent. Surpassing Shanghai, Beijing and other prosperous regions, Guangdong has now become the richest province in China in terms of per capita income.

While many studies have been devoted to investigating determinants of FDI (for example, Song and Zhang, 1998; Zhang, 2001), economic impacts of FDI (for example, Borensztein et al., 1998) and regional income disparity in China (for example, Tsui, 1996), few studies have been carried out to examine how inward FDI interacts with regional economic development in China. One critical question raised in the existing studies is how FDI and economic growth in host countries are simultaneously determined. A salient feature of the previous studies is that most of them specify and estimate a single equation model in which the effects of FDI on economic growth and the effects of economic growth on FDI were treated independently. This approach, while useful in exposing certain characteristics of individual effects of two issues, is deficient in the sense that variables considered exogenous in the analysis may be in fact endogenous. By failing to capture the interdependence of FDI and economic growth, the single OLS equation estimates are likely to be biased and inconsistent. As suggested in the theory, the simultaneity between FDI and economic growth should not be dismissed casually.

In this chapter, we provide evidence on the interaction between inward FDI and regional economic development in China using 1994 data on 619 cities. Establishment of the interactive link between FDI and growth has important implications for development strategies. If there exist strong effects of FDI on growth then it would lend credence to the FDI-led growth hypothesis that FDI not only leads to structural transformation and industrial upgrading, but also promotes the growth of national income in the host regions. If the effects of economic growth on inward were supported empirically, then it would imply that growth may be a prerequisite for a region to attract FDI and the amount of FDI into the region would depend on its absorptive capacity. If FDI and economic growth are interdependent of each other, then a virtuous cycle would be expected between FDI and economic growth.

Theoretical Framework

Three possible links between inward FDI and regional economic growth are identified here: distribution effects of regional economic growth on FDI, distribution effects of FDI on regional economic growth and simultaneous interactions between FDI and regional economic development.

Effects of Regional Economic Growth on FDI

The literature on FDI suggests three advantages for a firm to go multinational: ownership, location and internalization, which are called the 'OLI' framework (Dunning, 1981). Studies focusing on location factors, given the other two, concern how differences in economic performance across regions within a country, along with other factors, determine regional distributions of FDI.

Such growth-driven FDI may be seen from three aspects: (a) Viewed as a substitute for domestic capital, FDI inflows would increase with an expanding domestic demand for capital generated by growth. (b) Improvements in human capital, labor productivity and infrastructure through economic growth would increase the marginal return to capital thereby expanding the demand for investment including FDI. More importantly, a certain level of human capital, labor productivity and infrastructure facilities is required for host countries (regions) to absorb technologies, know-how and managerial skills embodied in FDI (Zhang and Markusen, 1999). (c) The growth in the market size of a region through economic growth makes it possible for multinational firms to exploit economies of scale. Multinational firms are characterized by increasing returns to scale and they will start investing and will increase their investment with the emergence of expanding markets. In sum, other things being equal, rapid economic growth in a region provides a better investment environment and greater opportunities for making profits and therefore attracts greater FDI (Zhang, 2000a).

The growth-driven FDI hypothesis thus suggests effects of regional disparity on FDI distribution within a country. Especially for a country with vast geographical disparities in economic structure, natural resources, human capital, and infrastructure, an uneven distribution of FDI inflows are definitely to be expected. Given a country has already been chosen as an investing location, the amount of inward FDI to *i*th city might be determined by income growth (g_i), market size (Y_i) and other locational characteristics (Ψ_i) such as labor costs, FDI incentives, and special links with foreign investors, as summarized in the following equation:

$$FDI_i = F(g_i, Y_i, \Psi_i).$$

Effects of FDI on Regional Economic Growth

Recent studies of the impact of FDI on host economies and the ongoing international tournament of FDI among developing countries have implied a FDI-led growth approach. For a large country like China, the theory of impacts of FDI on host countries can be directly applied to the regional level. Contributions of FDI to host regions may be analyzed in the context of the effects of FDI on the basic growth-driving factors. Studies of growth theories have identified the factors that play a critical role in promoting economic growth as follows: savings and investment in the Harrod-Domar model; technical progress in the Solow model; human capital and externalities in the Romer-Lucas models. These growth-promoting factors can be initiated and nurtured to enhance growth through FDI. In fact, FDI has been integrated into theories of economic growth and international expansion and there is a 'gains-from-FDI' approach being developed that parallels in many respects the long-standing 'gains-from trade' paradigm (Graham and Krugman, 1995).[2]

This leads to an augmented production function with FDI as an additional input as follows:

$$Y = A\Phi(L, K^D, K^F, \Omega)$$

where

Y is output or GDP,

L is labor,
K^D is domestic capital,
K^F is FDI inflows,
A captures the technology used in the production, and
Ω is a vector of ancillary variables.

FDI is typically seen as a way of filling in gaps between the domestically available supplies of savings, foreign exchange, government revenue and human capital and the desired level of these resources necessary to achieve growth and development targets. FDI may have similar growth effects as domestic investment, to the extent that FDI adds to the quantity of the existing capital stock. Thus viewed as one type of investment, FDI may directly enhance host-country (region) growth. FDI can not only alleviate part or the entire deficit on the balance of payments current account, but also function to remove that deficit over time if the foreign-owned enterprises can generate net positive flows of export earnings. By taxing the profits of multinational firms, host (countries or local) governments are better able to increase their tax revenues.

The presence of FDI in host economies may be more critical than the direct impacts of FDI, since FDI creates channels through which economic impulses such as technology and managerial skills can be transmitted.[3] The technology and productivity of local firms may improve as foreign firms enter the market and demonstrate new technologies, provide technical assistance to their local suppliers and customers and train workers and managers who may later be employed by local firms (for example, Rodriguez-Clare, 1996). The competitive pressure exerted by the foreign affiliates may also force local firms to operate more efficiently and introduce new technologies earlier than would otherwise have been the case (for example, Kokko, 1994). FDI also serves as an important agent in fostering host country growth through exports by setting up assembly plants and helping host firms access international markets for exports (for example, Aitken et al., 1994).

Simultaneous Interaction between FDI and Regional Economic Growth

An interesting question concerns how FDI interacts simultaneously with regional economic development or disparity. Regional economic disparity leads to uneven distribution of FDI within a country and the uneven FDI distribution in turn has a feedback on the regional disparity, though the feedback might be positive or negative. In the literature, however, few studies have examined the simultaneous interaction. The purpose of this chapter is to close the gap by testing the interactive link with Chinese city-level data.

Interaction between FDI and Economic Growth in China: An Overview

The most impressive characteristic of the FDI trend is the boom in the 1990s in contrast to the moderate growth in the 1980s. Although a surge of interest among foreign investors in China emerged, large FDI inflows did not occur during the period 1977–83 because of poor infrastructure and the lack of experience in dealing with foreign investors. The next eight years (1984–91) witnessed the first FDI wave with relatively large amounts. In 1992 China seemed to reach its critical threshold of attracting FDI on a large scale. China's market size measured by GDP in 1992 was ten times as large as in 1977 and its annual GDP growth rate during the period 1992–99 was over ten per cent, the highest in the world. The single-year FDI flow in 1993 ($26 billion) exceeded the cumulative flows ($23 billion) of the fifteen years from 1979–91. At the end of 1999, the cumulative FDI inflow was recorded as $305 billion (SSB, 2000).

FDI has significantly contributed to China's income growth through formatting capital, transferring technology and managerial know-how, generating employment and promoting exports. The share of FDI in China's total fixed investment rose from less than one per cent in the early 1980s to 12 per cent in 1996. The huge fixed investment has been a major source of China's income growth. Guangdong province, for example, hosted 24 per cent of total FDI in 1985–96 and thus achieved an average growth rate of 16 per cent per year during that period, much higher than the national rate of ten per cent (SSB, 1997). The presence of multinational enterprises not only has led to a transfer of technology and management skills embodied in FDI but also has promoted competition, which has helped China in upgrading its industrial structure. FDI also has reduced significantly China's unemployment pressure. By the end of 1999, 17 million Chinese were employed in around 349,000 foreign affiliates (SSB, 2000). The role of FDI in China's exports has been even more prominent in both augmenting export volume and upgrading export structure. While China's exports in 1980 totaled $18 billion with 53 per cent in primary goods, the corresponding numbers in 1996 were $152 billion and 14 per cent. Exports by foreign affiliates in China rose 48 per cent annually in 1980–96 and exports in 1996 (mainly manufacturing goods) were $62 billion, comprising 40 per cent of China's exports in that year (SSB, 1999).[4]

The interaction between FDI and economic growth can also be observed at the regional and city level. At the regional level, China is usually divided into eastern, central and western parts. In the eastern part there are eight provinces, one autonomous region and the three central government municipalities. In the central part there are eight provinces and one autonomous region. In the western part there are six provinces and three autonomous regions. Table 7.1 presents the distribution of population, GDP and FDI in 1994 across these three regions (SSB, 1995). Relative to population, eastern cities have a higher proportion of GDP, indicating that there exists economic disparity across the three regions. The last column of Table 6.1 suggests that FDI is highly concentrated in the eastern cities. The eastern cities alone took more than 90 per cent of total FDI in 1994, with less than ten per cent for those central and western cities. Relative to population and GDP, FDI is much more unevenly distributed across Chinese regions, with almost all in the eastern part.

Table 7.1 Distribution of urban population, GDP and FDI, by region, 1994

Region	Population (million)	Share (%)	GDP (¥ billions)	Share (%)	FDI ($ millions)	Share (%)
Eastern cities	247.2	51.7	2029.1	65.0	26516.8	90.3
Central cities	156.6	32.8	746.5	23.9	5115.1	7.2
Western cities	74.1	15.5	344.8	11.1	750.6	2.6

Source: *Urban Statistics Yearbook of China, 1995.*

When aggregated to the provincial level, the data reveal a very uneven distribution of FDI across provinces. Table 7.2 shows the distribution of population, GDP and FDI among municipalities, provinces and autonomous regions. In 1994, Guangdong Province alone accounted for 28 per cent of total FDI. The next three largest FDI recipients were Jiangsu, Shanghai, and Fujian. These top four areas together accounted for 61 per cent of total FDI. That left less than 40 per cent of FDI for the remaining 25 central government municipalities, provinces and autonomous regions. In comparison, cities in these top four regions accounted 21 per cent of total urban population and 30 per cent of total urban GDP, respectively. It is interesting to note that the correlation coefficient between FDI and GDP is 0.78 at the provincial level, suggesting that FDI and GDP interact with each other very closely.

At the city level, the data show that FDI is highly concentrated in the four special economic zones (SEZ) and coastal open cities (COC). The four SEZs alone received 11.2 per cent of the total FDI in 1994. The 14 COCs accounted for 28.08 per cent of the total. The other 601 cities absorbed 60.7 per cent of the total FDI in 1994. In comparison, the four SEZs and 14 COCs together accounted 7.4 per cent of the total urban population and 17.7 per cent of the total urban GDP, respectively. In the next section, we will use city-level data to perform detailed analyses on the interaction between FDI and GDP.

Evidence of the Interaction between FDI and Economic Growth

As suggested in the preceding discussion, regional economic growth has significantly interacted with inward FDI flows in China. This section first examines two important issues related to FDI. (1) How do local characteristics, including GDP and government policies, determine inward FDI flows? (2) What role does inward FDI play in local economic development? Then we investigate how FDI and local economic growth are simultaneously determined.

Data used in this research come from the 1995 *Urban Statistics Yearbook of China* (SSB, 1995b). At the city level, this data set provides 1994 information on population, employment, capital assets, production, economic structure, government spending, infrastructure, investment, trade, tourism and many other categories. In the 1994 data there are 619 cities. Among them, four are special economic zones (SEZ) established by the Congress in August 1980, 14 are coastal open cities (COC)

Table 7.2 Distribution of urban population, GDP and FDI, by province, 1994

Province	Population 10000	Share (%)	GDP (¥ billions)	Share (%)	FDI ($ millions)	Share (%)
Beijing	724.1	1.5	97.2	3.1	1222.8	4.2
Tianjin	592.2	1.2	58.5	1.9	1015.0	3.5
Hebei	2045.7	4.3	124.0	4.0	377.0	1.3
Shanxi	1085.9	2.3	53.9	1.7	37.5	0.1
Inner Mongolia	727.0	1.5	37.1	1.2	68.0	0.2
Liaoning	2705.1	5.7	222.9	7.1	1445.7	4.9
Jilin	1599.7	3.4	73.2	2.3	179.7	0.6
Heilongjiang	1959.0	4.1	115.6	3.7	188.4	0.6
Shanghai	953.0	2.0	152.2	4.9	3247.3	11.1
Jiangsu	3701.0	7.8	291.4	9.3	3322.5	11.3
Zhejiang	2549.3	5.3	201.0	6.4	966.9	3.3
Anhui	1677.1	3.5	65.6	2.1	176.2	0.6
Fujian	1246.2	2.6	106.7	3.4	3014.3	10.3
Jiangxi	1177.9	2.5	44.4	1.4	204.0	0.7
Shandong	4664.2	9.8	317.7	10.2	2264.4	7.7
Henan	2447.8	5.1	117.7	3.8	369.2	1.3
Hubei	3038.4	6.7	153.9	4.9	665.9	2.3
Hunan	1943.1	4.1	85.1	2.7	226.4	0.8
Guangdong	4096.8	8.6	384.2	2.3	8202.2	27.9
Guangxi	1168.2	2.5	55.0	1.8	695.3	2.4
Hainan	274.8	0.6	18.4	0.6	743.4	2.5
Sichuan	3510.9	7.4	145.3	4.7	331.8	1.1
Guizhou	830.6	1.7	24.4	0.8	35.1	0.1
Yunnan	794.9	1.7	56.4	1.8	103.7	0.4
Shaanxi	920.1	1.9	43.8	1.4	199.3	0.8
Gansu	628.5	1.3	28.4	0.9	38.3	0.1
Qinghai	80.1	0.2	3.9	0.1	0.8	0.0
Ningxia	134.8	0.3	7.4	0.2	36.2	0.1
Xinjiang	484.9	1.0	35.2	1.1	5.6	0.0
Total	47761.3	100.0	3120.4	100.0	29382.5	100.0

Source: *Urban Statistics Yearbook of China, 1995* and author's calculation.

designated by the State Council in May 1984. In mainland China, there are three central municipalities (Beijing, Tianjin and Shanghai) and 27 capital cities of provinces and autonomous regions. In the data set, no information is provided for the two cities in Tibet. These two cities are excluded from our analysis.

Determinants of FDI

Hypotheses are first proposed, along with variable definitions. One set of hypotheses is that FDI is closely related to access to overseas Chinese. Previous studies (for example, Zhang, 2001 and 2000b) found that Hong Kong and Macao have far more business establishments in mainland China than any other areas or countries, followed by Taiwan, the United States and Japan. This research uses each city's number of overseas Chinese tourists (OCT) as proxy for its overseas Chinese connection. Overseas Chinese tend to visit their hometown or origins when they visit China and many of them would choose their hometown to make investments. The variable OCT includes all overseas Chinese tourists from Hong Kong, Macao, Taiwan and other countries.

The second set of hypotheses is related to government's role in FDI. Government affects FDI through its tax and open-door policies. For example, the Congress established four special economic zones (SEZ) in August 1980: Shenzhen, Zhuhai, Shandou, and Xiamen. To encourage foreign investment in these SEZs, the government offered many privileges to foreign investors in terms of taxation, land requisition, currency exchange and visas. In May 1985, the State Council designated 14 coastal open cities (COC). In these cities, the government offered an 80 per cent discount in corporation taxes for enterprises that are either joint ventures or solely foreign funded units. Due to the tax and other advantages in SEZs and COCs, FDI is expected to be higher in these cities. This research uses a dummy variable noted by the combination of letters 'SEZCOC' to represent these cities.

The third set of hypotheses is related to local economic conditions. One hypothesis is that FDI may be positively affected by the share of joint ventures (JV) of a local economy. This reflects the agglomeration effect on foreign investment. JV shows the ratio of workers in joint ventures to the total number of workers. Another hypothesis is that FDI may be related to some other factors such as labor quality and wage rates. More importantly, FDI could be related to market size and level of local economic development. Like other investment, FDI seeks high investment returns. If the polarization effect is strong in Chinese economic development, investment in more developed areas could be expected to yield higher returns. This research uses GDP to represent market size and local economic development.

Based on the hypotheses outlined above, a linear regression model is specified as follows:

$$LFDI = \alpha_0 + \alpha_1 LGDP + \alpha_2 X + \varepsilon, \qquad (7.1)$$

where *LFDI* and *LGDP* are the logarithms of FDI and GDP respectively
ε is an error;
and α_i ($i=0, 1, 2$) are vectors of coefficients.

X presents other factors affecting FDI, including *OCT*, *SEZCOC*, *JV*, and *WAGE* (annual city average wages for all workers).

In our regression, however, we found that *SEZCOC* and *JV* are highly correlated. *SEZCOC* is a dummy variable for special economic zones and coastal open cities, and *JV* is the ratio of workers in joint ventures to local total number of workers. Both show the degree of openness of the local economy, though *SEZCOC* may better reflect the efforts of local government in attracting FDI and *JV* may better reflect the results. Because of this high correlation, we only include *JV* in our final regression.

Role of FDI in Local Economic Growth

No doubt, FDI stimulates local economic development. First, it provides capital, which is scarce in every Chinese city. This enables local economies to start up many projects, generating multiplier impacts on local economic development. Second, new technology is introduced into China with FDI. The spillover impact of such new technology improves the productivity of the Chinese economy. Third, FDI may also bring new methods of management, which make production and services more efficient. With China moving toward a market economy, the functions of the market become more important in guiding investment and production. FDI could help Chinese firms better understand how a market economy works.

To investigate empirically the role of FDI in local economic development, this chapter uses a Cobb-Douglas type production function that relates gross domestic product (GDP) to FDI, domestic capital stock, population, human capital, local infrastructure, and local economy structure. A regression model is specified as the follows:

$$LGDP = \beta_0 + \beta_1 LFDI + \beta_2 Z + \xi \qquad (7.2)$$

where ξ is an error;

β_i $(i=0, 1, 2)$ are vectors of coefficients.

Z represents variables that also affect *GDP*, including *LK* (logarithm of domestic capital stock), *LPOP* (logarithm of population), *LB2* (labor share of the second, mainly the manufacturing sector, in the local economy), *PCPE* (population share of professional employees in the local total population), and *PCRD* (per capita paved road area).

Equations (7.1) and (7.2) are first estimated separately by using the ordinary least squares (OLS). Table 7.3 and Table 7.4 report the results. To reduce the multicollinearity problem and to improve the reliability of the statistical inferences of the individual variables, we limited the number of independent variables in our final regression models. The *t*-values are calculated based on asymptotically consistent variances. Hence, the problem of heteroscedasticity is addressed. The adjusted R^2-value of 0.50 for equation 6.1 indicates that the model is reasonably good in explaining FDI inflows in Chinese cities. The adjusted R^2-value of 0.88 for equation 6.2 indicates that the model fits the data very well for GDP and its determinants.

Table 7.3 Determinants of FDI: ordinary least squares results (dependent variable: LFDI)

Variable	Coefficient	T-Stat.
Constant	–30.9869	–9.045***
LGDP (Log GDP)	1.5301	13.529***
JV (Proportion of workers in JVs)	0.0458	6.271***
OCT (Overseas Chinese tourists)	0.0739	2.746***
LWAGE (Log of wages)	1.9932	4.579***

Notes: Adj-R^2=0.50. F-value=157.57. Number of observations=619. *** indicates that coefficient is significant at 0.01 level.

Table 7.3 shows that *LFDI* is positively and significantly affected by *LGDP*, with an elasticity of 1.5 (that is, a ten per cent increase in GDP would increase FDI by 15 per cent). This result strongly suggests that inward FDI is driven by domestic market size and the expanding domestic demand for capital generated by growth, confirming the growth-driven FDI hypothesis.

Table 7.3 shows a positive and significant coefficient for the variable *OCT*, indicating that hometown connection is an important factor attracting FDI. This hometown connection means that overseas Chinese investors find it much easier to negotiate and operate their businesses in China relative to western investors. In their hometowns, overseas Chinese investors share the same language and culture as the local people and often have relatives, friends and business ties there. All these, in turn, attract more FDI where this hometown connection is stronger.

The result for *LWAGE* shows an elasticity of 1.99, suggesting that FDI flow is higher in cities where average wages are higher. At first glance, this finding is unexpected because the theory predicts that multinationals seek lower labor costs However, lower cost for labor does not exactly mean lower wages. It is the combination of wages and labor productivity. Wages, on the one hand, represent money costs; on the other hand, they imply labor quality and incomes. The positive result for *LWAGE* suggests that benefits from better quality and higher incomes outweigh the negative impact of higher money costs. This finding shows that FDI goes to areas where wages are higher but labor quality and incomes are also higher.

The positive and significant coefficient for *JV* reflects the positive agglomeration economies in FDI in urban China. Foreign direct investment, like any other investment, has risks. By investing in areas where many joint ventures already exist, uncertainty and risks could be reduced. First, cities with more joint ventures have more experience with FDI and thus may have more comprehensive and stable policies toward FDI. Foreign investors are often concerned about the stability and continuity of Chinese policies on FDI. Observing more joint ventures in a city would make them feel more confident in investing in that city. Second, many FDI are made to produce similar products in a city, such as textile and toys. By locating closer, they can benefit from the agglomeration economies in production and the labor market. In turn, they are able to lower their production costs and thus increase their profits. Third, many foreign direct investments are export-oriented. They are highly dependent on customs services and responsive to markets in other countries. Locating in the same city enables these investors to share information in a more timely manner and to use services more efficiently. The practice of special economic zones and development triangles or districts provides opportunities for FDI to locate together. This tends to attract more FDI to the same locale.

Table 7.4 Determinants of GDP: ordinary least squares results (dependent variable: LGDP)

Variable	Coefficient	T-Stat.
Constant	6.2098	34.350***
LFDI (Log of FDI)	0.0802	15.794***
LK (Log of domestic capital stock)	0.2204	9.653***
LPOP (Log of population)	0.7255	25.286***
LB2 (Log of share of mfg labor in economy)	0.0053	3.795***
PCPE (Proportion of professional employees)	0.0101	1.447
PCRD (Per capita paved roads)	0.0328	5.294***

Notes: Adj-R^2=0.88. F-value=721.38. Number of observations=619. *** indicates that coefficient is significant at 0.01 level.

Table 7.4 shows that FDI plays a significant role in local economic development. The high t-value (14.5) confirms a statistically significant relationship between *LGDP* and *LFDI*, with an elasticity of 0.08 (that is a ten per cent increase in FDI would increase GDP by 0.8 per cent). Indeed, foreign direct investment stimulates local economies. As mentioned earlier, FDI brings in capital, transfers technology and managerial skills, creates jobs and promotes exports. It is worth noting that this research does not include exports in the GDP production function and regression due to the lack of data at the city level. In addition, we found that FDI and exports are closely related. For example, 40 per cent of China's exports in 1996 were contributed by foreign affiliates (MOFERT, 1998). Hence, excluding exports from our model would reduce the multicollinearity problem and would not cause significant changes in our regression results.

The results for Z show that *LGDP* is positively affected by capital stock (*LK*), population (*LPOP*), local economic structure (*LB2*) and infrastructure (*PCRD*, per capita paved road area). All these results are expected. For example, *LGDP* is found to be higher in cities where infrastructure is superior and local economy is more industrialized. It is interesting to note that the sum of elasticities for LFDI, LK, and LPOP is 1.03, suggesting that production is very close to constant returns to scale with respect (domestic and foreign) capital and population (labor).

To examine possible simultaneous interaction between FDI and GDP, equations (7.1) and (7.2) are estimated jointly with two-stage least squares (TSLS) using city level data. If there exists a simultaneous relationship between FDI and GDP, structural equations should be employed to perform regression analyses, meaning that equations (7.1) and (7.2) should be jointly estimated. Applying the ordinary least squares estimators directly to each equation would lead to biased and inconsistent results (Judge et al., 1982).

Table 7.5 presents the results. The results on variable *LFDI* and *LGDP* clearly suggest that FDI and GDP interact with each other simultaneously. The higher *t*-values of these two variables (15.79 and 13.53 respectively) show that this interaction is not only statistically significant but also simultaneous. With such close *t*-values, it is evident that causality goes both ways: from FDI to GDP and from GDP to FDI. This finding confirms our hypothesis of simultaneous interaction between FDI and economic development.

Table 7.5 Results using two stage least squares

Equation 6.1 Using log FDI as dependent variable			Equation 6.2 Using log GDP as dependent variable		
Variable	Coefficient	T-Stat	Variable	Coefficient	T-Stat
Constant	-30.5098	-8.883***	Constant	6.9178	29.617***
LGDP	1.3676	11.099***	LFDI	0.1669	14.517***
JV	0.0482	6.563***	LK	0.1673	5.895***
LOCT	0.085	3.129***	LPOP	0.614	16.578***
LWAGE	2.1744	4.949***	LB2	0.0035	2.013**
			PCPE	0.0162	1.897*
			PCRD	0.0179	2.328**
Adj-R2=0.50 F-Value=156.53			Adj-R2=0.82 F-Value=455.25		

Comparing the OLS regressions and the TSLS, we found some qualitative changes in estimated results. Using TSLS, the positive coefficient of PCPE become statistically significant, indicating that human capital plays a positive and important role in economic development (GDP). The FDI elasticity for GDP (equation 7.2) has been doubled from the OLS estimate to the TSLS estimate. Given the nature of the simultaneous relationship between FDI and GDP, OLS estimates are biased and inconsistent (Judge et al., 1982). Hence, our TSLS results should be more reliable. It is worth noting that care must be exercised in drawing conclusions regarding the total impact of changes in the explanatory variables because the two equations are simultaneously related.

Concluding Remarks

Since economic reform and the open door policies started in the late 1970s, China has been experiencing rapid economic growth with GDP growing at ten per cent per year on average during 1977–97. This rapid growth was accompanied by a boom in inward FDI, especially after 1992. In fact, inward FDI has interacted positively with economic growth in China. On the one hand, FDI contributes to China's economic growth through formatting capital, transferring technology and managerial skills, creating jobs and promoting exports. On the other hand, economic growth increases demand for foreign capital, expands the domestic market for FDI and improves capacity to absorb technologies embodied in FDI.

Using 1994 city-level data, the analysis found that more than 90 per cent of total FDI went to the more developed eastern region, with less than ten per cent of total FDI left for the central and western regions. At the provincial level, we found that most FDI went to rich provinces and cities such as Guangdong, Jiangsu, Shanghai, and Fujian. These top four areas together accounted for more than 60 per cent of total FDI. That left less than 40 per cent of FDI for the remaining 25 central government municipalities, provinces, autonomous regions. At the city level, the chapter has shown that FDI is highly concentrated in the four special economic zones and 14 coastal open cities. These 18 cities received 39 per cent of the total FDI in 1994, with the other 601 cities absorbing 61 per cent of the total FDI.

This chapter has empirically examined the interaction between FDI and regional economic development in China. It found that FDI is attracted by market size (GDP) and other factors including overseas Chinese investors hometown connections, the existing scale of foreign affiliates (joint ventures), and workers wages and quality. The chapter also found that GDP is determined by FDI, domestic capital, population, human capital, infrastructure quality and local economy structure. More importantly, the two-stage least squares regression results confirm that FDI and GDP interact with each other simultaneously. FDI positively and significantly contributes to local economic development and GDP is an important factor attracting FDI. Because of this simultaneity, the TSLS provides more reliable and consistent results on the impact of each factor in attracting FDI and promoting local economic development. It also better reflects the relationship between FDI and GDP.

Notes

1 This is a revised version of the paper presented at the conference of 'Developing through Economic Globalization: China's opportunities and Challenges in the New Century' in July 2000, at Shanghai, China.

2 The other theoretical view suggests that inward FDI is likely to be detrimental to host country economic growth. For more discussion of the issue, see surveys by Helleiner (1989) and Caves (1996).

3 FDI has long been recognized as a major source of technology and know-how for developing countries (for example, Caves, 1996). Indeed, it is the ability of FDI to transfer production know-how and managerial skills that distinguishes it from all other forms of investment, including portfolio capital and aid. The new growth theory typically

stresses that technology spillovers and learning by doing from FDI are important benefits for the host countries.

4 FDI has brought extra gains to China in facilitating its transition toward a market economy that started in the late 1970s and which in turn has enhanced income growth. These gains include stimulating the move towards a market economy by introducing a market-oriented institutional framework; contributing to changes in the ownership structure towards privatization by promoting competition and facilitating the reform of state-owned-enterprises and by facilitating the integration of China into the world economy.

References

Aitken, Brian, Hanson, Gordon and Harrison, Ann (1997), 'Spillovers, Foreign Investment, and Export Behavior', *Journal of Development Economics*, Vol. 43, pp. 103–32.

Caves, Richard E. (1996), *Multinational Enterprises and Economic Analysis*, 2nd edition, Cambridge University Press, Cambridge, Ma.

Dunning, John H. (1981), *International Production and the Multinational Enterprises.* George Allen and Unwin, London.

Graham, and Krugman (1995), *Foreign Direct Investment in the United States*, 3rd edition, Institute for International Economics, Washington, DC.

Helleiner, G. K. (1989), 'Transnational Corporations and Direct Foreign Investment', in Chenery, H. and Srinivasan, T. (eds.), *Handbook of Development Economics*, Elsevier Science Publishers, pp. 1441–80.

Judge, G. G., Hill, R.C., Griffiths, W.E., Lutkepohl, H., and Lee, T.C. (1982), *Introduction to the Theory and Practice of Econometrics*, John Wiley & Sons, New York.

Kokko, Ari (1994), 'Technology, Market Characteristics, and Spillovers', *Journal of Development Economics*, Vol. 43, pp. 279–93.

Ministry of Foreign Economic Relations and Trade (MOFERT) (Various years), *Almanac of China's Foreign Economic Relations and Trade*, MOFERT Press, Beijing, China.

Rodriguez-Clare, Andres (1996), 'Multinationals, Linkages and Economic Development', *American Economic Review*, September.

Song, Shunfeng and Zhang, Kevin H. (1998), 'The Spatial Pattern of Foreign Direct Investment in the People's Republic of China', in C. Jayachandran and G. Lin, *Advances in Chinese Industrial Studies*, JAI Press, London, UK.

State Statistical Bureau (SSB) (1992–2000), *China Statistical Yearbook*, China Statistics Press, Beijing.

State Statistical Bureau (SSB) (1995b), *Urban Statistical Yearbook of China*, China Statistics Press, Beijing.

Tsui, Kai-yuen (1996), 'Economic reform and inter-provincial inequalities in China', *Journal of Development Economics*, Vol. 50, pp. 156–72.

United Nations Conference on Trade and Development (UNCTAD) (1999), *World Investment Report 1999*, United Nations, New York.

Zhang, Kevin H. (2000a), 'Human capital, country size, and North-South manufacturing multinational enterprises', *Economia Internazionale/International Economics*, Vol. LIII (2), pp. 237–60.

Zhang, Kevin H. (2000b), 'Why is US direct investment in China so small?' *Contemporary Economic Policy*, Vol. 18 (1), pp. 82–94.

Zhang, Kevin H. (2001), 'What explains the boom of foreign direct investment in China?' *Economia Internazionale/International Economics*, Vol. LIV (2), pp. 1–24.

Zhang, Kevin H. and James R. Markusen (1999), 'Vertical Multinationals and Host-Country Characteristics', *Journal of Development Economics*, Vol. 59, pp. 223–52.

Chapter 8

Closing the Productivity Gap: The Role of Globalization in Shanghai's Economic Transformation

Kevin H. Zhang

Introduction

In more than fifty years since 1949 Shanghai's economy has shifted dramatically from agriculture to industry and more recently, services. Among the factors that have contributed to the transformation is foreign trade (particularly exports) and foreign direct investment (FDI). In the two decades since economic reform began, especially in the 1990s, the role of exports and FDI in Shanghai has burgeoned in ways that no one anticipated. With the highly touted Pudong new district open for business and the systematic effort to turn Shanghai into the nation's trade and financial center, Shanghai fever has been rising since the early 1990s, with a dramatic rise in the volume of foreign trade and inward FDI flows. The real GDP of Shanghai grew at 14 per cent per year from 1990 to 1998, much higher than national average during that period (SMSB, 1999). The city once again was seen as a shining example of 'roaring economic development'. In fact, Shanghai has gained back its status as the most important economic center, symbol of rapid economic growth and deep institutional reforms and prospective major financial center not only for the East Asia but also for the entire world.

Export orientation and FDI, along with human capital, have received widespread attention in the literature on economic growth. Exports have been singled out as an engine of economic growth with the presumption that higher exports can lead to more efficient allocation of resources, greater capacity utilization, economies of scale, adoption of more efficient technology or increased foreign exchange as a vehicle for importing superior capital goods and raw materials (Krueger, 1984; Din, 1994; and World Bank, 1993).

Recent studies suggest that FDI has been able to enhance the economic growth of host countries through spillover efficiency and technology transfer, in addition to capital formation, export promotion and employment augmentation (Das, 1987; Dutt, 1997; and Rodriguez-Clare, 1996). The spillover efficiency occurs when the advanced technologies embodied in FDI are transferred to domestic plants because of the presence of multinational firms. According to the new growth theory, the spillover affects host economies through changes in the nature of market concentration, and transfer of technological, managerial and financial practices in the industries that multinational firms enter.

The so-called new growth theory suggests that sustained long-run growth is largely driven by investment in human capital (Romer, 1986; Lucas, 1988). While investment in R&D and knowledge may be subject to diminishing returns, the utilization of such knowledge in production activities results in increasing returns. The new growth theory also emphasizes learning by doing, because input of human capital exhibits increasing returns to scale in the presence of these growth-promoting ingredients. In sum, human capital and learning by doing form the main springs of endogenous growth theory.

An assessment of the role of exports and FDI in Shanghai's economic transformation is of obvious importance. While some work has examined the effects of exports and FDI on the Chinese economy, few studies have been done to investigate the issue in the context of Shanghai using a reasonable theoretical framework and a reliable estimation approach. The purpose of this chapter is to shed further light on the role of exports and FDI, along with human capital, in determining the long-run economic growth of Shanghai. We find strong and robust evidence of positive effects of exports and FDI on economic growth and an interaction between human capital and growth in the export/GDP ratio and FDI/GDP ratio, which previous empirical studies have not considered. These results indicate not only the significant role of exports and FDI in Shanghai's productivity growth, but also a high degree of complementarity between globalization (through exports and FDI) and human capital accumulation. The results provide new empirical support for the hypothesis that FDI, as well as export orientation, contributes to economic growth through increasing returns to scale, more rapid adoption of foreign technology or more efficient utilization of scarce resources. In addition, we find that growth in manufactured exports has a strong influence on economic growth, whereas growth in primary commodity exports has a negligible influence. The results thus suggest that increasing returns and other efficiencies are mainly concentrated within the manufactured export sector. The policy implications from these findings are therefore supportive of a development strategy that stimulates long-run economic growth by simultaneously promoting manufactured exports and inward FDI, along with investment in human capital.

Exports and FDI in Shanghai

Exports in Shanghai during the past five decades show a sharp increase since 1972 relative to the moderate growth during the period from 1950 to 1971. (See Figure 8.1). While exports grew from \$104 million in 1950 to \$981 million in 1971 (9.4 times), the growth accelerated since then with exports of \$16328 million in 1998, resulting in a rise of 16.6 times. This point is also quite obvious by looking at the ratio of exports to GDP. Exports rose faster than GDP in both periods, but much larger increases in the export-GDP ratio took place from 1972 to 1998 (from 14 per cent to 37 per cent), contrasting with those from 1950 to 1971 (from ten per cent to 14 per cent). Another significant feature is the dramatic changes in the export-commodity composition, suggesting a rapid transformation in Shanghai's economic structure. Exports of manufacturing products rose from \$38 million in 1950 to \$652 million in 1971 and to \$15529 million in 1998. At the same time, the share of

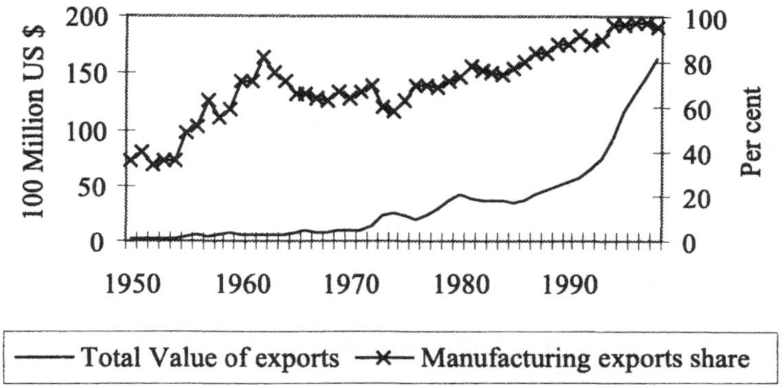

Figure 8.1 Shanghai's exports and manufacturing export share in total

manufacturing exports in total exports expanded from ten per cent in 1950 to 66 per cent in 1971 and eventually to 95 per cent (SMSB, 1999).

As happened in exports at the national level, changes in Shanghai's exports, particularly since the 1970s are the result of changes in international politics (the improvement in the relationship between China and the US in 1971) and China's economic reforms since 1979. The economic reforms, especially the reforms in the pricing of traded goods, led to the dramatic surge in Shanghai's exports and substantial changes in the commodity composition of exports in the reform era. These changes in exports and structure not only moved Shanghai's pattern of exports to one more congruent with its underlying comparative advantage than had been the case in the pre-reform era, but also greatly enhanced Shanghai's economic growth.

Figure 8.2 depicts the FDI trend in Shanghai over the period from 1981 to 1998 through its annual flows and its share in GDP. The most impressive characteristic of the trend is the FDI boom in the 1990s relative to the moderate growth in the 1980s. Three stages may be identified. The first stage (from 1981 to 1984) is characterized by a surge of interest among foreign investors in Shanghai, but not much actual investment. Large foreign investment inflows did not occur at this stage because both the demand and supply sides were perhaps trying to gain an understanding of each other. The second stage, from 1986 to 1991, was the first FDI wave and showed steady growth and a relatively large amount. FDI inflows stepped up noticeably in 1987 and continued to be strong until 1989, due in part to the extension of the special economic zones from four to another fourteen cities including Shanghai in 1984 and the increased incentives for FDI introduced in 1986. The next three years, from 1989 to 1990, showed slow growth due to a variety of factors. The Tiananmen Square incident in 1989 definitely hurt foreign investment because investors began to doubt China's political stability. The third stage, from 1991 to 1998, was the second wave and showed a sharp rise in both volume and the ratio of FDI to GDP, which has been heralded as a 'miracle'. FDI flows in the single year 1998 ($4.8 billion) exceeded the cumulative flows ($1.6 billion) for the eleven years

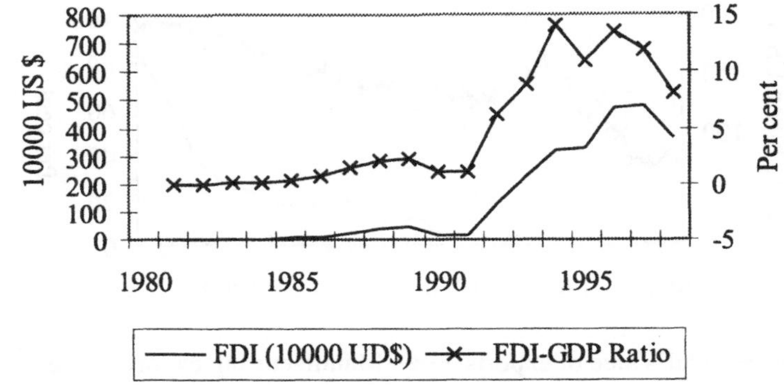

Figure 8.2 Shanghai FDI flows and ratio of FDI flows to GDP

from 1981 to 1991 by three times. The eight-year inflows from 1991 to 1998 amounted to $23.2 billion and accounted for 94 per cent of total FDI over the entire period from 1981 to 1998. At the end of 1998, the cumulative FDI inflows were recorded as $24.8 billion (SMSB, 1999). The boom in the 1990s was largely associated with Shanghai's Pudong new district as a special economic development zone and further liberalization of Shanghai's market to foreign investors.

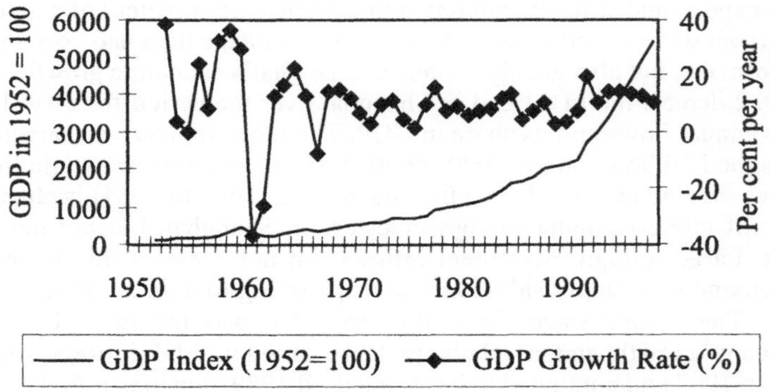

Figure 8.3 Shanghai GDP index and growth rate

Shanghai has experienced a dramatic transformation since the early 1950s. As indicated in Figure 8.3, Shanghai's GDP in 1998 represents a rise of 53 times over 1952 in constant prices, or annual growth rate of 9.1 per cent. Per capita GDP increased at a rate of eight per cent per year over the period from 1952 to 1998, and reached $3400 at the end of 1998, much higher than average level of the country. The important position of Shanghai in the national economy over the period from 1952 to 1998 may be seen from following indicators: Shanghai produced one twelfth of the country's industrial products; its port handled one fifth of national shipping cargoes; it made one fifth of the country's total exports; its fiscal revenue accounted for one ninth of the nation's total and 23 per cent of national college students were educated in Shanghai (SMSB, 1999).

The Model Specifications

Exports as an Engine of Growth

The role of exports in economic growth can be analyzed using the framework of a production-function model that treats exports as additional production inputs. Many studies have considered various circumstances in which total factor productivity is higher in export-oriented industries than in non-export-oriented industries. These include more efficient allocation of resources, greater-capacity utilization, economies of scale, more efficient adoption of foreign technology, and strong incentives for efficiency due to competitive pressures abroad (e.g. Balssa, 1978). One can then specify an aggregate production function fairly simply as:

$$Y = AL^{\beta_1}K^{\beta_2}, \qquad A = B\left[1 + \theta\left(\frac{X}{Y}\right)\right]X^{\alpha} \tag{8.1}$$

where
Y = real gross domestic product,
L = labor input,
K = capital stock,
H = human capital stock,
X = exports and
A = total factor productivity level.

This specification permits total factor productivity (A) to be endogenously determined by the volume of exports and the share of exports in GDP, as well as exogenous influences represented by the residual productivity factor (B) (Feder, 1982; Levin and Raul, 1997). Following the standard procedure in the literature, we take the total derivative in equation (8.1), dividing through by Y and slightly manipulating items in the right-hand side. Then we obtain the following expression describing the determinants of the growth rate of GDP:

$$\dot{Y} = \beta_0 + \beta_1\dot{L} + \beta_2\left(\frac{I}{Y}\right) + \beta_3\dot{X} + \beta_4\Delta\left(\frac{X}{Y}\right) + \varepsilon \tag{8.2}$$

where a dot over a variable indicates its rate of growth. β_1 and β_3 are output elasticities of L and X, β_2 is marginal product of capital, and β_0 as the constant term.

It has been recognized for long time that the productivity differential associated with the export sector is actually concentrated within the manufactured export sector (MX) rather than the primary commodity export sector (PX). This suggests following modification

$$A = B\left[1 + \theta_m\left(\frac{MX}{Y}\right) + \theta_p\left(\frac{PX}{Y}\right)\right]X^{\alpha}$$

where (MX/Y) and (PX/Y) are the ratios of manufactured export and primary export to GDP, respectively. The above specification leads to the following modified version of equation (7.2):

$$\dot{Y} = \beta_0 + \beta_1\dot{L} + \beta_2\left(\frac{I}{Y}\right) + \beta_3\dot{X} + \beta_4\Delta\left(\frac{MX}{Y}\right) + \beta_5\Delta\left(\frac{PX}{Y}\right) + \varepsilon \qquad (8.3)$$

where Δ in $\Delta(MX/Y)$ and $\Delta(PX/Y)$ indicates annual changes.

The coefficient on primary export share growth is likely to be statistically insignificant and very small in value relative that on manufacturing-export share growth. For comparison we also estimate the following model in which β_5 is assumed to be equal to zero.

$$\dot{Y} = \beta_0 + \beta_1\dot{L} + \beta_2\left(\frac{I}{Y}\right) + \beta_3\dot{X} + \beta_4\Delta\left(\frac{MX}{Y}\right) + \varepsilon \qquad (8.4)$$

Human Capital and its Interaction with Exports

The effects of human capital on economic growth may be captured by the following specification:

$$\dot{Y} = \beta_0 + \beta_1\dot{L} + \beta_2\left(\frac{I}{Y}\right) + \beta_3\dot{X} + \beta_4 H + \varepsilon \qquad (8.5)$$

where H is the value of the human capital that may be measured by various indices of human capital investment and attainment (such as a ratio of secondary school enrollment).

We postulate that export industries can utilize human capital more efficiently than non-export sectors. Educated workers, for instance, may be able to adapt more quickly to the sophisticated technology and rapid production changes required for competitiveness in world markets. The productivity in the export sector would thus rise with the level of education H. This leads to the following form of A in equation (8.1):

$$A = B\left[1 + \theta_0 + \theta_1 H\left(\frac{X}{Y}\right)\right]X^{\alpha}$$

By taking the natural logarithm and then the first difference of this equation and allowing for a direct impact of human capital on GDP, we obtain the following equation

$$\dot{Y} = \beta_0 + \beta_1\dot{L} + \beta_2\left(\frac{I}{Y}\right) + \beta_3\dot{X} + \beta_4\Delta\left(\frac{X}{Y}\right) + \beta_5 H\Delta\left(\frac{X}{Y}\right) + \beta_6 H + \varepsilon \qquad (8.6)$$

Now we reexamine the hypothesis mentioned before that the productivity differential is actually concentrated within the manufactured export rather than the primary export sector. Thus the total factor productivity A becomes

$$A = B\left[1 + \theta_0 + \theta_m H\left(\frac{MX}{Y}\right) + \theta_p H\left(\frac{PX}{Y}\right)\right]X^{\alpha}$$

Taking natural logarithms and first differences, and imposing the restriction that $\theta 0 = 0$, we then obtain the following equation.

FDI and its Interaction with Human Capital

$$\dot{Y} = \beta_0 + \beta_1\dot{L} + \beta_2\left(\frac{I}{Y}\right) + \beta_3\dot{X} + \beta_4 H\Delta\left(\frac{MX}{Y}\right) + \beta_5 H\Delta\left(\frac{PX}{Y}\right)_0 + \beta_6 H + \varepsilon \quad (8.7)$$

The role of FDI in economic growth might be analyzed in the framework of a production-function model that treats FDI as additional production input. Let Y be aggregate real output, L be the labor input, and K_D and K_F be stocks of domestic and foreign capital (K_F is from FDI flows), respectively. With the addition of a constant term (α_0) and a stochastic component (μ), we obtain the following expression, which is similar to equation (7.2).

$$\dot{Y} = \alpha_0 + \alpha_1 \dot{L} + \alpha_2\left(\frac{I_D}{Y}\right) + \alpha_3\left(\frac{I_F}{Y}\right) + \mu \quad (8.8)$$

where *ID* and *IF* are annual flows of domestic and foreign direct investment, respectively, $\forall_l$ is the output elasticity of labor, and α_2 (defined to be $\partial Y/\partial K$) and α_3 ($\equiv \partial Y/\partial K_F$) are the marginal physical product of domestic and foreign capitals, respectively. It is noted that many studies of economic growth in the literature include exports as production input in the production function (for example, Ram, 1987). In the case of Shanghai, however, exports are strongly correlated with FDI flows (the correlation index in the period 1981–98 is 0.92). This is because many FDI projects had been export-oriented under China's FDI regime in which FDI was invited exclusively for exports except offshore oil exploration and the real estate sector (UNCTAD, 1999).

Following the same procedure as in the case of exports, we specify following two equations with human capital and its interaction with FDI.

$$\dot{Y} = \alpha_0 + \alpha_1 \dot{L} + \alpha_2\left(\frac{I_D}{Y}\right) + \alpha_3\left(\frac{I_F}{Y}\right) + \alpha_4 H + \mu \quad (8.9)$$

$$\dot{Y} = \alpha_0 + \alpha_1 \dot{L} + \alpha_2\left(\frac{I_D}{Y}\right) + \alpha_3\left(\frac{I_F}{Y}\right) + \alpha_4 H + \alpha_5 H\left(\frac{I_F}{Y}\right) + \mu \quad (8.10)$$

In the following analysis, the estimated coefficient of I_F/Y (α_3) is of particular interest because it will indicate the direction and magnitude of the impact of inward FDI flows on economic performance.

The Data and Main Results

All data on *Y, L, I, X, H,* I_D, I_F and *X* are taken from *Statistical Yearbook of Shanghai* (1999) by Shanghai Municipal Statistical Bureau (SMSB), which contains five decades of historical data on the new Shanghai from 1952 to 1998. The descriptive statistics for the major variables used in the study are presented in Table 8.1.

To capture structural changes between the reform and pre-reform eras, a time dummy, which is equal to one for the period from 1979 to 1998 and takes a value of zero for the period from 1952 to 1978, is included in the estimations. A positive coefficient for the dummy is expected since exports would have large effects on economic growth in the reform period. The impact of exports on economic growth is tested with time-series data for the period from 1952 to 1998, while the effects of FDI on economic growth are estimated with time-series data for 1981 through 1998.

The parameter estimates of equations (8.2)(8.3) and (8.4), which focus on effects of exports and manufacturing exports on income growth, are given in Table 8.2. The main results of the models with human capital and the interaction with exports, equations (8.5)(8.6) and (8.7), are presented in Table 8.3. Table 8.4 reports estimation results for the three different specifications on the economic impact of FDI in Shanghai.

Table 8.1 Sample statistics: characteristics of Shanghai, 1952 to 1998

Variables	Mean	Stand. Dev.	Max	Min
GDP growth rate (%)	0.0990	0.1279	0.3850	–0.3690
Population growth rate (%)	0.0195	0.0586	0.3697	–0.0598
Investment/GDP	0.2696	0.1784	0.6700	–0.0200
Total export growth rate (%)	0.1267	0.1845	0.7414	–0.1669
Total export share of GDP	0.2222	0.0780	0.3967	0.0964
Total export share growth	0.0056	0.0347	0.1153	–0.0913
Manufactured export share of GDP	0.1697	0.0929	0.3827	0.0435
Manufactured export share growth	0.0068	0.0278	0.1298	–0.0326
Primary export share of GDP	0.0532	0.0267	0.1256	0.0100
Primary export share growth	–0.0011	0.0157	0.0446	0.0157
Secondary school enrollment (%)	5.9683	2.2746	11.8500	2.2746

The following points are easily discerned from Tables 8.2 through 8.4. First, in all relevant cases, the export and FDI variables have relatively large and statistically significant coefficients. The overall picture of the estimates in Table 8.2 is very similar to that of the panel estimates in Table 7.3, except for the larger explanatory power in the models with human capital and its interaction terms with exports. This is also true for estimations of the three FDI equations. Comparison of estimations from the specifications including export-human capital terms and FDI-human capital terms with those without exports and FDI variables highlights the superior explanatory power of the former in terms of adjusted R^2. The results thus lend strong support to the widely held observation that exports and inward FDI flows, along with improvements in human capital, have had the positive impact on Shanghai's economic performance. The finding of positive effects of exports and FDI on economic growth is quite consistent with previous studies such as Balassa (1978), Feder (1982), Ram (1987), Balasubramanyam, Salisu and Sapsford (1996), and Borensztein, DeGregorio and Lee (1998).

Table 8.2 Linear effects of exports on GDP growth: 1952 to 1998

Independent Variables	Model 7.2	Model 7.3	Model 7.4
$\dot{L}$	0.74 (1.97)*	0.68(1.82)*	0.76(1.75)*
I/Y	0.21(0.65)	0.17(1.01)	0.19(0.77)
$\dot{X}$	0.14(2.65)**	0.16(3.40)***	0.20(2.38)**
D (dummy)	0.65(2.64)**	0.54(2.78)**	0.57(2.41)**
(X/Y)	0.38(2.01)*		
(MX/Y)		0.42(2.60)**	0.42(4.08)***
(PX/Y)		-0.09(-1.00)	
Adjusted R^2	0.65	0.68	0.70
DW-Statistic	2.01	1.97	1.86

Notes: The dependent variable is growth rate of real GDP (%). Number of observations is 46 for all estimations. Figures in parentheses are t-statistics. The asterisks ***, **, and * indicate levels of significance at 1%, 5%, and 10%, respectively. The estimates of coefficients of constant terms and time trend are omitted to save space.

Table 8.3 Interaction between human capital and exports, 1952 to 1998

Independent Variables	Model 7.5	Model 7.6	Model 7.7
$\dot{L}$	0.70(1.77)*	0.71(1.60)	0.74(1.95)*
I/Y	0.21(0.69)	0.17(0.75)	0.19(0.38)
$\dot{X}$	0.14*(2.80)**	0.16(5.35)***	0.20(2.38)**
D (dummy)	0.45(2.50)**	0.41(2.33)**	0.50(2.71)**
)(X/Y)		0.37(2.66)**	
H	–0.05(–1.21)	–0.04(–0.87)	0.42(0.52)
H•)(X/Y)		0.19(4.16)***	
H•)(MX/Y)			0.26(4.02)***
H•)(PX/Y)			–0.07(–1.03)
Adjusted R^2	0.69	0.72	0.74
DW-Statistic	1.88	1.90	1.75

Notes: The dependent variable is growth rate of real GDP (%). Number of observations is 46 for all estimations. Figures in parentheses are t-statistics. The asterisks ***, **, and * indicate levels of significance at 1%, 5%, and 10% respectively. The estimates of coefficients of constant terms and time trend are omitted to save space.

Table 8.4 Effects of FDI and human capital on GDP growth, 1981 to 1998

Independent Variables	Model 8	Model 9	Model 10
$\dot{L}$	1.08(1.89)*	1.00(1.77)*	1.12(1.81)*
DI/Y	0.11(1.39)	0.14(0.92)	-0.17(1.01)
FDI/Y	0.46(2.44)**	0.43(2.60)***	0.32(2.33)**
H		-0.33(1.02)	-0.36(-0.98)
H•(FDI/Y)			1.09(1.75)*
Adjusted R^2	0.65	0.71	0.73
DW-Statistic	2.22	1.98	1.82

Notes: The dependent variable is growth rate of real GDP (%). Number of observations is 17 for all estimations. Figures in parentheses are t-statistics. The asterisks ***, **, and * indicate levels of significance at 1%, 5%, and 10% respectively. The estimates of coefficients of constant terms and time trend are omitted to save space.

These results indicate that Shanghai's experience is similar to that of the so-called high-performing economies of East Asia. That is, the rapid growth of manufacturing exports, combined with improvements in human capital, led to high rates of growth of total factor productivity. As the World Bank (1993) suggests, this is because exports help Shanghai adopt and master international best-practice technologies. At the firm level, labor with high levels of education is better able to adopt, adapt, and master technology. Therefore, exports and human capital interact to provide rapid growth in total factor productivity.

Second, the effect of exports on economic performance is clearly larger in the reform period (from 1979 to 1998) than in the pre-reform era (from 1952 to 1978), as suggested by the significant and positive coefficients of the dummy variables in Tables 8.2 and 8.3. The result is anticipated from the consideration that the reform in trade regimes and prices based on comparative advantage might have resulted in an improvement in production efficiency in both trade sectors and non-trade sectors and therefore had a greater impact on economic growth. At the start of its economic reforms in the late 1970s, China (including Shanghai) was an insignificant participant in international trade and international capital markets. Since the reforms began in 1978 Shanghai as well as China has emerged as major trading economies and exports have begun to exert a greater influence on domestic economic activity than at any other period in the history. Shanghai's outward-orientation is successful not simply in terms of the sustained growth of exports and rising inward FDI flows, but also a significant increase in the growth of Shanghai's economy. As indicated, Shanghai's GDP indeed grew fastest in China in the 1990s, while China as a whole was the fastest growing economy in the world.

Third, the results from models (8.3) and (8.4) of Table 8.2, and (8.7) of Table 8.3 show that the contributions of exports to economic growth concentrate on manufacturing exports rather than primary exports. The coefficient of change in manufacturing export share in GDP has the right sign and is statistically significant in Table 8.2, while the coefficient for changes in primary exports share in GDP is negative but not statistically significant. The interaction of manufacturing exports with human capital in Table 8.3 has positive and significant effects on economic growth. The large share of manufacturing exports in total exports indicates a successful transformation of economic structure from agricultural to industry, and more recently to services.

Fourth, the coefficients of FDI are numerically much larger than those of domestic investment in the three models of Table 8.4. This result is consistent with the predictions of the FDI theories that marginal product of foreign capital should be greater than that of domestic capital, because a multinational firm must possess some special advantages such as superior technology to overcome inherent disadvantages and high costs of foreign production (Caves, 1996; Zhang and Markusen, 1999, and Zhang, 2000).

Concluding Remarks

This study attempts to assess the impact of exports and FDI on Shanghai's economic performance, based on the augmented production function approach with time-series data for the period from 1952 to 1998 (for exports) and the period from 1981 to 1998 (for FDI). The estimates indicate that both exports and FDI do seem important to Shanghai's economic growth and the importance of exports seems to have increased from the period 1952 to 1977 to the period 1978–1998, as we might have suspected. While the impact of exports on growth seems to be larger, the contribution mainly comes from manufacturing exports rather than primary product exports. Finally, FDI has been shown to be critical to the increase in total factor productivity and the marginal product of foreign capital seems to be significantly larger than that of domestic capital, which is quite consistent with theories of FDI.

Shanghai's success in globalization through exports suggests that good export performance could make a major contribution to economic growth through the following channels: increasing specialization and expanding the efficiency-raising benefits of comparative advantage; offering greater economies of scale due to an enlargement of the effective market size; affording greater capacity utilization and inducing more rapid technological changes.

While Shanghai's case in using FDI reported here might be similar to the coastal region of China, Shanghai's experience should be considered within the entire Chinese economy, which is somewhat unique in the sense of its large country-size, its strong government, and its on-going transition from a planned to a market economic system. China's advantages over many developing countries in country-size plus centralized and strong government have provided it with negotiating power in the world trade system and control to some extent over adverse effects and the opportunity to realize positive effects of trade and FDI. In fact, opening-up (especially attracting FDI) does not necessarily lead to rapid economic growth. As mentioned by Helleiner (1988) and Caves (1996), inward FDI is likely to be detrimental to host economic growth because, for example, (a) FDI might lower domestic savings and investment and lead to shrinking of indigenous industries; (b)

FDI may reduce a host country's welfare when multinational firms manipulate market power and transfer pricing and (c) FDI may create enclave economies within a host country, widen income gaps, and bias the host economy toward an inappropriate technology and product mix.

The experiences of Shanghai as well as China are definitely a successful story. In addition to the benefits generated in capital formation, employment augmentation, export promotion and human capital development, FDI seems to have brought extra gains to Shanghai as well as China in facilitating its transition toward market systems, which in turn have enhanced Shanghai's income growth. These gains include stimulating the transition by introducing a market-oriented institutional framework; contributing to changes in the ownership structure toward privatization by promoting competition and facilitating the reform of state owned enterprises; and facilitating the integration of Shanghai into the world economy. As a result, FDI seems to have been the engine of Shanghai's economic growth.

It should be noted that other forces that affect Shanghai's economic growth may exist but were excluded from the investigation. This work, therefore, should not be treated as an exhaustive study of economic growth in Shanghai but, rather, as a narrowly focused investigation of the merits of FDI.

References

Balassa, B. (1978), 'Exports and economic growth: further evidence', *Journal of Development Economics*, Vol. 5, pp. 181–9.

Balasubramanyam, V. N., Salisu, M. and Sapsford, David (1996), 'Foreign direct investment and growth in EP and IS countries', *The Economic Journal*, Vol. 106 (January), pp. 92–105.

Borensztein, E., De Gregorio, J. and Lee, J-W (1998), 'How does foreign direct investment affect economic growth?', *Journal of International Economics*, Vol. 45, pp. 115–135.

Caves, Richard (1996), *Multinational Enterprises and Economic Analysis*, 2nd edition, Cambridge, MA: Cambridge University Press.

Das, Sanghamitra (1987), 'Externalities, and technology transfer through multinational corporations: A theoretical analysis', *Journal of International Economics*, Vol. 22, pp. 171–82.

Din, Muslehud (1994), 'Export processing zones and backward linkages', *Journal of Development Economics*, Vol. 43, pp. 369–85.

Dutt, Amitava K. (1997), 'The pattern of direct foreign investment and economic growth', *World Development*, Vol. 25 (11), pp.1925–36.

Feder, Gershon (1982), 'On exports and economic growth', *Journal of Development Economics*, Vol. 12, pp. 59–73.

Helleiner, G. (1989), 'Transnational corporations and direct foreign investment', in Chenery, H. and Srinivasan, T. N. ed., *Handbook of Development Economics*, Elsevier Science Publishers B.V., pp. 1441–80.

Levin, Andrew, and Lakshmi, Raul (1997), 'Complementarities between exports and human capital in economic growth: Evidence from the semi-industrialized countries', *Economic Development and Cultural Changes*, Vol. 46 (1), pp. 155–74.

Lucas, Robert (1988), 'On the mechanics of economic development', *Journal of Monetary Economics*, Vol. 22 (1), pp. 3–42.

Ram, Rati (1987), 'Exports and economic growth in developing countries: Evidence from time-series and cross-section data', *Economic Development and Cultural Changes*, Vol. 36 (1), pp. 51–72.

Rodriguez-Clare, Andres (1996), 'Multinationals, linkages and economic development', *American Economic Review*, Vol. 86 (4), pp. 852–73.

Romer, Paul (1986), 'Increasing returns and long-run growth', *Journal of Political Economy*, Vol. 94 (5), pp. 1002–37.

Shanghai Municipal Statistical Bureau (SMSB) (1999), *Shanghai Statistical Yearbook 1999*, China Statistics Press, Beijing, China.

United Nations Conference on Trade and Development (UNCTAD), *World Investment Report 1999*, United Nations, New York.

World Bank (1993), *The East Asia Miracle: Economic Growth and Public Policy*, Oxford University Press, New York.

Zhang, Kevin H. (2000), 'Human capital, country size, and North-South manufacturing multinational enterprises', *Economia Internazionale / International Economics*, Vol. LIII (2), pp. 237–60.

Zhang, Kevin H. and Markusen, James (1999), 'Vertical multinational and host-country characteristics', *Journal of Development Economics*, vol. 59, pp. 233–52.

Chapter 9

China's Health Care System Reform under Globalization

Ling Li and Peter Yuen

Introduction

Recently, health care and health care system reform have become dominant economic and political issues around the world. On the one hand, as living standards improve, people's life expectancy is rising. The demand for health care is increasing rapidly. On the other hand, due to the adverse incentives that exist in current health care systems, there are many instances of unnecessary services, waste and fraud in heath care. All these cause escalating health care costs and limited access to health care services in many countries. How to control health care costs and provide comprehensive health care coverage for the people is a worldwide unsolved problem.

As China enters the WTO, the opening of its financial and insurance market will bring new opportunities and challenges for reforming China's health care system. In a sense whether China can successfully catch the chance and reform its health care system will determine whether it can maintain its long-term economic growth and social stability. Ever since the start of economic reform, the Chinese government has introduced a number of experiments aimed at reforming its health care system (World Bank, 1996; Liu and Hsiao, 1995; Yuen, 1996). Based on the results of these experiments, the model of China's future health care system consists of individual medical savings accounts and social pooling funds.

While China is painstakingly reforming its health care system, western countries, most noticeably, the United States, are reforming their health care systems. Although President Clinton's universal coverage plan failed, the debate over health care reform has never stopped. The Clinton administration tried various ways and passed many bills to reform the US health care system. Under 'The Health Insurance Portability and Accountability Act', which became effective in 1997, more than one million people have already become part of an experiment testing the controversial arrangement known as medical savings accounts (Li, 1999).

Widespread application of individual Medical Savings Accounts (MSA) in providing efficient health care for a country's citizens is just a recent phenomenon. In the MSA program, instead of paying health insurance for their employees, enterprises contribute a fixed amount of money into their employees' medical savings accounts. Employees will pay for their routine health care expenses out of their MSA. The MSA fundamentally changes the patients' incentives and behavior. This program is widely considered as an effective way of controlling health care cost and reducing waste.

Historically, China and the US have had very different health care systems. However, both systems are being reformed and both countries have experimented with individual medical savings accounts. In this chapter we will briefly review the heath care systems and efforts at reform around the world. More attention will be given to the US health care system, efforts at reform and possible lessons for China. Facing the opportunity that China will join the WTO, we will further analyze China's health care system reform under globalization and make a few policy proposals accordingly.

We believe that adopting an MSA approach has merit for reforming China's health care system, since this approach follows the trend of health care reform, namely, decentralization and incorporating market mechanisms. MSA could significantly reduce the abuse and over-consumption of medical service caused by lack of incentives to control costs on both the patients' side and the health care providers' side. For the treatment of major illnesses, the current experiment is mainly financed by citywide pooling of funds. There are many disadvantages to this scheme:

- For the citywide pooling funds, the risk-sharing function is very limited.
- The management of the medical pooling funds is controlled by government and is inefficient.
- The citywide pooling funds hamper labor mobility.

Since China's financial market and insurance markets are still underdeveloped, there are not many choices but to use the pooling funds to pool the risk in the previous experiment. Now WTO and globalization will speed up the development of Chinese financial and insurance markets, which will enable China to adopt market mechanisms to diversify the risk associated with major illness. Therefore, we suggest that the Chinese government should abolish the current social pooling scheme and adopt catastrophic insurance through private insurance companies.

We propose that China's new health care system should consist of the MSA and catastrophic insurance, which are portable when workers change jobs and locations. Then the MSA and catastrophic insurance will provide a nation-wide health care system. The government will no long get involved in the provision of health care and the management of pooling funds, but will enact and implement laws and rules. Government regulation and market competition will force insurance companies to provide high quality services at cheaper prices. In this way, health risk will be spread out and effectively shared across the population. Labor mobility will not be tied to the job and location. Such a system can balance the cost containment and risk sharing function. Also it is flexible, manageable and can quickly adjust to a new market environment.

The rest of the chapter is organized as follows: The next section briefly reviews the current trend of health care system reform around the world. The section after that reviews the US health care system and efforts at reform. The section after that reviews China's health care system. The final section discusses the reform of China's health care system and provides some suggestions.

The Current Trend of Health Care System Reform Around the World

Currently, there are four basic types of health care systems in the world:

- Traditional sickness insurance, which is the private insurance market approach, with state subsidy. Coverage is basically employment related. The countries that have this type of health care system are Germany, Austria, Belgium and France.
- National Health Insurance, which is a national-level health insurance program established by the state. Canada, Sweden, Norway, and Spain have this system.
- National Health Service, which involves the state directly providing health care to its citizens and residents. The UK, Denmark, Greece and the former socialist countries have this system.
- Mixed systems, which combine elements of the above programs. The US, Japan, South Korea and Switzerland have these systems.

Table 9.1 shows average health spending as a proportion of GDP in selected OECD countries in 1997, the latest year for which comparative data are available. The US is still, by far, the largest spender on health care, outspending other OECD countries on an average per capita basis by 2.5 to 1 (Table 9.1). The annual per capita spending on health in the U.S. amounted to $4,095 in 1997, compared with an average of $1,615, calculated on a purchasing power parity basis, for the OECD as a whole and $1,698 in the European Union. Switzerland was the second highest spender per capita on health care after the US, followed by Germany and Canada. Higher expenditures on health in individual countries appear to be related mainly to the level of average incomes in these countries, regardless the health care system. No matter what type of health care systems they have, many countries have faced runaway health care costs and limited coverage problems, especially during the 1970s and 1980s. After a decade or more of health-care reforms in many OECD countries, the percentage of GDP devoted to health care declined slightly from 1996 to 1997 in several countries, while in other countries it stabilized, marking a pause or reversal in a previously rising trend that had caused concern among policy analysts. In many cases, modest declines were related to both economic upswings in countries and reforms that have limited the rate of increase in health spending in relation to the rate of GNP growth.

The trend of health care reform in OECD countries is toward decentralization and installing more elements of competition in the health care sector. For example the UK has the National Health Service system. In order to introduce market mechanisms, the government lets hospital and community health services become self-governing trusts, and district authorities become purchasers of care. This separation of the purchaser and provider roles has created an internal market. A hospital would now survive only if it could attract sufficient patients (Ham and Brommels, 1994).

Since the US combines all the different health care systems, let us take a brief look at its system and reform.

Table 9.1 Total expenditure on health in 1997 and trends from 1970–1996

	Spending per capita $PPP	Growth of Expenditure per capita (NCU at 1995 prices)			Health spending as % GDP	
		Average annual growth rate				
		1970–80	1980–90	1990–96	1996	1997
Australia	1909	3.3	2.6	3.0	8.0	8.3
Canada	2175	3.1	2.5	0.4	9.3	9.2
Denmark	2042	7.4	0.6	2.6	8.1	8.0
Finland	1525	5.0	3.1	–2.3	7.8	7.4
France	2047	6.6	4.5	2.3	9.8	9.6
Germany	2364	5.6	1.3	2.2	10.8	10.7
Greece	1196	n/a	n/a	n/a	8.4	8.6
Italy	1613	7.8	1.9	0.9	7.8	7.6
Japan	1760	n/a	2.3	3.7	7.1	7.2
Korea	870	n/a	n/a	n/a	5.9	6.0
NZ	1357	–1.1	–0.7	–1.3	7.3	7.6
Norway	2017	7.9	2.3	1.8	7.8	7.5
Spain	1183	5.8	5.3	2.6	7.4	7.4
Sweden	1762	n/a	n/a	n/a	8.6	8.6
Switz	2611	2.1	3.0	1.6	10.1	10.0
UK	1391	4.7	1.8	2.2	6.9	6.8
US	4095	3.6	2.8	1.1	14.1	13.9

Source: OECD Health Data 1999.
Notes:
a. Total expenditure on health includes public and private spending.
b. Purchasing power parities (PPPs) provide a means of comparing health spending between countries on a common base. PPPs are the rates of currency conversion that equalize the cost of a given 'basket' of goods and services in different countries.
c. NCU National Currency Unit.
d. n/a not available.

The US Health Care System and Reform

The US health care system is a mixed system. Health insurance is provided by employment-related insurance, the private insurance market, and government insurance programs. The distribution of health care resources is mainly determined by the market forces.

Government Health Insurance Programs

In 1965, the US Congress enacted Medicare and Medicaid programs to provide health insurance for the aged and the poor. These two programs are similar to the national insurance system.

Medicare is a federal program that primarily serves the aged and physically disabled. There are two parts to Medicare: Part A and Part B. Part A covers acute hospital care, skilled nursing home care after hospitalization for rehabilitation, home health services and hospice care for the terminally ill. All of the aged are automatically enrolled in Part A, when they reach age 65. Part A is financed by an earmarked Medicare Social Security Health Insurance (HI) tax. Medicare Part B is a supplemental medical insurance (SMI) program that covers physician and outpatient services. Those eligible for Medicare are not automatically enrolled in SMI, which is a voluntary program. However, more than 90 per cent of the aged are willing to pay around \$40 a month as a premium to join the program.

Unlike Part A, Medicare Part B does not have a trust fund. If Part B expenditures exceed projections, the shortfall is covered through the federal budget. Currently, about 75 per cent of Part B is financed by federal tax revenue and the remaining 25 per cent is financed by premiums. The growth of Part B expenditure has become an important contributor to the current federal deficit (Feldstein, 1994).

Medicaid is a welfare program for the poor. It is administrated by each state, but the federal government pays between 50 per cent and 80 per cent in matching funds (on average 57 per cent) based on each state's per capita income. Medicaid benefits cover hospital and physician services in addition to other services. Medicaid is one of the major payers of nursing home care. In 1998, over 60 per cent of Medicaid's federal-state budget was spent on the elderly or disabled.

Since their establishment in 1965, Medicare and Medicaid have contributed to the improvement of the people's welfare in the U.S. But the cost of financing these two programs has been increasing much more rapidly than most people had expected. Table 9.2 shows the pattern of expenditures over the 33–year period.

As shown in Table 9.2, the percentage increases in expenditure on both programs have been in double digits for most years. There were many reasons causing the increase in cost. First, growth in the enrolled population contributed to the rising cost. The number of Medicare enrollees grew at an average rate of 3.3 per cent. For the Medicaid program, since the federal government pays a large portion of the cost, state officials have the incentive to expand the Medicaid coverage to get more federal matching dollars. Medicaid has become one of the nation's fastest growing entitlement programs, with an average annual increase rate of around 20 per cent. Second, costly new technological improvements increased the cost of per unit of health care. Third, when the government acts as a big insurer and insurance covers a very substantial portion of the health care bill, the health care providers have less incentive to control the cost. On the contrary, both health care providers and insurance recipients have incentives to abuse the system. The increased inefficiency of Medicare and Medicaid programs has a significant effect on the rising costs. In the state of Florida, it is estimated that Medicare fraud is as high as two billion dollars each year.

Table 9.2 Federal government spending on health, fiscal year 1965–1998 (billions of dollars)

Spending	1965	1970	1975	1980	1985	1990	1992	1995	1998
Total Federal	118.2	195.6	332.3	590.9	946.3	1251.7	1381.9	1574.5	1839.1
Federal Health	3.1	13.9	29.5	61.8	108.0	168.0	222.7	320.2	434.2
Medicare	n/a	6.2	12.9	32.1	65.8	98.1	119.0	171.7	239.3
Medicaid	0.3	2.7	6.8	14.0	22.7	41.1	67.8	105.0	145.9
Veterans	1.3	1.8	3.7	6.5	9.5	12.1	14.1	16.2	18.0
Other	1.5	3.2	6.1	9.2	10.9	16.6	21.8	27.3	31.0
**	2.6%	7.1%	8.9%	10.5%	11.5%	13.4%	16.1%	20.3%	23.6%

** Federal health spending as a percentage of total federal spending.
n/a not available.
Source: U.S. Congressional Budget Office.

Since the late 1970s, the US government has implemented various plans to regulate Medicare and Medicaid programs. However, since these two huge government programs lack cost control incentive mechanisms, the effect of government regulations is very limited. Rising Medicare and Medicaid costs put tremendous financial pressure on federal and state governments to reform the system.

Employer Provided Health Insurance and Private Insurance in The US

For those less than 65 years old, the main source of health insurance coverage comes from their work place. About 65 per cent of all private health insurance is purchased by employers on behalf of their employees. Employer provided health insurance has tax advantages.

The US health insurance system primarily depends on the private insurance market, which provides coverage to roughly 70 per cent of the population. The private health insurance market consists of three different types of health plans:

a) Nonprofit insurance companies, such as Blue Cross & Blue Shield
b) Commercial insurers, which are typically for-profit; and
c) Managed health care systems, such as health maintenance organizations (HMOs).

Blue Cross & Blue Shield and commercial insurers belong to the traditional fee-for-service health insurance system, in which patients pay health insurance premiums to the insurance company, health care providers deliver health care services to the patient and the insurer reimburses the health care expenditures to the providers. This system creates incentives for substantial overconsumption. The insured individual is only concerned with the out-of pocket cost of health care but not the full cost of the services. Thus, the insured has incentives to consume more than he normally needs. Furthermore, the health care provider also has an incentive to induce the insured to consume more health care services than he actually needs. The fee-for-service remuneration system lacks incentives to control costs.

HMOs appear to be able to overcome the incentive problem inherent in fee-for-service health care system. HMOs are a form of health care organization in which the functions of insurance and provision of care are combined. HMOs provide care to their enrollees at a capitated rate. Thus hospitals, physician groups, clinics, and nursing homes must manage to stay under a fixed budget. As a result, HMOs have an incentive to lower the health care costs of their enrollees, such as by emphasizing prevention and health promotion practices; by treating patients in the most cost-effective way; by reducing hospital use, etc.

The drawbacks of the HMO system are that patients have limited freedom in choosing doctors and hospitals and that doctors tend to ration or under-provide medical services for the sake of cutting costs.

Reform of the US Health Care System

Despite the enormous amount of resources devoted to the health care sector, there are still 40 million people in the U.S. without insurance. Public opinion polls also indicate that majority people in the US are not satisfied with the current health care system.

Since the 1970s, the US government has tried various ways to control rapidly rising health care expenditure. Medicare utilization review programs were instituted, hospital investment in new facilities and equipment was put under control, and physician fee increases were limited under Medicare and Medicaid. However, the government controls proved to be ineffective and health care expenditures continued their rapid rise.

Studies by Ira Magaziner, President Clinton's appointed lead man on health care reform, show that up to two-thirds of insurance premiums were retained by insurance companies for administrative costs and profits. A proposal to resolve this problem was to let the employer give each employee an additional $4000 to $5000 in annual wages, which is the amount that would have gone to pay health insurance premiums. These so-called Medical Savings Accounts are used to pay for routine health costs. The individual would be allowed to save what he does not spend and the balance would accumulate in the same account, which could then be used to pay those inevitable medical bills later in life. This proposal would eliminate waste, fraud and abuse from the current health care system by introducing a market-driven force that would result in doctors and hospitals lowering costs and would allow the patient to determine his doctor and the quality of his treatment.

In August 1996, Congress passed and President Clinton signed the Health Insurance Portability and Accountability Act of 1996. In 1997, the Federal Government implemented a highly restrictive program to offer MSA to 100,000 people employed by companies with 50 or fewer workers. The pilot project was well received especially among the young and healthy. By late 1999, 95,000 policies had been sold. A government study showed that the program is effective in bringing in those previously uninsured to the health insurance system (*Wall Street Journal*, 5 October 1999). Many people argue that MSAs are an easy way to reduce the number of uninsured without higher taxes or a big bureaucracy (Li, 1999; Pauly and Goodman, 1995; Folland et al., 1997). However, the liberals suspect that the MSA program is just another gimmick used by the conservatives to kill the nationwide health insurance programs. They also have doubts about the effectiveness of the MSA in controlling health care spending, protecting the welfare of the less wealthy people and sharing risks in the whole population (Carey, 1997).

China's Health Care System

From 1950 to 1980, China had a National Health Insurance system in urban areas, which consisted of two programs. One was the Government Employee Medical Insurance Program (GEMIP) and the other was the Industrial Labor Medical Insurance Program (ILMIP). In rural areas, there was the Rural Cooperative Medical Service Program (RCM).

The Government Employee Medical Insurance Program (GEMIP) was established in 1952 according to the State Council's 'Regulations on Providing Public Medical Insurance to Employees of Central and Regional Governments, Party, and Their Affiliated Businesses'. Its actual coverage includes not only employees of governments and the Party, but also those of certain social groups, disabled veterans and college students. The medical cost is paid by direct state finance based on a per capita annual quota. The GEMIP is jointly managed by the Ministry of Health (MOH) and the Ministry of Finance (MOF).

The Industrial Labor Medical Insurance Program (ILMIP) was established in 1951 according to the State Council's 'Regulations on Labor Insurance'. Beneficiaries are employees of state-owned enterprises and their families The ILMIP is managed by various labor departments and the funds are drawn from the individual enterprise. Since each individual firm has an incentive to spend more on its medical care program, the central government has designed strict regulations on each firm's medical care program (Zhu and Zhang, 1995).

The Rural Cooperative Medical Service Program (RCM) is the peasants' voluntary co-operative system. It started in the mid-1950s. As China's agriculture was gradually collectivized, the RCM rapidly became very popular. Peasants, organized into villages or townships, contribute small amounts to the RCM; the collectives match the peasants' contribution by using their own collectively owned welfare funds. The RCM covers a fixed proportion of the medical expenses of its members, who are responsible for the rest of the expenses. The RCM significantly helped alleviate shortages of medical services in rural China during the early stages of economic development. However, since 1978, there has been a large shrinkage of the RCM system due to the advent of economic reform and decollectivization. Currently, the RCM only covers about ten percent of China's rural population (The World Bank, 1996).

In this chapter, we shall concentrate on China's urban health care, that is, the GEMIP and the ILMIP. Given that the provisions of these programs are similar, we shall refer to both as the Employee Medical Insurance Programs (EMIPs).

Since its inception in China over 40 years ago, the EMIP has made significant contributions in alleviating the medical risks faced by employees and improving their general health status. As a result, China's public health level was greatly improved, with its major health indicators being higher than those of an average developing country and in some cases, close to those of many developed countries. For example, before 1949 the life expectancy in China was 35. In 1957 it was 57 and currently, it is over 70. However, after the initiation of economic reform, there have been increasing numbers of problems with the EMIP that are threatening to slow China's overall economic development. Major problems are discussed below.

Insufficient Sharing of Medical Risk

The EMIP only plays the role of diversifying medical risk among employees within a single enterprise. Each enterprise is virtually responsible for its own medical expenses. Apparently, there is essentially no risk sharing across employees of enterprises of different operation, age, size, industry and performance. In general, older enterprises have more retirees than younger enterprises. This gives rise to the situation that older enterprises are less competitive than newer ones in the market place. Moreover, this creates a vicious circle in that enterprises with a large number of retirees and ill employees are uncompetitive and perform poorly while poorly performing enterprises are the more likely to have trouble covering their medical expenses, causing lower morale and poorer market performance. In fact, in many money-losing enterprises, the EMIP is non-existent and each employee is responsible for his own medical expenses. Clearly, the current structure of the EMIP is undesirable.

Rapidly Rising Costs and Insufficient Funding

The EMIP system lacks an efficient cost control mechanism. In the new market environment, health care providers become profit oriented. Although prices of health care are still controlled by the government, doctors seek to augment their own economic payoff by inducing patients to have unnecessary tests and treatments. On the other hand, patients with EMIP have no incentive to check the medical care cost and the doctors' behavior. On the contrary, the patient has incentives to over-consume health care services since he is spending 'other people's money'. The government and the enterprises, as the EMIP providers, lack effective methods to control health care costs. Statistics show that per capita health care costs had been constant from 1952 to 1978. However, since economic reform starting in 1978, health care costs are out of control. During the 1980s, the health care costs of EMIP increased around 20 per cent annually. In the 1990s, China's health care costs increased over 30 per cent annually (Jiangsu, 1996). Over the same period, real GNP grew about eight per cent per year. The increase in health care expenditures is far more than the GNP growth rate. Therefore, a severe problem with the existing EMIP program is the huge gap between ever increasing medical expenses and the limited sources of funding for the EMIP.

Reforming China's Health Care System

Restructuring the health care system is a major component of China's overall economic reform. A proper medical insurance system would provide effective medical services for employees, prevent rapid increases of medical expenses, minimize the financial burden of enterprises and employees, improve labor mobility and competitiveness of enterprises in the market place and therefore, help induce long term economic development and social stability.

How to reform China's health insurance system under the globalization environment? In this section, we shall provide a few suggestions for China, based on the experience of other countries, especially the US health insurance system.

The US experience tells us that relying only on market mechanisms cannot efficiently allocate resources and provide universal health care. Under the market mechanism, insurance companies are only concerned with profits so that they would restrict their sales to relatively healthy people. Those who are more exposed to poor health and in more need of medical care often cannot afford to pay for health insurance. Hospitals and doctors, motivated by increasing their profits, tend to mislead their patients by providing expensive and unnecessary tests and treatments. Patients also have an incentive to abuse the medical care system. All these adverse incentives lead to a waste of medical resources, drastic increases in insurance costs and therefore, tend to decrease potential medical coverage and quality.

The US experience also tells us that government provision alone cannot provide effective allocation of medical resources and provide medical coverage for the whole population. In the US, the government provided medical assistance for the aged and the poor is inefficient. Both the users and providers of medical services have incentives to over-spend government medical funds, resulting in rapid increases in medical expenses.

The US experience indicates that it is not wise that the government promises to take the national medical insurance system on its own shoulders. In the short run, using tax revenues to finance medical care expenses is an easy and quick way to balance the nation's medical funds. However, in the long run, this is not a good practice. The reason is that with the increase of living standards, the demand for medical care increases disproportionately. Population aging and the emergence of new diseases will both push up medical expenses. All of these potential increases in medical care expenses will quickly outpace any well-designed tax system. In fact, in the US the current expenses on Medicare are around 50 times higher than what was originally expected. Given China's huge area and enormous population, if the government takes over the nation's whole health insurance program, the administrative and managerial costs will be unimaginably high and the resulting waste of resources will be out of control. Moreover, once such a program is in place interest groups will make it very hard to phase out or to reform the program. In the US, the 1996 Republican presidential candidate Robert Dole lost many votes from the old population by simply raising the issue of reforming the US Medicare system. Thus, the US government is facing an enormous dilemma with its two large medical insurance programs.

During the past twenty years, there have been various experiments aimed at reforming the health care system in many localities in China (Hsiao, 1984; Hu,

1984; 1988; The World Bank, 1997; Henderson et al., 1994; Liu et al., 1994; Liu and Hsiao, 1995). Based on the previous experiences, since January 1995 the State Council (the central government) has been experimenting with MSA in Jiujiang city of Jianxi province and in Zhenjiang city of Jiangsu province. The main principle of these experiments is that each city should be an independent unit for providing medical insurance, which consists of the individual MSA and is supplemented by a citywide medical pooling of funds.

In the Zhenjiang program, employees will contribute one per cent of their salaries to their own individual medical accounts; the enterprise (employer) will contribute a sum equivalent to ten per cent of the employee's salary. Of the ten per cent, one half goes to the employee's individual account and the rest enters the citywide pooling fund. The pooling fund will be administered by a city government agency. A participant in the program is issued an Employee Medical Insurance ID card and goes to a pre-assigned hospital for medical service. The medical expenses should first be paid by his individual account. When the individual account is exhausted, the participant pays out of his/her pocket. However, if the extra payment is over five per cent of the participant's annual salary, the pooling fund will cover, together with co-payments by the participant. The ratio of the co-payment to the total extra payment varies with the amount of the extra payment, very much in the way of a regressive income tax. The co-payment rate is ten per cent for the part of the extra payment between five per cent of the annual salary and 5,000 RMB; eight per cent for the part between 5,000 RMB and 10,000 RMB; two per cent for the part over 10,000 RMB. For retirees, if the individual account is insufficient, the pooling fund pays. Moreover, the retiree's contribution to his individual account is only one half that of active workers (Jiangsu, 1996). There are several advantages to such a system.

First, because of the cost-sharing feature in the MSA and the pooling funds, the tendency toward abuse and overconsumption of medical services is under control, while medical risks are shared among the population. In the old EMIP system, all medical expenses were fully covered by the enterprise (or the insurance fund) and the patient (consumer) did not fully realize the cost incurred. Thus, the tendency toward abuse and overconsumption in the health care system was rampant. In the new system, when one uses the individual account for medical services, it is as if he is using his money for other consumption goods. As a result the cost must be taken into account. The patient also pays part of the costs when he uses the pooling fund. The MSA are effective in reducing the cost. According to a survey conducted by the Ministry of Health in Zhenjiang city, after the implementation of the new medical insurance system, there was a significant reduction in the consumption of medical services. Among the seven hospitals, visits of patients with medical insurance were only 17.1 per cent and the usage of CT (Computed Tomography imaging) examinations decreased 208 patient times (Yu and Ren, 1995).

Second, patients have incentives to monitor the behavior of their doctors. In the old EMIP system, since the patients do not pay for any cost of medical service, doctors and hospitals have an incentive to induce the patient to over-consume medical services so as to generate more benefits for the doctors and hospitals. In other words, the demand for medical services is to a great extent determined by the doctor which results in a lot of unnecessary tests, drugs and in-patient care being prescribed. According to Chinese statistics on health care, the per-capita medical expenses of those patients having medical insurance are twice as large as those without insurance and the duration of in-patient care of those with medical insurance was 12.4 to 60.8 per cent longer than those without insurance. (Yu and Ren, 1995). On average, a woman with medical insurance delivering a baby stayed in a hospital for seven days (in the US, the average is 48 hours). In hospital, the patients also received many redundant supplies, such as wash basins, thermos bottles and spittoons, which were all paid by the patients' insurance.

When a patient pays for health care costs from his personal MSA plus a portion of the cost from his own pocket, he has more incentive to monitor the doctors' treatment and to choose more efficient treatment methods. This will lead to an overall improvement in efficiency and lower medical costs.

Third, treatment of major illnesses is mainly financed by the pooling fund and therefore, health risks are spread out and shared across the population in one city. In the new program, each firm's contribution only depends on the amount of its total salary but independent from the health status and age distribution of its employees. The system reduces the competitive disadvantage to the firms with many employees exposed to risks of poor health. This will reduce discrimination against older and less healthy people in the society and lead to increases in social productivity.

An empirical study (Liu and Yuen et al., 1999) presents a preliminary assessment of Zhenjiang's experiment. Major findings show there are significant changes in health care cost and utilization patterns after implementation of the MSA. First, the incidence of using any health care services increased by 12 per cent among the general population. Second, when looking into changes in the composition of services, there was a shift from the likelihood of using inpatient care to outpatient care. Third, total health care expenditures decreased by eight per cent among the general population and 18 per cent among users. And fourth, among respective service-specific users, the utilization rates consistently decreased by 14 per cent for outpatient visits, 11 per cent for inpatient admissions, and 17 per cent for length of stay (LOS) per admission. Based on these findings, the experimental plan appears to be more cost effective than the previous health care programs.

Because of the successful experiment in Zhenjiang city, the Chinese government has advocated the MSA scheme for the urban health care reform. In July 2000, at the conference of China's Health Care and Insurance System Reform, Vice Premier Li Lanqing declared that China would reform its health care system by relying on the MSA combined with citywide social pooling funds. The government wishes to extend the MSA scheme to all the cities in China by the end of this year (People's Daily, 26 July 2000). We believe this approach is appropriate for China. But regarding social pooling funds, there are a few issues that need to be improved.

First, for the citywide pooling funds, the risk-sharing function is very limited. One reason is that the majority of Chinese cities are small cities. The citywide social pooling funds are not enough to provide adequate risk sharing. Another reason is that there are huge distribution disparities of income, age, and health status among Chinese cities. Currently, in the newly developed cities, like Shenzhen, the medical social pooling funds show a large surplus because of the high income, younger and healthy population. But in the old large cities, like Shenyang, a heavy industry city, many state owned enterprises are bankrupt. The citywide pooling funds show a big deficit and can not provide risk sharing.

Second, the management of the medical pooling funds and individual medical savings accounts is controlled by the government and is inefficient. In the medical reform experiments in Zhenjiang and Jiujiang, each city's metropolitan labor medical insurance management commission manages the cities medical pooling funds. Under the supervision of the commission, each city sets up a medical pooling fund management center, which is responsible for the MSA and fee collection, daily operation and management. The pooling funds and individual accounts are deposited in banks. The return rate is very low. If a single agency controls all the medical insurance funds, it is difficult to avoid the inefficiencies caused by the bureaucracy. In practice, due to the system's excessive complexity, loopholes, and non-standardized management, the current system's management is inefficient.

Third, citywide pooling funds hamper labor mobility. As China is moving into the WTO, the whole economy will merge into the world's track. During this process, many traditional industries might be out of the market, while many new technology industries might emerge. All these changes foster labor movement. Labor mobility is crucial for economic development. However, the current citywide medical pooling funds could not facilitate the labor movement. If workers leave a city, they can only bring their individual medical savings accounts with them, but they would lose all the benefit from the social pooling funds. So the citywide pooling funds that tie health insurance coverage to certain cities hamper labor mobility.

The U.S. has been experimenting with individual medical savings accounts. The basic principle is very similar to the Chinese practice. But the management of the US system relies more on the market mechanism. Treatments for major illnesses are not managed through a government agency, but by buying catastrophic insurance through private insurance companies. Individuals have freedom to choose providers of insurance services. Facing market competition, insurance providers have to decrease their management costs and increase the quality of their services to attract customers. Those insurance companies have nationwide networks. Whenever people change jobs, their individual medical accounts combined with catastrophic insurance will go with them. Then people can change jobs and locations without jeopardizing their health benefits.

Since the Chinese financial market and insurance market are still underdeveloped, it is risky to let medical pooling funds and individual accounts go to the market. There are not many choices other than letting the government control the funds. But the WTO will give China an opportunity to change the management of the funds. After China joins the WTO, the financial market and insurance market will open their doors for foreign companies, which will greatly expose Chinese medical funds to the international market and bring many new opportunities for health care system reform. China should catch this opportunity to reform its health care system through globalization. Based on the experiences of other countries, our suggestions for reforming China's health care system are as follows.

Following the world-wide trend of health care system reform, including decentralization and incorporation of market mechanisms to control the adverse incentives, China's health insurance system should consist of the MSA combined with catastrophic insurance. This will provide nation-wide insurance coverage, while the provision of insurance and management of medical accounts are decentralized. Such a system is portable, flexible, and manageable and is able to balance the goals of risk sharing and cost containment.

The government should not be directly involved in providing health care services and managing medical pooling funds. The government should enact laws and rules to regulate health care market.

The MSA should be the core of the health care system. Employers and employees will pay a certain share of the salary to set up the individual accounts, which will be responsible for routine health care cost. Individuals can invest the MSA in the financial market and achieve a higher return. In the Zhenjing experiment, the enterprises contribute a sum equivalent to 20 per cent of the employee's salary. Of the 20 per cent, one half goes to the employee's individual account and the rest enters the citywide pooling fund. We believe that the percentage contribution rate going to the MSA should increase to 12–15 per cent of the salary, the remaining eight–five per cent will be used to buy catastrophic insurance through private insurance companies.

Instead of medical social pooling funds, major illnesses will be taken care of by catastrophic insurance. Those insurance companies should be strictly regulated by the government, which should insure the insurance companies are large enough to gain economies of scale, provide nationwide coverage and effectively diversify financial risk. At the same time, the government should maintain enough market competition among different insurance companies. Individuals have the freedom to choose the providers of the insurance services. The market competition will force insurance companies to learn and adopt new technology and management skills quickly and to provide higher quality services at cheaper prices to attract consumers. Because the price elasticity of demand for catastrophic insurance is very inelastic, the abuse and overconsumption of health care services problems could be significantly reduced. Overall, this type of setting will improve efficiency. The MSA combined with nationwide catastrophic insurance will simulate labor mobility. As workers change jobs and cities, their health care benefits, the MSA and catastrophic insurance, will go with them. It will greatly enhance labor mobility and economic development.

In conclusion, how to control the health care costs and provide comprehensive health care coverage for the people is a worldwide and unsolved problem. The experience of the OECD countries, especially the US, in reforming health care systems is highly illustrative for China. The US experience tells us that relying only on market mechanisms or the government cannot efficiently allocate resources and provide universal health care. The trend of health care system reform is to decentralize health care systems and to incorporate market mechanisms to control the adverse incentives embodied in the health care sector.

China and the US have had very different medical insurance and medical care systems. However, both the systems of both countries are being reformed. The reforms in both countries have included experimenting with MSA. The US experience of using market mechanisms to manage pooling funds provides a valuable lesson for China.

Given the opportunity that China's economy will integrate with the world's economy, China should catch the chance to reform its health care system. We suggest that China's health care system should consist of the MSA combined with catastrophic insurance, which will provide nationwide insurance coverage, while the provision of insurance and management of medical accounts are decentralized. The government should not be directly involved in providing health care services and managing medical pooling funds. The government should enact laws and rules to regulate the health care market. Such a system is portable, flexible, manageable and can balance the goals of risk sharing and cost containment.

References

Carey, Mary (1997), 'Medicare Conferences Prepare for Savings Account Fight', *Social Policy*, 5 July, pp. 1580–1.

Feldstein, Paul (1994), *Health Policy Issues*, AUPHA/Health Administration Press.

Folland, S., Goodman, A. and Stano, M. (1997), *The Economics of Health and Health Care*, Prentice Hall.

Ham, Chris and Brommels, Mats (1994), 'Health Care Reform in the Netherlands, Sweden, and the United Kingdom', *Health Affairs*, Vol. 13, pp. 106–19.

Henderson, G., et al. (1995), 'Distribution of Medical Insurance in China', *Social Science and Medicine*, Vol. 41 (8), pp. 1119–30.

Hsiao, W. C. (1984), 'Transformation of Health Care in China', *New England Journal of Medicine*, Vol. 310 (14), pp. 932–6.

Hu, The-Wei, Ong, Michael, Lin, Zi-hua, and Li, Elizabeth (1999), 'The Effects of Economic Reform on Health Insurance and the Financial Burden for Urban Workers in China', *Health Economics*, Vol. 8, pp. 309–21.

Jiangsu Province Bureau of Health (1996), *Zhengjiang Employee Medical Insurance Systems Reform Studies*, Nanjing, Jiangsu, China.

Li, L. (1999), 'Reforming United States' Health Care System', *International Journal of Public Administration*, Vol. 22 (3 and 4).

Liu, Xingzhu and Hsiao, William C. L. (1995), 'The Cost Escalation of Social Health Insurance Plans in China: Its Implication for Public Policy', *Social Science and Medicine*, Vol. 41 (8), pp. 1095–101.

Liu, G., Yuen, P. et al (1999), 'Urban Health Care Reform Initiative in China: Findings from Its Pilot Experiment in Zhengjiang City', *International Journal of Economic Development*.

Pauly, M., and Goodman, J. (1995), 'Tax Credits for Health Insurance and Medical Savings Accounts', *Health Affairs*, Vol. 14, pp. 126–39.

The U.S. Congressional Budget Office (1998), *A CBO Study of Trends in Health Spending*, The US Congressional Budget Office Press, Washington, DC.

The U.S. Department of Commerce (1998), *Statistical Abstract of the United States*, Washington, DC.

World Bank (1996), *China: Issues and Options in Health Financing*, The World Bank, Washington, DC.

Yuen, P. P. (1996), 'Reforming Health Care Financing in Urban China', *International Journal of Public Administration*, Vol.19, pp. 211–232.

Yu Wei and Ren Minghui (1995), 'The Important Issue of Enterprise Reform: Health Care Insurance System', Chapter 26 in Xu, D. and Wen, G. eds., *Reforming China's State-owned Enterprises*, China Economic Press, pp. 433–458.

Zhu, Jiazhen and Zhang, Sai (1995), *The Handbook of China's Social Insurance*, China Statistics Press, Beijing, China.

Chapter 10

Where Will China's Internet Regulation Go after WTO Accession?

Qingjiang Kong

Introduction

With no escape from the age of information, China has chosen to embrace the Internet without a lot of fanfare.[1] As in the West one big issue facing the government is the regulation of the Internet.[2] As a result recent years have seen the promulgation of numerous regulations on the Internet.[3]

The WTO negotiations, in addition, served as a catalyst to strengthen and consolidate liberalizing forces in the economic arena. While international observers habitually notice that the Chinese government has already taken measures to regulate the Internet, they fail to perceive the inter-linkage between the new rules and the bureaucratic obstacles to open market competition in the telecommunication industry. It is also easy to underestimate the inherent power of the Internet and particularly, to ignore the ambition of the Chinese government to adapt to the technological opportunity. As the government is readily embracing the information technology (IT) revolution and preparing for WTO accession, the Internet rules would not be so restrictive as to deny free access to the Internet. It is undoubtedly meaningful to have an overview of the Chinese approach to the regulation of the Internet with the advent of WTO accession.

An Overview of the Internet Rules

It is not difficult to find that the rules regulating the Internet come from two sources: specific rules for Internet regulation and general rules for telecommunications regulation. Among the specific regulatory rules, the Interim Provisions on the Administration of International Wiring of Computer Information Networks (*jisuanji xinxi wangluo guoji lianwang guanli zhanxing guiding*), which the State Council promulgated on 1 February 1996, are the principal rules from which the rest are derived. As the term 'administration' or '*guanli*' indicates, the purpose of the regulations is to strengthen the administration of international wiring of computer information networks.

The Regulations on Telecommunications, which the State Council promulgated on 20 September 2000, have been the only comprehensive governing rules in the field of telecommunications regulation. The Regulations on Telecommunications basically focus on the operation of telecommunications services, and the operation of Internet services naturally falls within the Regulations' scope of application.

In general, rules regulating the Internet can largely be divided into three inter-related categories: rules governing Internet content censorship, rules governing operations of Internet service and rules governing users of Internet services.

Rules for Internet Content Censorship

Of the three categories of Internet rules, the most controversial are those relating to Internet content censorship. In this regard, particular attention should be paid to the Administrative Provisions on Secrecy of Computer Information Systems (*jisuanji xinxi xitong baomi guanli guiding*), which deal with state secrets on the Internet. The Administrative Provisions, which some international observers see as 'a disaster for the Chinese Internet revolution'[4] ban individuals and institutions from discussing or disseminating any information that is considered 'state secrets'.[5] As to what 'state secrets' mean, the Administrative Provisions fail to provide any definition. Presumably, the State Secrecy Law should be referred to in this regard, since this provides that 'state secrets are matters relating to the national security and benefits whose access is, in accordance with the legal procedures, limited to persons of a certain scope in a certain period'.[6]

It is intriguing that the Administrative Provisions on Secrecy of Computer Information Systems provide that state approval should be obtained from the relevant authorities for the distribution of information on the Internet.[7] This requirement probably is most likely to give rise to criticism in the Administrative Provisions on Secrecy of Computer Information Systems in that, among other things, it fails to take account of the difference between information flow over the Internet and information transmission over traditional media such as newspapers and television. It dictates as tight censorship on Internet contents as on traditional media materials.[8] In letter it is so prohibitive to the ISPs that the implementation of this requirement would mean not only devastating China's emerging Internet industry but also a giant backlash.[9] However, as observed by numerous Internet analysts, it would be too costly and impractical to do.[10] Nevertheless, the self-censorship among the ISP can also be an expected result of the strict implementation of the requirement.[11]

In addition to state secrets, pornographic information is also on the list for Internet content censorship.[12] However, while dictating rigid censorship, the Internet rules are far from complete. A clear indication is that they fail to address the issue of privacy protection, which in western democracies is viewed as crucial to the human rights of individuals. Apparently the drafters of the Internet rules realized that transmission of both state secrets and pornographic information is harmful to state interests or the public good but overlooked privacy protection. The adoption of censoring state secrets and pornographic information by the Internet rules and its failure to incorporate rules for protection of privacy in a similar way clearly reflect the values of the typical oriental rule makers.[13]

Rules Governing Operations of Internet Service

Rules governing the operation of Internet services are divided into two categories: rules governing licensing or registration and rules governing wiring. As pointed out before, the Regulations on Telecommunications regulate the operation of telecommunications services. Pursuant to the Regulations on Telecommunications, the State Council adopted the Administrative Measures for the Internet Information Services (*hulianwang xinxi fuwu guanli banfa*) on 20 September 2000 to further specify the conditions for the licensing and registration of the Internet services.

According to the Administrative Measures for the Internet Information Services, Internet services are divided into two categories: profit-making services and non-profit-making services. While non profit-making services providers need to file registrations with the competent authorities before operating, profit-making services providers must obtain licenses from the authorities.[14] For the profit-making Internet services, the Administrative Measures set forth stiff licensing requirements in addition to those stipulated in the Regulations on Telecommunications.[15] These additional requirements include: a business development blueprint, a corresponding technical support plan and 'healthy and complete' network security safeguard measures. The vague licensing requirements seemingly leave much room for the authorities, thus creating difficulty for the starters.

The Interim Provisions on the Administration of International Wiring of Computer Information Networks establish a complex four-tier system for international wiring. The first is the gateway for International wiring. The Interim Provisions require that all traffic to the computer networks outside China be effectuated through the gateway maintained by the public telecommunication networks, that is, the networks maintained by China Telecom and the other approved public networks.[16] The Rules for the Administration of International Wiring Gateway for Inbound and Outbound Computer Information (*jisuanji xinxi wangluo guoji lianwang churukou xindao guanli banfa* http://www.mii.gov.cn/mii/zcfg/hy/law456.htm" \t "_blank), adopted by the former MPT, reaffirms the privileged role of the China Telecom network as the gateway.[17] No persons or units may establish or use other gateways for Internet traffic without prior approval from the government.[18] In addition to the ChinaNet of China Telecom, the approved networks include the CERNET of the Ministry of Education, the CSTNET of the Chinese Academy of Sciences, the GBNet of China Jitong, the UNINET of China Unicom, the CNCNET of China Netcom, the CIET of the Ministry of Foreign Trade and Economic Cooperation, the CMNET of China Mobile, the CGWNET of the People's Liberation Army and the CSNET of China Satcom.[19] Nevertheless, this international gateway requirement facilitates the filtering of information that may be offensive to the regime.

The second is those computer information networks directly wired with the gateway. It is required that only those approved 'inter-wired networks' can carry out international wiring directly through the gateway. The third is 'wired networks' that are defined as computer information networks that carry out international wiring through the 'inter-wired networks'.[20] In practice, most maintainers of inter-wired networks also act as those that maintain wired networks. They both constitute the ISPs21.[21] The Interim Provisions require that any entity intending to be connected with the Internet has to file an application with the relevant government agencies for Internet wiring; an entity intending to operate a business on the Internet has to procure a license.[22] Individuals are excluded from the scope of ISP. The last tier consists of the Internet users that are individuals or entities.

According to the Interim Provisions, individuals and entities engaging in international wiring, shall, in compliance with the relevant state laws and administrative regulations, not commit violations or crimes concerning endangering national security, disclosing state secrets, and must refrain from making, checking, copying and transmitting pornographic information.[23] Also, according to the Regulations on the Safeguarding of the Computer Information System, endangering the security of computer networks is also punishable.[24]

It is worth noticing that the Interim Provisions here suggest that the other laws of China, the Criminal Law in particular, also apply to the ISPs. Moreover, the vaguely worded provision may even leave room for the government to deal with cases that otherwise may be dealt with on other grounds, for example, tort. Moreover the NPC Standing Committee adopted the Decision on Safeguarding the Internet (*weihu hulianwang anquan de jueding*) on 28 December 2000. The Decision provides in detail that 15 online acts are criminal offences and thus has remedied the defect in this regard. However it is noteworthy that the Decision on Safeguarding the Internet goes so far as to provide that a website keeper who links to pornographic information websites is criminally chargeable.[25]

Nevertheless, there is a risk for the police, that is, the Ministry of Public Security (MSB) and its local branches, the Public Security Bureaus (PSBs), to tend to charge the violating businesses on the intimidating ground of endangering national security.[26] An example is that of a private Internet service provider who was prosecuted for alleged endangering national security by disclosing the e-mail addresses of his clients to an overseas institution identified as an anti-government organization.[27]

Fortunately, there are signs that the Chinese courts are not always willing to support the accusations of the ISPs based on the 'endangering national security' provisions. It is interesting to note a high-profile case in Fujian Province. The Chen brothers, who are Internet users of China Telecom, set up a phone service via the Internet, selling calls to the United States at a fraction of the state monopoly's price.[28] Acting on requests from China Telecom, the local police arrested the brothers, seized their property, including their computer and accused them of 'endangering national security' and committing 'a new type of crime'. The brothers responded by suing the police, arguing that their actions were not criminal because there was no law banning Internet phone service.[29] The brothers won the case.[30]

In this regard it should be pointed out that the Regulations on the Administration of Commercial Encryption, which govern the development, production, sale and use of commercial encryption has also an adverse, indirect impact on the operation of the online services. On 7 October 1999, the State Council adopted Administration of Commercial Encryption Regulations governing the sale, distribution, use and production of commercial encryption products in China, including a ban on the sale of all foreign products.[31] On 31 January 2000, the Chinese government began to implement the Encryption Administration. As originally proposed, the rules were viewed to have a stifling effect on the development on the Internet and e-commerce in China and foreign companies seeking market access. The Chinese government, realizing the practical and commercial implications of implementing such a broad regulatory regime, recently issued a statement clarifying its commercial encryption policy. According to the March 2000 statement by the National Commission on Encryption Code Regulations (NCECR), the Encryption Administration would be limited to 'specialized hardware and software products for which encryption and decoding operations are its core functions'. Wireless phones, 'Windows' software, and browser software are not covered. Registration requirements are also relaxed. In addition, the regulations are being researched and will be revised 'in accordance with WTO regulations and promises to foreign governments'.

Rules for Users of Internet Services

In regard to users of Internet service, individuals and entities, intending to plug in to the Internet are required to register with the police. Failure to register may result in forced de-wiring by PSBs.[32]

Internet users are also not allowed to publish, discuss and spread any 'state secrets' through the e-mail systems, chat rooms or electronic bulletin boards.[33] The MII even adopted the Administrative Measures for Services on Electronic Bulletin Boards (*hulianwang dianzi gonggao fuwu guanli guiding*) to specify the conditions for the provision and use of services through electronic bulletin boards. For example, operation of services through electronic bulletin boards must be approved or registered[34] and the operators must keep the service records for 60 days for official inspection.[35]

Departments in Charge of the Administration of the Internet

It should be borne in mind that in practice the unstreamlined Chinese bureaucratic structures make the regulation of the Internet in China a more complicated situation.

According to the Interim Provisions on the Administration of International Wiring of Computer Information Networks, an agency that is the Leading Group of Informatization (LGI) under the auspices of the State Council, was established. The LGI is entrusted with a wide range of powers, including making detailed rules for the implementation of the regulations, regulating the rights and duties of channel providers, ISPs and users, and supervising and inspecting the international wiring of networks.[36] It had the Office of the Leading Group of Informatization as its administrative body. In 1998 the Office of the Leading Group of Informatization and the former State Radio Regulatory Committee became two divisions of the newly established MII. Recently, the LGI was reorganized into a higher-ranking State Leading Group of Informatization (SLGI). Premier Zhu Rongji is its head.[37]

However, as shown from the Internet regulations that come from various ministries, the LGI is not the sole responsible administrative authority on the Internet. Among the competent authorities, the MII, the MSB and the State Secrecy Bureau (SSB) are particularly worth mentioning. Though regulatory power has been shifted officially from the Ministry to the IWLG in the field of Internet administration, these bodies are, to some extent, still intertwined. MII is the governing department of China Telecom and is vested with the power to regulate the telecommunication industry. It is believed that drafting the regulations to govern operations of ISPs actually rests with MII rather than with the IWLG, which is only in charge of writing rules for Internet content providers. As for the MSB and PSBs, which are traditionally seen as 'dictatorship organs (*zhuanzheng jiguan*)', they are empowered with a wide range of administrative and quasi-judicial authorities on the Internet.[38] With the Administrative Provisions on Secrecy of Computer Information Systems one has reason to believe that the police work in close collaboration with the SSB in patrolling the Internet. It is fair to argue in this regard that the enforcement of the Interim Provisions on the Administration of International Wiring of Computer Information Networks rests primarily on the police.

In this context it is important to bear in mind that in China rules and their implementation often differ. For example, registration and annual renewal with the police is a prerequisite in many localities for end users to plug in to the Internet.[39] However, the personal experience of the author, an enthusiastic user of the Internet, shows the reality is not the same. The author has never renewed his registration since 1997 and no de-wiring has been imposed by the local PSB. In other words, there is a possibility that, though the Internet rules feature the usual restrictive rhetoric, they might not generate unwanted consequences.

Hidden Agenda behind the Tight Internet Rules

Indeed, governments tend to favor regulation although others see the Internet in a different way.[40] In the West, the government has traditionally had an interest and is allowed to regulate access to such issues as indecency in that it can block out minors as long as it keeps access open for adults.[41] The background to this is that the government may serve the good of the society as a whole. However, anti-government and political content has been limited or outlawed mainly in nations that traditionally have either not recognized, or given little protection to, freedom of speech.[42] From the perspective of these governments, controls are needed to reduce to a minimum the adverse effect of the Internet on the society as a whole.

In China, government regulation of the Internet is taken for granted. The justification should be traced back to the unique and delicate Chinese culture. In China, the advent of new forms of technology is always a cause for public anxiety and unease. The age-old mantra was *zhongxue weiti*, *xixue weiyong*, or, 'Chinese thinking for our essence, western learning for application', is evidence. Historically, the government has never hesitated to block access of the people to information it deems politically or culturally suspect. For the Chinese government that deems maintaining stability as its paramount challenge, it is understandable that it attaches ever-greater importance to what it calls security of information inflow. Tight censorship has long been established to control the traditional media. The Internet, with its staggering ability to disseminate information quickly and to give an amplified voice to minority views, would pose a fundamental challenge to China's tightly run society. In this connection, it is the natural reaction of the government to attempt to address politically sensitive issues and combat 'spiritual pollution'.[43]

However, the Internet rules are also a result of pressure from the telecommunication industry. China Telecom, which used to be the commercial arm of the MPT, has long enjoyed monopoly status. Facing the enormous potential that the Internet will bring forth, it is naturally reluctant to lose its monopoly. Its ambitions are reflected in the new regulations,[44] both because of the influence of the monopoly and its allies in the administration and because of the vesting of the regulatory power in the industry.

External Pressure for Liberalizing the Internet Regulation: Implications of China's WTO Accession

According to the Provisional Regulations for Guiding the Direction of Foreign Investment and its companion Catalogue for Guiding Foreign Investment in Industry, the telecommunications industry is one of those where foreign investment is prohibited. Although both the Regulations on Telecommunications and the Administrative Measures for the Internet Information Services have been promulgated, neither of them has answered the crucial question of how China should open the telecommunications and Internet sectors to foreign investment. In principle, therefore, there has been almost no direct role for foreign companies in Internet service provision, although foreign portfolio investments have been active in the state-controlled Internet service companies.[45]

In the effort to join the WTO, China has made substantial commitments regarding opening, *inter alia*, the Internet services to foreign participation. As initially negotiated in the bilateral agreements with the United States and the EU and later incorporated in the Accession Protocol, the main accession terms relevant for the Internet services sectors, are as follows:

1 Permit up to 50 per cent foreign ownership in value-added and paging services (including Internet, e-mail, voice mail, online information, data retrieval, and enhanced fax) four years after accession (30 per cent upon accession) and remove all geographic restrictions on the participation by foreign companies in such services two years after accession.
2 Adhere to the pro-competition and level–playing–field regulatory principles embodied in the Agreement on Basic Telecommunications Services (ABTS) concerning pricing, interconnection rights, technology-neutral scheduling, domestic leased-circuit services, and independent status of the regulatory authority.

In addition, China agreed to eliminate all current restrictions on domestic distribution and trade, as well as import and export quotas applicable to foreign companies operating in China, by 2003, remove all export requirements, as well as local content restrictions on foreign-invested companies upon accession, and apply all taxes and tariffs uniformly to companies regardless of ownership upon accession.

The long-term social, political, financial, and economic consequences of full implementation of China's commitments are likely to be great. China's pending WTO accession will fundamentally change the landscape of Internet services and the Chinese market for Internet services will be one of the most open in developing countries.

If fully implemented, China's commitments will also enhance competition. Currently, state-owned telecommunications companies, which are regulated and controlled by the MII, dominate the market for ISPs. The dominant ISP is ChinaNet of China Telecom, which controls 83 per cent of all current Internet connections. Many small, local Internet companies exist, but most are struggling financially, in part because of the high rates charged by China Telecom. In the post-WTO era, with foreign participation, the monopoly on the Internet service is unlikely be maintained in the long run. In fact, in order to gain a strategic foothold, many major multinational telecommunications and Internet companies in the world have already begun making investment in China's Internet services sector.[46]

Unsettled Issues

Given the restrictive features of the Internet regulations, a question naturally arises whether there are any risks that China will build the electric equivalent of the Great Wall or that the Chinese government will facilitate all sorts of filtering of all sorts of content, at any level on the distributional chain, turning the Internet from this great space of freedom and openness into a space of maximum regulation.

The question has to be explored in the context of market-oriented reform and the technological aspects of the Internet. It is fair to assert that the Chinese government envisions its relationship with the Internet as one entirely geared towards business, where it serves as a tool to spur China's economic development. In the tech-minded leadership, the Internet is considered a technological area *vis-à-vis* the traditional media that is more restricted. Early in the 1990s the Chinese government began introducing and promoting the application of the Internet, seeing it as strategic in restructuring the economy towards gaining a competitive edge. As a matter of fact the above-mentioned ministerial level body LGI was accordingly established to ensure the widespread application as well as the regulation of the Internet. Given that technology and competitiveness are deeply linked and that the Internet can serve the purpose of making China competitive, what concerns the leadership most is how to get China onto the Internet in an orderly way and how best to explore the Internet, not how to keep the Internet out altogether.

From the technological point of view, it is unlikely that China would be able to resort to the same tight censorship as it used in the traditional media to design an Internet whose essence is the control of access and content.

Still, another issue remains to be clarified. While China has pledged to allow 30 per cent global stakes in the Internet, paging and other value-added services upon accession, rising to 49 per cent after one year and 50 per cent after two years most web start-ups in China have upwards of 90 per cent outside capital. Will they readjust their portfolio structure in the post-WTO era? Will they survive loopholes and slack enforcement? Almost none of China's major web sites began as Chinese firms with pre-existing revenues. It is noted that lower incomes, lack of well-established payment infrastructure and consumer reluctance to pay for content have been the main hurdles to the development of the Internet industry, and that all have depended mainly on other investment to survive.

Concluding Remarks

As China is readily embracing the IT revolution, it has to deal with an accompanying problem, namely, the regulation of the Internet. This in turn cuts to the heart of issues that are key to China's future, such as how much market competition will be allowed and whether the free flow of information, crucial for economic development, will be hindered by political concerns. China's WTO accession provides a badly needed dimension for Internet regulation. With foreign participation guaranteed by WTO commitments, the Chinese rules on the Internet, though featuring the usual restrictive rhetoric, should not be so restrictive as to deny free access to the Internet.

In concluding, the Internet regulations in China will serve more than merely as the legal techniques of political control on the Internet in that the government perceives the Internet as a means to its economic end. However, the real challenge is for the Chinese government to balance the need to promote Internet development and its efforts to control the information flow.

It is proposed, in relation to the regulation of the Internet, that special information zones be established with open competition and uncensored Internet access, much like the special economic zones of the 1980s that allowed China to experiment with western ideas and institutions. This has to be prompted by the desire of the government to tap the benefits of the Internet and shows the most revolutionary features of China's information openness. It is also inspiring to note that the Chinese government has reportedly granted the News Corporation and AOL Time Warner, two leading media giants in the world, the concession to access the media market in Guangdong Province, which might signify a gradual relaxation of control on the Internet.[47]

Notes

1 Some small, local Internet experiments started in 1987. China's Internet was formally launched in 1991. It was initially limited to interconnections between university research laboratories, but it has since been expanded nationally. According to China Internet Network Information Centre, in 1994 the use of the Internet was only limited to a small group of computer scientists and students. By 31 December 2001 there were already 33.70 million Chinese with access to the Internet. The Internet monitoring company expects that China will become one of the leading Internet-related markets in the world in ten years.

2 For the past 25 years, the US government administered the overall activity of the Internet with the actual work parcelled out to DOD contractor think tanks. During most of this period, the arrangement worked well, since the Internet was owned and operated first exclusively by DOD, then later jointly by DOD together with government science agencies. For important national security and research reasons, network-wide policies were established, registrations accomplished, databases maintained and public directory services made available.

3 Among them are the Regulations on the Safeguard of Computer Information System (the State Council, 18 February, 1994), the Interim Provisions on the Administration of International Wiring of Computer Information Networks (1 February 1996, revised on 20 May 1997), the Rules for the Administration of International Wiring Gateway for

Inbound and Outbound Computer Information (Ministry of Post and Telecommunication, 9 April 1996), Circulars of the Ministry of Public Security on the Recording of the Internationally-wired Computer Information System (29 January 1996), the Interim Rules on the Connection between Specialized Networks and the Public Network (Ministry of Post and Telecommunication, 24 July 1996) and the Administrative Provisions on Secrecy of Computer Information Systems (State Secrecy Bureau, 1 January 2000).

4 Jasper Becker (2000), 'Mainland clamps down on Net', *South China Morning Post*, Internet Edition, 27 January.

5 Article 6, the Administrative Provisions on Secrecy of Computer Information Systems.

6 Article 2 of the State Secrecy Law.

7 Article 9 of the Administrative Provisions on Secrecy of Computer Information Systems.

8 It is no secret that in China not only is the traditional media used by the CPC and the government as state instruments for blatant political propaganda, but it is also put under strict monitoring. According to a study all materials are reviewed by the CPC officials. See Suzanne Ogden (1995), *China's Unresolved Issues* (3rd edition), Prentice Hall, Englewood Clifts, N.J., p. 150.

9 For instance, it may frighten off foreign investment that is badly needed to nurture the nascent Chinese Internet industry and kill hopes that China's entry into the World Trade Organization will signal a new openness to technological advance and Internet use.

10 For instance, see Ong, Carolyn *et al.* (2000), 'Taming the web', *South China Morning Post*, 27 January.

11 A member of the News Department of Sina.com, a leading Chinese ISP, admitted that it had to wait for an official organization to release sensitive news before it could upload the information on its website. See O'Neill, Mark (2000), 'Battle of new and old media, *South China Morning Post*, the Internet Edition, 19 February. As a matter of fact, the self-censoring is also a natural response of the ISPs in the context that it is up to the government to determine whether or not to approve the listing of the ISPs, which are start ups and badly need capital from the financial market.

One Chinese scholar even proposed that besides self-censorship ISPs should have the following obligations: 1) Regular Checks. The ISPs shall check the on-line information released by their domestic clients to ensure that it is proper; 2) Monitoring and Screening. ISPs shall monitor regularly foreign websites or on-line information sources and screen 'politically reactionary' or pornographic or 'not really useful' materials; 3) Notification and Reporting. ISPs shall notify the relevant government authorities of any release of prohibited information and 'unfit' foreign websites, the fate of which will be left at the disposal of the government; 4) Cooperation. ISPs shall cooperate with the relevant authorities in regulating the Internet and investigating on-line crimes. See Sun Tiecheng (1999), 'Legal Problems of Computer Networks', *in The Editing Group of Jurisprudence Frontiers* (in Chinese), Beijing: Law Press, 1999, pp. 99–100.

12 Article 13, the Interim Provisions on the Administration of International Wiring of Computer Information Networks.

13 It suffices to mention that same rigid censorship applies on the Internet in Singapore. See Rodan, Garry (1998), 'The Internet and Political Control in Singapore', *Political Science Quarterly*, Vol. 113, pp.71–6 and Tan, Zixiang (Alex) and Lu, Ding (1998), 'The State Borderline in the Cyberspace', in Erik Bohlin and Stanford L. Levin (eds.), *Telecommunications Transformation: Technology, Strategy, and Policy*, IOS Press, Netherlands.

14 Article 4, the Administrative Measures for the Internet Information Services.

15 Article 6, the Administrative Measures for the Internet Information Services.

16 Article 6, the Interim Provisions on the Administration of International Wiring of Computer Information Networks. When the Interim Provisions on the Administration of International Wiring of Computer Information Networks were promulgated, China

Telecom was a department of the MPT, which was later renamed 'MII'. Therefore, Article 6 referred to the 'public network maintained by the MPT' as the international gateway.

17 Article 2 of the Rules for the Administration of International Wiring Gateway for Inbound and Outbound Computer Information.

18 Article 6 (2), the Interim Provisions on the Administration of International Wiring of Computer Information Networks.

19 When the Interim Provisions on the Administration of International Wiring of Computer Information Networks were promulgated, there were only four gateways, that is, ChinaNet, CERNET, CSTNET and GBNet. Therefore, Article 7 recognized these four existing inter-wired networks.

20 Article 10, the Interim Provisions on the Administration of International Wiring of Computer Information Networks.

21 By the end of 1999 there were 520 ISPs in China. Reuters, 15 February 2000.

22 Article 8, the Interim Provisions on the Administration of International Wiring of Computer Information Networks.

23 Article 13, the Interim Provisions on the Administration of International Wiring of Computer Information Networks.

24 Article 7, the Regulations on the Safeguard of Computer Information System.

25 Article 3.5, Decision on Safeguarding the Internet.

26 According to the Criminal Law, a person may be sentenced to ten years imprisonment or even life imprisonment.

27 The facts were reported by the media in China and abroad. See *generally*, Lianhe Zaobao, 6 December 1998, the Internet edition. It may be interesting to observe that it is apparently illegal even in the West for a business to disclose, without prior consent, its clients' information obtained through commercial channels. However, the difference in approach, taken by China and the West in dealing with this issue, is striking. It should be noted that the competent Chinese authority would not find itself in a position to charge the violating business because there is no applicable rule of torts.

28 The Chen Brothers apparently violated the provision that only entities are entitled to act as ISPs.

29 Unfortunately, such a regulation was approved, apparently only to maintain the telecommunication monopoly, in September 1998, nine months after the business of Chen brothers was shut down.

30 Pomfret, John (1999), 'China's Telecoms Battle', *International Herald Tribune*, 26 January.

31 Article 13 of the Order provides that imported Commercial Encryption Codes (CEC) products, imported equipment containing CEC technologies and exported CEC products must be approved by the National Commission on Encryption Code Regulations (NCECR) and that no work units or individuals may sell foreign CEC products. Article 15 further provides that foreign organizations or individuals using CEC products or equipment containing CEC technologies within the borders of China are required to report these products and their use to the NCECR and obtain approval.

32 Article 20 (2), the Regulations on the Safeguard of Computer Information System.

33 Article10, the Administrative Provisions on Secrecy of Computer Information Systems; Article 2, the Decision on Safeguarding the Internet.

34 Article 5, the Administrative Measures for Services on Electronic Bulletin Boards.

35 Article 14, the Administrative Measures for Services on Electronic Bulletin Boards.

36 Article 5, the Interim Provisions on the Administration of International Wiring of Computer Information Networks.

37 See Ming Pao News, 27 September 2001.

38 The police are vested with the quasi-judicial power to issue warnings, order the cessation of wiring, and impose a fine of no more than RMB 15,000 *yuan* (US$1,800) for, among

other things, violations of the requirement to use the public gateway for international wiring, violations of the requirement that wired networks must carry out international wiring through an interconnected network; and violations of the requirements that Internet users must carry out international wiring through a wired network. See Article of 14, the Interim Provisions on the Administration of International Wiring of Computer Information Networks.

39 For instance, Zhejiang Province. Apparently, these local measures (*tu banfa*) regarding annual renewal are further restraints in addition to the Article 20(2), the Regulations on the Safeguard of Computer Information System.

40 For them cyberspace is itself a regulator and governmental regulation is redundant and therefore conventional politics should not apply to the Internet. Technically, if unfettered access to the Internet is being threatened, the dream of universal access will remain only a dream. Politically, without free and unfettered access to the Internet, this exciting new medium could become little more than a souped-up television network. Internet is 'the most participatory form of mass speech yet developed', and should be entitled to 'the highest protection from governmental intrusion'. In view of this, they firmly hold that government censorship of the Internet violates the freedom of speech.

41 Pornography is almost universally criticized. Governments of almost every nation which has access to the Internet have pronounced certain limitations on the transmission of pornographic materials over the Internet. For instance, on 8 February 1996 the US President, Bill Clinton, signed into law the Telecommunication Act of 1996, which includes the Communications Decency Act of 1996 (CDA), an exclusively Internet-related section. The CDA declared that ISPs would be criminally liable for transmitting 'indecent' material without restricting access to minors. In 1997 the Federal Republic of Germany adopted a similar law on the Internet, which authorizes the punishment of ISPs failing to comply with the 'decent' rule. See U.S.C. § 223 (a)-(h); Compuserve Deutschland GmbH case, see, *generally*, Determann Lothar (1998), 'The New German Internet Law', *Hastings International and Comparative Law Review*, Vol. 22, pp. 117–24.

42 See, for instance, Arnold, Wayne (1996), 'Cyberpatrols: Censoring the net isn't easy, but it can be intimidating', in: *Asian Wall Street Journal*, 11 September, p.1.

43 The term 'spiritual pollution' normally refers to, among other things, political dissent and pornography.

44 For instance, Article 2, the Administration of International Wiring Gateway for Inbound and Outbound Computer Information.

45 For instance, all the three major Internet portals, that is, Sina.com, Sohu.com and Netease.com, are primarily financed by foreign venture capital and have been listed in Nasdaq over-the-counter market. The scenario is even more impressive if consideration is taken of the Hong Kong initial public offerings of China Telecom, through which the government decided to sell more of the shares it holds in this state-controlled Internet gateway and services giant.

46 On 24 September 1999, the US Internet player Yahoo! launched Yahoo! China. This enterprise is a joint venture between Beijing Founder Electronics Co., a leading Chinese computer company, and Yahoo! to provide Chinese online information and advertisement services. See Reuters 24 September 1999. On 11 June 2001, AOL Time Warner, the largest media corporation, and the Chinese computer maker Legend Holdings set up a joint venture to provide online services in China. The venture is 51 percent owned by Legend and 49 percent owned by America Online, a subsidiary of AOL Time Warner. Reportedly, the joint venture partners hope to combine AOL's marketing and technology expertise with Legend's leadership and brand recognition in the Chinese market for personal computer for consumers. However, since China has so far prohibited foreign ownership of content providers, AOL will initially have to provide technical support and consultation. See *China Daily*, 12 June 2001.

47 *The New York Times*, 5 September 2001, Internet Edition, available at http://college1.nytimes.com/guests/articles/2001/09/05/866101.xml.

References

Annoymous (2001), *The New York Times*, Internet Edition, 5 September.

Becker, Jasper (2000), 'Mainland clamps down on Net', *South China Morning Post*, Internet Edition, 27 January.

China Internet Network Information Centre, <http://www.cnnic.net.cn/>.

Lothar, Determann (1998), 'The New German Internet Law', *Hastings International and Comparative Law Review*, Vol. 22, pp. 117–24.

O'Neill, Mark (2000), 'Battle of new and old media, *South China Morning Post*, the Internet Edition, 19 February.

Ong, Carolyn *et al.* (2000). 'Taming the web', *South China Morning Post*, 27 January.

Pomfret, John (1999), 'China's Telecoms Battle', *International Herald Tribune*, 26 January.

Rodan, Garry (1998), 'The Internet and Political Control in Singapore', *Political Science Quarterly*, Vol. 113, pp. 71–6.

Sun Tiecheng (1999), 'Legal Problems of Comupter Networks', *in The Editing Group of Jurisprudence Frontiers* (in Chinese), Beijing: Law Press, 1999.

Tan, Zixiang (Alex) and Lu, Ding (1998), 'The State Borderline in the Cyberspace', in Erik Bohlin and Stanford L. Levin (eds.), *Telecommunications Transformation: Technology, Strategy, and Policy*, IOS Press, Netherlands.

Zheng Chengsi (1998), Intellectural Property Studies, Chinese Fangzheng Publishing House, Beijing, Vol. 5.

Chapter 11

Challenges and Opportunities for China's Agriculture after its WTO Accession

Guanzhong James Wen

Introduction

Among scholars, China is known to be exceptional with respect to many laws and norms that apply to most other nations. The exceptionality of China has doomed many predictions in the past. They are often proven to be too optimistic or too pessimistic. While people can have widely different opinions about China's future, it seems, however, that most agree on the following observations that can serve as our starting point for evaluating the impact of China's joining WTO on its agriculture and the lives of its farmers. First, relative to its population, most of China's natural resources are not abundant. In terms of per capita possession of main resources such as water, arable land, timber, oil, etc., China is, just like Japan, one of the poorest nations on earth. For example, China's per capita arable land and fossil fuel reserves are only 25 per cent and one-third of the global average respectively (Kym and Chao, 1998). China is also poorly endowed with fresh water. Its per capita water resources are only one-third of the world average. To make it worse, 81 per cent of national water resources are concentrated in an area (mostly southeast and southwest) where the arable land only accounts for 36 per cent of China's total arable land (Veeck and Li, 2002). That means that the areas that have 64 per cent of China's arable land and hundreds of millions of population have only 19 per cent of China's water resources. China's per capita forest possession is also alarmingly low. According to China's official data, forest only covers 13.9 per cent of its total territory, conspicuously low if compared with the world average of 26.0 per cent. Its per capita forest possession is merely 17.2 per cent of the world average (*The Statistical Yearbook of China*, SYOC, 2000).

Second, the overall ecological and environmental situation that China is facing is severe.[1] For the last several centuries, China saw rapid deforestation, desertization, salinization, frequent sandstorms, and rampant water shortages. One of the main causes of the environmental degradation used to be the rampant reclamation and overgrazing in areas where ecology was fragile and water resources were scarce. While overreclamation and overgrazing are yet to be reversed, as is reflected in rapid desertization in many areas of China[2] now, rural China is facing new types of environmental problems. Chemical pollution used to be concentrated in China's urban areas. However, because of the rapid development of township and village enterprises (TVEs) and the lack of regulations on discharge of solid, liquid and air wastes, pollution has been increasingly spread to China's vast rural areas.

Third, in order to raise its per capita income, China has to reduce the absolute number of its farmers so that it can transform itself from a farmer nation to a modern nation. Currently about 70 per cent of its population is living in rural areas. Because of its huge population base and limited arable land resources, the average farm scale in China is among the smallest in the world. Farmers are constrained in their income not only by the extremely small operating scale of farms, but also by the fact that many of these farms are located in remote and barren areas. In other nations where arable land resources are rich, people do not need to reclaim the meager land for agricultural purposes. However, the population pressure built up over the last several centuries forced a significant amount of the population to migrate into these areas to find a living in the farming sector. Unless the marginalized population can be removed from these areas, the hope of raising their per capita income and at least stopping, if not reversing, the worsening trend of China's GINI coefficient is very dim.

The cruel reality of its poor resource endowment relative to its already huge and still growing population dictates that the tough tasks faced by China will not go away no matter how China chooses between opening its door to the rest of the world and closing its borders, as it often did in the last few centuries. Now that China has decided to let itself be fully integrated into the world by choosing to enter the WTO, the relevant question is will China's WTO accession ease or further aggravate the pressures that China will feel in its modernization effort. In this chapter I will mainly focus on China's WTO accession on its agriculture and its rural population.

The organization of the chapter is as follows. The next section comments on China's main commitments to liberalize its trade and production of agricultural goods. The section after that discusses the short-term impacts on China's agriculture of its WTO accession. The section after that discusses the long-term impacts of China's WTO accession on its agriculture. The section after that explores the possible alliance of China and the US that may emerge out of their own interest to jointly push for further liberalization of agricultural production and trade within the framework of the WTO. The section after that explains why China's WTO accession will greatly accelerate its urbanization and help China absorb most of its surplus labor that will be released from its rural areas. The last section concludes.

China's Main Agricultural Commitments

China's main commitments can be summarized as follows.[3]

1 With WTO accession, by 1 January 2004, China's average tariff on agricultural imports will fall to 17.5 per cent from 22 per cent. China will set up a tariff-rate quota (TRQ) system on major agricultural products such as wheat, rice, corn, barley, cotton and soybean oil. For imports within the quota, the tariff rates will be no more than three per cent for grains and nine per cent for soybean oil. Not only the tariff rates within quotas are low, the quotas themselves are generous. For example, in 1999 China only imported two million tons of wheat. But in order to get into the WTO, China agrees to set up a TRQ of 7.3 million tons of wheat immediately on entering the WTO and promises to raise it to over 9.6

million tons. Overall China promises to import 21.8 million tons of grain including wheat, corn, and rice by the year 2004.[4]

2 The above quota tariff rates are also relatively low. According to D. G. Johnson (2001), China's tariffs for above quota imports will be only 65–77 per cent. US, Europe and Canada usually set their above quota tariff rates in the range of 144 per cent to 297 per cent on imports such as sugar, dairy products and poultry.

3 China will allow private traders, including foreign traders, to have the right to import and distribute agricultural products. China specifically agrees that the private traders will obtain a share of the TRQ. This arrangement will make it no longer possible for China to continue its government monopoly over marketing and distribution of important agricultural goods.

4 China agrees to eliminate the SPS barriers (Sanitary and Phytosanitary Measures) that are not scientifically grounded and to eliminate export subsidies as required by the WTO.

Based on these commitments, main grain producers such as the US will have good opportunities to increase immediately some of their agricultural export to China. For example, the US has comparative advantages in land-intensive products such as corn, wheat, and soybean oil. Currently, developed nations such as the US, European Union, Canada and Australia have some advantages in high quality meat and some fruit products (Economic Research Service or ERS/USDA, 2001). In the long run, the US, Canada and Australia may very likely continue to maintain their comparative advantages in land-intensive crops, but it is unclear whether they will continue to have an edge over China in most fruit products, vegetable products, and certain types of meat products such as pork and poultry. If agricultural protection can be reduced, EU will lose its edge immediately in many agricultural products.

Short Term Impacts on Chinese Agriculture – Challenges

According to trade theory, a nation can greatly benefit from specialization on products that it has a comparative advantage and then trade them for products that it has a comparative disadvantage. China has a comparative advantage in producing labor-intensive products such as rice, fruits, vegetables and flowers, and aquatic and meat products. These products use less land input per unit product, but use more labor input, a factor of production in which China is richly endowed. However, China has a comparative disadvantage in producing land-intensive products such as wheat, corn, and soybeans, etc. Unfortunately, China's current agricultural product mix is very far from the mix that would mean that China would benefit according to trade theory. China is not only the world largest rice producer, as it should be according to trade theory, but also the world largest wheat producer, the world second largest corn producer and the world third largest soybean producer. The current production structure in China's agriculture strongly suggests that China will gain enormously if China can find a way to restructure its product mix according to the trade theory. The present production structure has been shaped historically by the belief that China, as the most populous nation in the world, must be self-sufficient in satisfying the demand of its population for all farming produces. With this type of mindset, China has been producing many products that have no comparative advantage in terms of its factor endowments. As China opens up to the world market after the WTO accession, these products will face increasing pressure from foreign competitors. Therefore, in the short run, China's WTO accession immediately exposes it to serious challenges. This prospect triggers heated debates within China. Many are worried about the nightmarish prospect of the influx of foreign products that are cheaper, better, and more attractive.

These concerns can be summarized as follows. First, whether or not Chinese agricultural production will simply collapse in front of a sudden surge of agricultural imports. Second, whether or not the agricultural imports will greatly depress the income of the Chinese farmers and the income disparity between rural and urban areas get worse than now. Third, whether or not the number of the displaced farmers will become so large that they will threaten the social stability or become a burden that neither the Chinese government can bear nor China's urban areas can absorb.

The answer to the first concern is simply no. There are several strong reasons why such a concern is not grounded because most Chinese farmers will be protected by China's market power, underdeveloped social infrastructures, and geographical distance. As a nation, China has 1/5th of the world population and that gives China a big leverage in determining world grain prices. In other words, world grain prices are endogenous to China. Currently China is enjoying almost 100 per cent food self-sufficiency. Any significant changes in China's self-sufficiency rate, say from 100 per cent down to 85 per cent,[5] will sharply raise the food grain prices at the international market and will make it profitable to grow these crops in China again. This is because an 85 per cent self sufficiency rate, while still very high compared with many nations, represents a need to import 75 million tons of grain from the international market assuming China's total demand for grain is 500 million tons.[6] The consequent and much higher world market price will induce Chinese farmers to continue to produce most of the food grain that it needs in years to come.

Most Chinese farmers will also be protected by China's backward infrastructure and geographical remoteness. It is simply too costly to ship a large amount of foreign grain to China's vast inland, given that the grain price is so cheap. To residents living in China's inland, a mark-up to cover the shipping and handling cost will immediately make the imported grain less attractive to them than the locally produced products. Since rural residents represent the majority of China's population, it is obvious that if most of them will continue to consume their own grain products, then China will continue to produce most of the food grain that it needs. In addition, the WTO allows the safeguard mechanism. In case of a sudden surge in the influx of foreign grain import that is more than the TRQ allows, thus disrupting and damaging China's own grain production, China is entitled to impose much higher tariff rates on the above TRQ import.

The answer to the second concern is not that clearly cut. Broadly we can divide the Chinese farmers into three groups. Group I, whose population is growing rapidly, as a result of the on-going urbanization, is mostly living in the coastal areas and in areas close to urban centers where the per capita is rising rapidly. Group II is mostly living in South and Southwest where the main crops such as rice still have comparative advantage. Group III is mostly living in Northeast, North and

Northwest where the main crops are land-intensive crops such as corn, barley, soybean and wheat, that are losing comparative advantages.

As consumers, all of them will benefit from cheaper and better imports. However, as producers, Group I will benefit most from urbanization and industrialization that is creating an ever expanding domestic market for vegetables, flowers, sea food, and meat and dairy products. Farmers in this group also show strong competitiveness in producing these products in the world markets (Huang and Rozelle 1998). They will, if not yet, switch gradually to producing these products for domestic market first, and eventually for world markets in the future.

Group II may not benefit as much as Group I, but will also not see much harm done by increases in imports. This is because their staple crop is rice, a food grain that is labor-intensive and in which China still has comparative advantage. Overall, this area is endowed with fertile land, warm climate, and most importantly in China's context, rich rainfalls, and many big lakes and rivers. Therefore, this area is very suitable for vegetables, fruits, and aquatic and meat products.

Group III seems to be the only group that will see its income falling gradually as a result of increased imports. But the situation will not be as disastrous as some claim. Given the semi-subsistence nature of Chinese agriculture, as was pointed out above, farmers in this group will continue to grow what they need for their own consumption. Therefore, even for Group III, production will not collapse. However, the amount of their surplus products that they can otherwise sell to markets will fall as a result of increased foreign competition and so will their cash income.

The answer to the third concern about the sudden surge in the number of homeless and landless farmers is also highly unlikely. The reason is simple. Protected by the geographic distance, China's market power and by the safeguard mechanism permitted by the WTO, agricultural imports simply will not surge suddenly and dramatically.[7] Therefore, most Chinese farmers will not be displaced immediately. However, the pressure on farmers in Group III will gradually build up.

In summary, we can say that in the short run, China will continue to produce most of its grain crops and other products and most Chinese farmers will continue to work in the field. Increasingly farmers will be pushed out or attracted away from the farming sector. This process will proceed gradually, and will not immediately cause major social instability in the short run. While small-scale and scattered conflicts or clashes are happening everyday, as they were happening even before China's WTO accession, the WTO itself alone cannot be a major factor to lead China to disorder or collapse, as some claim. These rural conflicts and clashes have been mainly caused by corruption and power abuse rampant among rural officials, and land disputes and feuds widely reported among farmers in some areas. So far these conflicts and clashes have never escalated into social instability. However, the income disparity between rural and urban areas will continue to grow. The situation of farmers in North, Northeast and Northwest will be exacerbated particularly.

Long Term Impacts

While the short-term impacts of WTO accession on agriculture could be painful and strenuous, China's long-term prospects for growth will never be so favorable as after its WTO accession. WTO is an institutional arrangement to allow its members to share their resources through peaceful competition in the world market. Its institutional arrangement is a response to colonialism and imperialism that the world experienced in the earlier rounds of globalization. During that period of time, more powerful nations obtained the resources that they were scarcely endowed by force, occupation and plunder. Only after paying the high price of two world wars did most nations, including the main powers, come to realize what Ricardo revealed more than one hundred years ago that nations did not need to get the resources in the battlefields through colonization and occupation. If they choose to vent what they have in surplus in the world market in exchange for what they are in short supply through division of labor, specialization and trade, all the nations will gain much more from such exchanges. After World War II, led by North America, Western Europe and Japan gave up all their colonies and accepted GATT, the predecessor of WTO. The whole world witnessed unprecedented prosperity and growth in these areas. The foresight of the free trade theory thus has been evidenced and its vision accepted by the rest of the world. Unfortunately, during this period, China chose to stay away from this free trade system, and its gap with the world average was widened and its environment was further deteriorated.

WTO accession will allow China to have access to the global resources, technology, physical and human capital peacefully and will allow China to pursue its own comparative advantages. In particular, the WTO accession will allow China to change gradually its agricultural product mix by reducing the share of land-intensive products such as corn, wheat, soybeans, barley, etc. and gradually increasing the share of labor-intensive products, such as rice, vegetables, fruits, flowers, herbs, aquatic and meat products. China has great potential in producing these products. It has already become the world's largest vegetable producer and a leading fruit and meat producer (Bottelier 1999, Du). In the future, China can easily expand its production and export of these products for the following reasons. Given the vast land base, abundant labor resources, diverse soil and climate endowment, China actually can produce almost any vegetables and fruits that can be found from tropical areas to the very cold zones. In addition, China can produce pork and poultry at lower cost than many developed economies. China also has long but underutilized seashores and, to a lesser extent, river shores and lakeshores, that can be used to raise aquatic products.

China will greatly benefit from moving toward this new product mix. First, vegetable, fruit, aquatic and meat products have higher value added than grain crops and can bring higher income to producers. For the last decade or so, farmers in the suburbs of urban centers already greatly benefited from growing vegetables for urban residents. Second, China will be able to switch the hilly land that is currently used to grow corn, wheat, or rice to produce fruit and to raise cattle by using imported feed. China can slow down erosion on slopes and grazing land. Third, higher income from the new product mix will make water-saving techniques such as greenhouses, dripping or sprinkler systems become affordable to farmers. Currently, the total areas using greenhouse or sprinkler system are expanding rapidly around the major urban centers. Fourth, China's farming sector can absorb more rural laborers when China's product mix becomes more labor-intensive than now and will help reduce the growing unemployment pressure in China's urban areas.

A Big Contributor to Liberalizing World Agricultural Production and Trade

The timing for China to grow into a powerful free agricultural trader is very good. Many Asian economic powers turned to protectionist policies when they had finished becoming industrialized and when the share of farmers in the total population fell significantly. In China industrialization and urbanization is going on rapidly and citing the examples from Japan, South Korea, and Taiwan, many have started to talk about the need to protect agricultural production, particularly the need to provide protection to grain production. In the mid 1990s, the government implemented the governor responsibility system that required that each province be self-sufficient in grain supply. Later, the government adopted new measures to monopolize the purchase and marketing of grain by providing some price floors to grain growers. Such a policy has been proved to be a big failure (Lu, 1999) because it cost the government more than 500 billion yuan. The protectionist policy partially also contributes to the gluts of grain supply, that in turn, hurt farmers income.[8] The earlier phasing out of this policy and China's promise to phase out other protectionist policies will save the government from incurring even bigger deficits and better prepares China for new rounds of negotiations on liberalizing agricultural production and trade within the framework of the WTO.

The good thing is that China does not need to overcome major barriers to become a natural promoter of free trade of agricultural products. Evidences from Japan, Europe and the US have demonstrated that once interest groups are formed, it is very difficult to eliminate protectionist policies without meeting strong resistance from the interest groups that are affected by such policy changes. For the last five decades or so, instead of subsidizing its agriculture (in net terms), China transferred a significant amount of agricultural surplus to develop its industries (Lin et al, 1996).[9] This situation has not been fundamentally changed. Therefore, the overall net protection that the Chinese government has been providing to the Chinese farmers is minimal, often negative.[10] Therefore, unlike Japan, the European Union and some other nations such as South Korea, China does not have a protection edifice to be dismantled. What is more encouraging to those who believe that nations should organize their domestic production according to their true comparative advantages and then trade is that the Chinese government promises to liberalize gradually its agricultural trade. Thus, Chinese agriculture as one of the largest in the world is poised to become one of the most market oriented. Assume that the US is serious in making it one of its global goals to further liberalize world agricultural production and trade, then China is a natural ally to the US in achieving this goal. The US has comparative advantages in many agricultural products. If the US works closely with China and other nations to dismantle the rampant agricultural protectionism and high trade barriers we see now in many areas, especially in Europe and Japan, both nations have little to lose, but a lot to gain. China will find a huge market in Japan, Korea, Taiwan and some other Asian economies, where the taste of the local people is closer to that of China. The US farmers will find a much friendlier market for their products in Europe. Many developing nations, whose main exports are agricultural products, will also find more opportunities to sell their goods in the world markets.

However, before China becomes a major exporter of agricultural products, it has some serious technical barriers to overcome. First, China needs to increase the range of varieties in its vegetable and fruit exports. Second, China needs to learn how to raise the quality of its products to the international standard. Third, China needs to learn how to package and promote its products worldwide. Fourth, China needs to learn how to meet sanitary and phytosanitary standards. It remains to see if China can retain its comparative advantages in these products after it meets the international standards for quality and sanitary measures.

WTO and Urbanization – An Historical Opportunity

In the Introduction, I raised the question of whether China's WTO accession will ease or further aggravate the pressures that China faces in its modernization effort. Now the answer seems clearer to me. The WTO, as a multilateral trade arrangement, will make China feel much secured in obtaining through peaceful and commercial ways the world resources that it badly needs for its modernization. Especially, China's food supply, a major concern of the Chinese government for the last several centuries, will be much more secure, because the WTO rules will make it highly unlikely for any nation to use food as a weapon to impose food sanctions on China unilaterally. Once China feels secure about its food supply, it no longer needs to maintain an almost 100 per cent food self-sufficiency rate and can move to a new product mix that better reflects its resource endowments and comparative advantage. China's fragile environment and ecology will get a precious opportunity to have a long due break and the majority of its population need not be tied to often barren land to make a meager living. More specifically, WTO accession will greatly facilitate China's modernization for the following reasons.

First, by producing a new product mix which is more labor-intensive, China's agriculture, even after it is modernized, will absorb more laborers than if China had to live in autarky and had to produce all it needed for survival, including all the land-intensive crops. Second, the new product mix requires that China import more land-intensive crops, that will alleviate the pressure on land in the North, Northeast and Northwest, the areas where erosion and environmental problems are most serious and water shortage is rampant. Third, the rest of the world will help absorb a part of China's rural laborers by further opening up their markets to the labor-intensive products from China, as required by WTO. Fourth, and most important, China will have better chances to absorb most of its own surplus labor by accelerating its urbanization.

The importance of accelerating urbanization can never be overestimated in China's context. Urbanization is different from industrialization, although in most nations they go hand in hand. Up to now, China's urbanization is lagging behind its industrialization. Experiences from most nations show that first the share of the farming sector and then that of the manufacturing sector, fall in the total labor force as a society modernizes. It is only the service sector that sees its share rising continuously. However, the precondition for the rapid growth of service sector is the concentration of population in a relatively small space, i.e., urbanization. The delay in China's urbanization has seriously aggravated China's unemployment situation.

Worrying about food security in its urban areas, the Chinese government was very hesitant, often even hostile, to urbanization. Even after reforms started in 1978, the government still did not allow the floating population to settle down in urban areas and prohibited TVEs from moving closer to urban centers.[11] Currently, TVEs are hiring more than one hundred million laborers and the floating population amounts to about one hundred million. However, they are yet to be accepted as urban residents officially under the household registration system. This policy not only deprived TVEs of the opportunity to benefit from the agglomeration effect that urban areas can generate by allowing all the residents and firms to share urban infrastructure, including transportation, communication, sewage, water and electricity supply, but also delayed the growth of service sector, consequently aggravated unemployment.

With the accession to the WTO, China is now in a position to reform its household registration system and encourage urbanization. The population who are living in areas where rampant water shortage has been developing will have the opportunity to move to areas where water resources are relatively abundant, such as the coastal areas and South. By moving to these areas, people from the inland, especially from China's North, Northeast and Northwest, will have the chance to share the growth and prosperity in the coastal areas and in China's South. This is an effective way to reduce the spatial income disparity.

Concluding Remarks

In summary, while the accession in WTO will not make many of the century-long thorny problems that China faces disappear over night, it seems to me that it will help China gradually get out of the trap that it has been locked in for the last several hundred years. That is, in order to reach food self-sufficiency, it had to compel the majority of its population to tie themselves to land. This choice was out of necessity when China had no other way to secure its food supply. China has achieved this goal, using only nine per cent of world arable land to feed more than 20 per cent of the world population. But to achieve this, the environmental and ecological prices are simply too high for China's future generations to bear. By forcing the population to spread out so they can have a piece of meager land, China also seriously delayed its urbanization, aggravated its unemployment situation and marginalized a significant fraction of its rural population.

WTO accession provides China a way out of the trap that it has been locked in and enables China to face a more favorable external economic environment than China faced in the past. Whether or not China can translate this opportunity into reality depends on whether or not China can successfully reform its socio-economic institutions. Without such reforms, China cannot maximize the potential benefits that can come from its WTO membership; it also cannot minimize the potential social-economic costs that it has to pay.

Notes

1 There is a report on *Renmin Ribao* (*Overseas edition, 6/1/2002*) that provides a summary of the Communique on China's Environmental Situation in the year 2001.

2 China is one of the countries that has been threatened by desertization most severely. According to *Renmin Ribao* (*People's Daily* overseas edition), desertization is most concentrated in China's Northwest and North. The areas that have already been desertized or are desertizing are increasing annually by 3000 square kilometers, and causing direct economic losses in the amount of 54 billion yuan every year (28 May 2002).

3 This summary is based on Whitehouse Facts Sheet (2 February 2000), Protocol on Accession of the People's Republic of China provided by WTO (WT/L/432, 23 November 2001), and the paper No. 00–02 by D. Gale Johnson. See References for more detailed sources.

4 This amount is still less than what China originally planed to import. China publicly promised to set its self-sufficiency rate at 95 per cent. That is equivalent to an import of 25 million tons of grain if we take China's annual average grain output of 500 million tons as a base. Therefore, China's commitment is no more than what it originally planed to do.

5 According to OECD statistical data for the period 1979–1988, the grain self sufficiency rates in Italy, Holland, Switzerland, and Japan are 80 per cent, 28 per cent, 53 per cent, and 22 per cent respectively. See Table 18 in 'Can China feed its own?'by Ying Liang (1996).

6 According to Brown (1995), on average, the total amount of grain available in the world grain market during the 1980s and 1990s was about 230 million tons. If China were to import 75 million tons of grain, or one-seventh of the world total grain export, the world grain price would be driven up inevitably.

7 According to the WTO rules on safeguard, a nation is entitled to set a much higher tariff rate on any good whose import experiences a sudden surge surpassing what TRQ allows, and leads to the disruption in the domestic production of that good (Eglin, 2002).

8 Because of the low income elasticity of demand for grain food, the drop in the free market price of grain products as a result of surplus grain induced by the protectionist policy might hurt farmers' income more than help them. It is not accidental that farmers' income has become stagnate in recent years exactly when China has enjoyed unprecedented good supply of almost all types of agricultural products.

9 Having a monopoly of purchasing and marketing before 1978, the government was in a position to push down the procurement prices of agricultural goods, at the same time to raise the prices of the industrial goods that were used as intermediate goods by agriculture. Through such price differences, the Chinese government channeled away almost all the agricultural surplus to developing China's industries, especially the heavy industries that otherwise could not have been developed under a free market system.

10 The Chinese farmers are not only subject to agricultural taxes, high intermediate input prices, low output prices as a result of the contract or quota system, but also to illegal fees and levies collected by local officials. Farmers heavy financial burdens are increasingly receiving attention from the central government, but little has been done to alleviate the situation because of the competing demands for limited financial resources at the disposal of the central government and the much less assertive voice from the traditionally underprivileged farming section.

11 During that period, China was even convinced to think that it found a new path to modernization — the so-called rural industrialization in the forms of TVEs. It took two long decades for China to realize that this so-called new path has very little future. China still can not avoid urbanization if it wants to reduce the cost of industrialization, to provide more job opportunities to its farmers, and to have pollution under better and more efficient control.

References

Bottelier, Pieter (1999) 'China's Economic Transition and the significance of WTO Membership', Center for Research on Economic Development and Policy Reform, Stanford University.

Du, Ying (2000) 'China's Agricultural Restructuring and System Reform under its Accession to the WTO'; ACIAR China Grain Market Policy Project Paper No. 12, Canbera, Australia.

Economic Research Service, USDA (2001) 'China's Fruit and Vegetable Sector: A Changing Market Environment', *Agricultural Outlook*, June-July issue, pp.10–13.

Eglin, Richard (2002) 'Challenges and Implications of China Joining the WTO: What WTO Accession Means'. Collected in *'The Globalization of the Chinese Economy'*, ed. by Wei, Shang-Jin, Wen, Guanzhong James and Zhou, Huizhong. Edward Elgar, forthcoming.

Huang, Jikun and Rozelle, Scott (1998), *'China's Grain Economy to the Twenty-First Century.'* Beijing, China Agriculture Press.

Johnson, D. Gale (2000), 'China's Agriculture and WTO Accession'. Paper No. 00–02, Office of Agricultural Economic Research, the University of Chicago.

Kym, Anderson and Chao, Yang Peng (1998), 'Feeding and Fueling China in the 21st Century', *World Development*, Vol. 26, No. 8, pp.1413–29.

Liang, Ying (1996), 'Can China feed its own?', Economic Science Publishing House, Beijing.

Lin, Justin Yifu, Cai Fang and Li Zhou (2002), *The China Miracle: Development Strategy and Economic Reform*, The Chinese University of Hong Kong Press.

Lu, Feng (1999), 'Three Gluts of Grain — An Alternative Interpretation of Changes in China's Grain Circulation Policies',Working paper No. C1999003, CCER, Peking University.

Renmin Ribao (*People's Daily* overseas edition), 'The Emergency Situation of Our Country's Desertization', 28 May 2002.

Veeck, George and Li, Zhou (2002), 'Environmental Degradation and Natural Resource Conservation in Rural China', RDT-CASS (Chinese Academy of Social Sciences) White Paper.

Whitehouse Facts Sheet 2000. 'Summary of U. S. – China Bilateral WTO Agreement'. http://www.uschina.org/public/wto/ustr/generalfacts.html.

Chapter 12

Recent Claims of China's Economic Exceptionalism: Reflections Inspired by WTO Accession

Wing Thye Woo

Introduction

The phenomenal growth of China in the last two decades is not in much dispute. What has been the subject of vigorous research and even more vigorous debate are the causes of this phenomenal growth. While there is broad agreement that the most important part of the answer is the marketization of the economy and its integration into the international division of labor, there is much less agreement over the relative contributions of the many economic mechanisms that were put into motion by these two policies. For example, while virtually all economists would agree with the proposition that complete price flexibility is to be preferred over complete price fixity, there can be disagreement over the optimal speed at which price flexibility is to be introduced and the economic mechanism through which a given speed is to be implemented.

Suppose that, even if agreement could be reached, 20 per cent of prices are to be decontrolled in each of the first two years instead of five per cent or 50 per cent each year, there still remains the choice of totally freeing the prices of 20 per cent of the commodities or of allowing 20 per cent of each commodity to be sold at freely-determined prices. In this case, there is agreement over the general principle of price flexibility, but not necessarily over the implementation of this principle.

Of course, there is then the more difficult issue of whether the same economic mechanism can be applied successfully across different economic sectors. This is clearly the case in the use of the 'contract responsibility system' (CRS) to implement the principle of decentralized decision making. Many researchers will agree that the household responsibility system unleashed sustained productivity improvements in the agricultural sector that boosted economic growth substantially, especially in the 1978–84 period. But many fewer researchers can agree that the enterprise responsibility system generated impressive productivity gains in the state enterprise sector that lifted the overall growth rate significantly, even in the 1984–88 period. Clearly, the difference in outcomes could be due to a combination of the differences in the way that CRS was implemented in each sector and in the structure of agricultural and industrial production. While descriptive differences are obvious and many on the implementation front and on the structural front, our priors are that the production relationships in agriculture and industry are so different that there is a different optimal economic mechanism for implementing the 'decentralized decision-making' principle in each sector.

The difference in sectoral outcomes to the CRS mechanism raises many intriguing but disturbing hypotheses. Possibly the most relevant of these hypotheses for China, on the eve of its WTO accession, is whether the optimal economic mechanism for a particular sector in a foreign country can also be the optimal, or even a useful, economic mechanism for the same sector in China. Specifically, is it possible that (almost) complete marketization and total internationalization of economic activities was optimal for the capitalist East Asian economies but would be disastrous for China's economy? Is this the reason for the vastly different output responses of China in 1979 and Poland in 1990, when they embarked on their market-oriented reform paths? More specifically, what is the optimal degree of marketization and the optimal degree of international integration for each country? In light of China's high growth since 1978, is China already at, or already close to, the optimal degree on these two fronts, such that entry into WTO and the harmonization of Chinese economic institutions to WTO-specified institutional forms will cause an overshooting of marketization and internationalization?

The aims of this chapter are to argue that China is still below the optimal degree of marketization and international integration and that the chosen method of WTO membership to advance marketization and integration is a desirable one, conditional upon supplementary policies being enacted to reduce the adjustment costs. In our view, even with WTO membership, China stands a much greater chance of undershooting on both fronts than of overshooting. Our case for China's WTO membership is based on the proposition that China's economic progress since 1978 was the result of China's institutional convergence to a prototype WTO market economy rather than the result of China's economic institutions being different from those of a prototype WTO economy. We will make our case by examining some claims in the literature that Chinese economic exceptionalism is the cause of the phenomenal growth.

It is important to state at the outset that we agree with some important parts in these claims of Chinese economic exceptionalism. While we recognize China has had the luxury of more than one feasible path to a prototype WTO market economy, we see that the costs and unsustainability of some of these alternative feasible paths have not been adequately laid out. Furthermore, while we also recognize that the prototype WTO market economy accommodates a variety of institutional forms, we hold that there are some key features of a prototype WTO economy that are important for China to converge to. These key institutional features include near absence of state intervention in price-setting, dominance of private ownership, primary reliance on capital markets to allocate investment capital and overwhelming even-handedness in legal treatment of state capital, domestic private capital and foreign capital. China has almost achieved the first feature, has made some big strides since 1993 on the second and is still largely amiss on the third and fourth.

Before starting the discussion, we would like to say a few words about the obfuscating terminology that the debate over transition strategies has generated. A wealth of oxymora has been conjured up because protagonists have sought to attach undeserved positive connotations to their viewpoints. A number of authors have labeled rapid, comprehensive reforms (big bang reforms) as top-down reforms, and slow, partial reforms (incremental reforms) as bottom-up reforms. Big bang reforms were hence associated with a reform style that is reminiscent of central planning coercion and incremental reforms with a democratic trial-and-error market-learning process. These two associations are largely false and self-contradictory as suggested by the following two considerations.

First, the reliance on markets to allocate resources represents decentralized economic management achieved by empowering individual initiatives. Markets are naturally occurring phenomenon because they render both buyers and sellers better off. The only time when markets are absent is when they are suppressed by the central plan of the state. Marketization means allowing the bottom-up process to run its natural course. Second, reform of a centrally-planned economy means the marketization of economic transactions and the deep entrenchment of market-supporting institutions such as the criminal justice system to maintain law and order, commercial courts to enforce contracts, bankruptcy courts to encourage prudent lending and enable fresh starts for entrepreneurs and social safety nets to lower the costs of resource reallocation. By its nature, marketization can be accomplished fairly quickly if desired, but the firm entrenchment of market-supporting institutions cannot be achieved quickly even if desired.

In short, big bang reforms (quick marketization) means the unleashing of the bottom-up process of individual initiatives on a grand scale, while incremental reforms (slow marketization) means incremental legalization of the bottom-up process. The amazing semantic sleight of hand that has happened is that the advocates of gradual reform have identified themselves as advocates of the bottom-up approach to economic management! It is time for the misleading terms of 'top-down reform' and 'bottom-up reform' to be dropped from the transition strategy debate.

The two words 'evolutionary' and 'path-dependent' are often encountered in the transition literature and while they are always accurate, they are not always useful. In the strictest sense, rational policymaking is evolutionary and path-dependent by necessity. Policymaking has to be evolutionary because new exogenous shocks are always appearing and it is nearly always path-dependent because reversals can be expensive, if not impossible. For example, China's tariff policy is contingent on whether China is already a WTO member or not.

There is one important sense in which the term 'evolutionary' is analytically useful. Take the case of bankruptcy procedures. They were not needed during the planning period and so they were non-existent prior to 1990. With the transition to a market economy, the state faces two policy choices. The first policy is to adopt the bankruptcy procedures of another country after modifying them to accommodate relevant differences in national circumstances and then to continue to modify them in light of experience. The second policy is to rely on the bottom-up process in the most fundamental sense by encouraging citizens to come up with private contractual arrangements that would cover the contingency of financial difficulties that the borrowers might encounter. Comparing these two policies, we see that the first promotes institutional evolution in the local sense and the second choice promotes institutional evolution in the global sense.

In practice, institutional evolution in the local sense entails a pro-active state in the sphere of institution building, where the usual operational principle is to adopt a foreign prototype and then modify it through practice.[1] Institutional evolution in the global sense, on the other hand, requires a state that is agnostic and passive about institution building because of its unbridled faith that the demand for institutions will inevitably induce the appropriate institutional innovations. Sachs and Woo (2000) called the first approach 'the convergence school of institution building' and the second approach, the 'experimentalist school of institution building'.

The misunderstanding over these two approaches to institution building has caused the biggest obfuscation in the debate over transition strategies *for China*. The transition debate for China has primarily been a debate over the origins of institutions and the desired direction for institutional evolution and only very secondarily, a debate over the speed of implementing the reform program, even though the debate did focus on speed in the beginning. The real question in the transition debate on China still remains whether a third way exists between socialist planning and capitalist markets.

In sharp contrast, the fundamental academic issue in the post-mortem debate on transition strategies *for Eastern Europe and the former Soviet Union* (EEFSU) is the desired speed for institutional changes. This is because leading EEFSU economists (such as Janos Kornai, 1992) take it for granted that there is no third way. There is clearly no simple answer to the speed issue because 'the transition from socialism to capitalism... is a curious amalgam of revolution and evolution'.[2]

Some reforms, such as macroeconomic stabilization, have to be done very quickly and some reforms, such as privatization, have to be done much slower. In all cases, the decision on speed has to take into account the administrative capacity of the state and the political situation in the country.

It is clear that most of the EEFSU have embraced the convergence school of institution building (albeit with different speeds in implementation). But would it be accurate to say that China has followed the experimentalist school of institution building, since many of the critics of quick marketization have explained the gradual pace of Chinese reform as being due to the time-consuming process of experimentation to discover policies and institutions that are optimal for China's economic situation? If the experimentalist interpretation of China's phenomenal growth is correct, then China's forthcoming WTO membership is a negative development because it could be a straitjacket that would constrain China's scope for experimentation. But if the experimentalist interpretation is wrong, then WTO membership is a positive development that will lock China on to the path of deepening economic reform and openness.

Sachs and Woo (2000) presented a comprehensive survey of China's performance up to 1994 and concluded that China's phenomenal growth had come from its convergence to a prototype WTO economy. Therefore, another objective of this paper is to assess several recent interesting additions to the literature to see whether the Sachs-Woo conclusion still holds and hence, whether optimism about China's WTO accession is still justified.

The Feasibility and Optimality of the Dual Track Reform Strategy

Strictly speaking, 'dual track' does not capture the complexity of China's reform policies. In different periods there was dual-track for the pricing of inputs, output, and foreign exchange; five-track for ownership in the service and light industrial sectors (individual, state, collective, private and foreign); multiple-track for revenue-sharing between the center and the provinces (Guangdong and Fujian signed lump sum revenue contracts with a five-year duration and the other provinces paid varying proportions of their revenue to the center); multi-track for international trade and foreign direct investments (with Shenzhen having the most liberal regime for the longest time); and a single-track, until recently, for interest rates and ownership in the banking sector.

In this section, we will focus mainly on the dual-track price reform.[3] The academic analysis of China's dual track price system (DTPS) has gone through two phases: the partial-equilibrium approach and the general equilibrium approach. Proponents of the DTPS describe it as a Pareto-improving way of introducing price flexibility that encourages growth without arousing political opposition from entrenched interest groups. We find this claim of gain-without-pain to be either factually wrong or politically implausible.

The Partial Equilibrium Analysis (PEA) of Dual Track Pricing

The analytics can be summarized by the following example when there is a light industrial good and a heavy industrial good, with the following supply and demand relationships in a free market setting.

For the light industrial good, we assume
supply curve (marginal cost curve): $P = 2 + Q$
demand curve: $P = 12 - Q$ where Q is in units of millions.

For the heavy industrial good, we assume
supply curve (marginal cost curve): $P = 3 + 2Q$
demand curve: $P = 12 - Q$ where Q is in units of millions.

Under the free market, see Figures 12.1 and 12.2, in the light industrial good market: $P = 7$ and $Q = 5$; and in the heavy industrial good market: $P = 9$ and $Q = 3$.

For the central plan situation, assume the modus operandi to be where the planner picks the output level in each industry and sets the plan price to equate revenue with production costs of the output quota. Furthermore, assume that the planner creates the typical Stalinist outcome where the light industrial good is under-produced vis-a-vis the free market situation and the heavy industrial good is over-produced vis-a-vis the free market situation.[4] Say, for light industrial goods, the planner picks $Q = 2$, and hence sets $P = 3$. The result is a black market price of 10 with the marginal cost being 4. And, say, for heavy industrial goods, the planner picks $Q = 4$, and hence sets $P = 7$. The result is a black market price of 8 with the marginal cost of 11.

The Dual-Track Price System (DTPS) is the situation where the producer is allowed to sell his above-quota output at a freely determined price. Then for the light industrial good, we have:

market price = 7

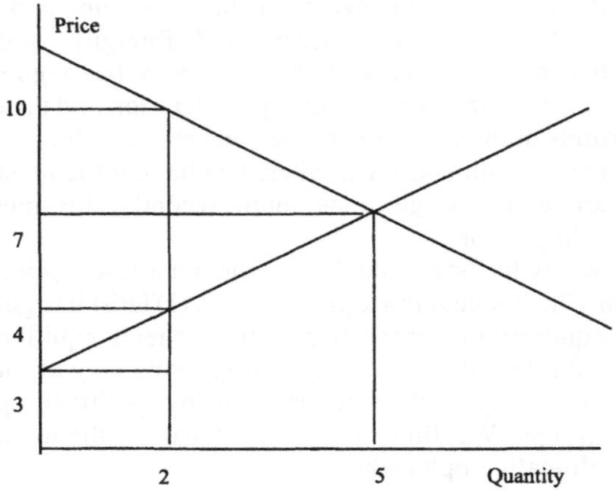

Figure 12.1 Light industrial good

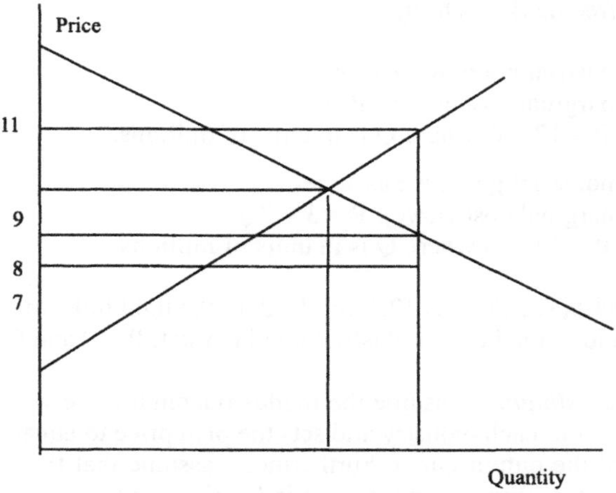

Figure 12.2 Heavy industrial good

market quantity = 3
plan price = 3
plan quantity = 2

The total quantity of five represents an increase in the output of the light industrial good, with no decrease in quantities sold at the lower plan price to the privileged buyers. This is a Pareto-improving situation.

For the heavy industrial good, we have:
market price = 8
market quantity = 0 because the marginal cost exceeds the market price,
plan price = 7
plan quantity = 4.

The total quantity produced remains at four with no losers and no winners. So the overall situation from the DTPS is a Pareto-improving situation.

Complete price liberalization (big bang reform), as is clear from Figures 12.1 and 12.2, is not Pareto improving because the privileged buyers of both goods under rationing will now have to pay higher prices and there will be laid-off workers in the heavy industrial goods sector. A big bang will cause a collapse in the production of heavy industrial goods and the resulting disorganization (*à la* Blanchard and Kremer, 1997) could cause a temporary drop in the production of light industrial goods as well. This is a situation that is reminiscent of Poland and Russia upon the marketization of their economies in January 1990 and January 1992, respectively. The key lesson from the partial equilibrium analysis (PEA) is that partial price flexibility is superior to total price flexibility.

The General Equilibrium Analysis (GEA) of Dual Track Pricing

The inadequacy of PEA is obvious if these two goods comprise the entire production structure and if there were full-employment and maximum production efficiency under the original central planning situation. In this context, the introduction of dual-track pricing cannot cause an increase in the output of the light industrial good unless there is a decrease in the output of the heavy industrial good. How could the occurrence of the latter still make the DTPS Pareto-improving?

Lau, Qian and Roland (2000) answered this question by claiming that the light industrial good supplier will execute the following sequence of actions:

(a) go into the market for the heavy industrial good and buy (at the free market price) the rights to some of the planned output that was allocated to privileged consumers (at the free market price). Say that he bought the rights to X units of the heavy industrial good.
(b) tell the heavy industrial good producer to reduce his production by X units and send the released workers to work in the light industrial good sector.
(c) hire the newly released workers from the heavy industrial sector and expand the production of the light industrial good by Y units.

The heavy industrial good producer is happy to cooperate because he now makes a positive profit from his costs having decreased more than his revenue. One of the possible outcomes is that X=1 and Y = 3, which makes the dual tracking outcome the same as the free market outcome. The important prediction is that the DTPS, in a general equilibrium setting, will cause one sector to expand and the other sector to shrink as in complete price liberalization and this DTPS-induced adjustment is contractual and mutually beneficial in nature.

For policy purposes, both PEA and GEA offer the same advice: limited price deregulation is better than complete price deregulation. Complete price deregulation might produce the same input allocation and output composition as the DTPS, but the former definitely generates resentment against the government while the latter does not.

Critique of the Preceding Two Analyses of the Dual Track Price System

It is ironic that the supposedly flawed PEA is factually more correct than the theoretically coherent GEA. Table 12.1 shows that the output of both the light and heavy industrial sectors went up every year following the introduction of the DTPS in 1985.[5] Light industrial output increased 64 per cent in the 1984–87 period and heavy industrial output increased 55 per cent. The Lau, Qian and Roland prediction of a (voluntary) contraction in heavy industrial output upon marketization of the economy is contradicted by the data, suggesting that their elaborate general equilibrium analysis could be an exercise in false precision. Clearly, we need an explanation other than the DTPS to explain why China grew so fast upon marketization.

Table 12.1 shows two interesting facts that suggest an alternative explanation for what really happened in China. First, output from industrial SOEs increased every year in the reform era, but the state sector's share of total industrial output declined secularly from 78 per cent in 1978 to 28 per cent in 1998. This means that the bulk of the increase in industrial output came from the non-state sector. Hence, fast growth of industrial output should not be attributed entirely to the incentive effect of dual-track pricing. Most of the credit, in our judgement, should be given to the legalization of the dual-track ownership system in the industrial sector in 1984. The legalization of non-state firms allowed non-state industrial enterprises to be established in the rural areas, the famous township and village enterprises (TVEs).

Second, the non-state sector did not grow by obtaining their labor from the state sector through contractual agreements, the key mechanism behind the Lau, Qian and Roland assertion of 'gain without pain'. State employment was 17.9 per cent of the labor force in 1984 (the eve of the introduction of the DTPS to the industrial sector) and it rose to 18.3 per cent in 1989 (the eve of the replacement of the DTPS with almost complete price decontrol). The state sector in 1989 employed 14.7 million workers more than in 1984 and 26.6 million more than in 1978. In employment terms, China was certainly not growing out of the plan either in absolute or in relative terms.[6]

The labor that fuelled the fast expansion of the non-state industrial sector came from agriculture, a sector that was not identified by Lau, Qian and Roland as an important contributor to China's high growth rates after 1984. Part A of Table 11.2 shows that employment in the primary sector declined from 71 per cent in 1978 to 50 per cent in 1998.[7] Therein, we have the *deus ex machina* of China's growth. The marketization and internationalization of economic activities generated substantial productivity increases, not only by enlivening the agricultural sector in the 1979–84 period and by creating a dynamic non-state sector from 1984 onward, but also by moving low-productivity agricultural growth. The marketization and internationalization of economic activities generated substantial productivity increases, not only

Table 12.1 Production of light and heavy industrial goods and state sector employment, 1978–1998

	Index of Gross Industrial Output 1978=100		Composition of Gross Industrial Output (%)		Proportion of Labor Force in S-O Units (%)	Proportion of Gross Industrial Output by S-O Units Current Prices (%)
	Light industry	Heavy industry	Light industry	Heavy industry		
1978	100.0	100.0	38.9	61.1	18.6	77.6
1979	110.0	108.0	39.3	60.7	18.8	78.5
1980	130.8	110.1	43.1	56.9	18.9	76
1981	149.5	105.1	47.5	52.5	19.1	74.8
1982	158.2	115.5	46.6	53.4	19.1	74.4
1983	172.9	130.6	45.7	54.3	18.9	73.4
1984	200.7	152.2	45.6	54.4	17.9	69.1
1985	246.3	182.9	46.1	53.9	18.0	64.9
1986	278.5	201.6	46.8	53.2	18.2	62.3
1987	330.3	235.3	47.2	52.8	18.3	59.7
1988	403.3	280.9	47.7	52.3	18.4	56.8
1989	436.4	305.9	47.6	52.4	18.3	56.1
1990	476.6	324.9	48.3	51.7	16.2	54.6
1991	548.0	372.0	48.4	51.6	16.5	56.2
1992	657.7	479.8	46.6	53.4	16.6	51.5
1993	835.2	611.8	46.5	53.5	16.5	57.3
1994	1,032.3	762.3	46.3	53.7	16.2	37.3
1995	1,268.7	899.5	47.3	52.7	16.1	34.0
1996	1,573.2	1,013.7	49.7	50.3	15.9	36.3
1997	1,801.3	1,132.4	50.3	49.7	15.5	31.6
1998	2,013.9	1,242.2	50.8	49.2	12.6	28.2

Source: Calculated from State Statistics Bureau (1999).

Table 12.2 Production in employment structure in China, Soviet Union and United States

Part A China – Change in production and employment, 1978–1998						
	Composition of GDP, 1995 prices, %			Composition of employment, %		
	Primary	Secondary	Tertiary	Primary	Secondary	Tertiary
1978	41.2	34	24.7	70.5	17.3	12.2
1979	40.9	34.2	24.9	69.8	17.6	12.6
1980	38.0	37.0	24.9	68.7	18.2	13.1
1981	38.4	35.6	26.0	68.1	18.3	13.6
1982	39.0	34.2	26.7	68.1	18.4	13.4
1983	38.1	34.2	27.8	67.1	18.7	14.2
1984	37.3	33.9	28.8	64.0	19.9	16.1
1985	33.8	35.9	30.3	62.4	20.8	16.8
1986	32.2	36.5	31.3	60.9	21.9	17.2
1987	30.3	37.5	32.2	60.0	22.2	17.8
1988	28.2	38.8	33.0	59.4	22.4	18.3
1989	28.0	38.4	33.6	60.0	21.6	18.3
1990	28.9	38.0	33.0	60.1	21.4	18.5
1991	27.2	39.7	33.0	59.7	21.4	18.9
1992	25.1	42.3	32.6	58.5	21.7	19.8
1993	23.2	44.8	31.9	56.4	22.4	21.2
1994	21.5	47.3	31.2	54.3	22.7	23.0
1995	20.5	48.8	30.7	52.2	23.0	24.8
1996	19.7	50.0	30.3	50.5	23.5	26.0
1997	18.8	50.7	30.5	49.9	23.7	26.4
1998	18.1	51.5	30.4	49.8	23.5	26.7

Part B Cross-country comparison of production and employment structure						
	Composition of GDP, 1995 prices, %			Composition of employment, %		
	US	Soviet Union	China	US	Soviet Union	China
	1986	1988	1978	1986	1988	1978
Agriculture	1.9	9.3	41.2	2.7	19.3	70.5
Industry	23.5	48.9	28.9	17.6	28.9	17.3*
Construction	6.1	10.7	5.1	4.6	11.5	**
Services	68.5	31.1	24.7	75.1	40.3	12.2

* = data includes construction, ** = data included in industry.

Source: China data from State Statistic Bureau (1999). Statistics for the United States and the Soviet Union are from Lipton and Sachs (1992).

by enlivening the agricultural sector in the 1979–84 period and by creating a dynamic non-state sector from 1984 onward, but also by moving low-productivity agricultural workers into higher-productivity jobs in the secondary and tertiary sectors.[8] In short, China's marketization and internationalization policies initiated the non-zero sum process of economic development, moving China away from a subsistence peasant economy and causing agriculture to drop from 41 per cent of GDP in 1978 to 18 per cent in 1998.

Part B of Table 12.2 explains why Russia's GDP fell upon marketization of its economy. The Russian industrial sector, especially the heavy industrial component, was much bigger than what a market economy would require.[9] Industrial output accounted for 49 per cent of Russia's GDP in 1988 compared to 24 per cent of U.S. GDP in 1986. Given the relatively small proportion of labor in Russian agriculture compared to China, 19 per cent versus 71 per cent, a substantial amount of the labor needed for the growth of new light industries and new service activities had to come from the heavy industrial sector. The collapse of Russia's heavy industries was necessary in order to release the labor put there by the central plan.[10] The salient point is that the marketization of the over-industrialized Russian economy triggered the almost zero-sum (certainly in the short run) process of economic restructuring.

The importance of how existing structural conditions shape the output response to marketization is captured in Figure 12.3, which shows a three-dimensional production possibility frontier of output from agriculture, light industry and services and heavy industry. Point B on plane NOP denotes the production mix of a developed private market economy that is integrated into the production mix of a developed private market economy that is integrated into the international division of labor. Point A, which is also on plane NOP, represents Russia on the eve of its

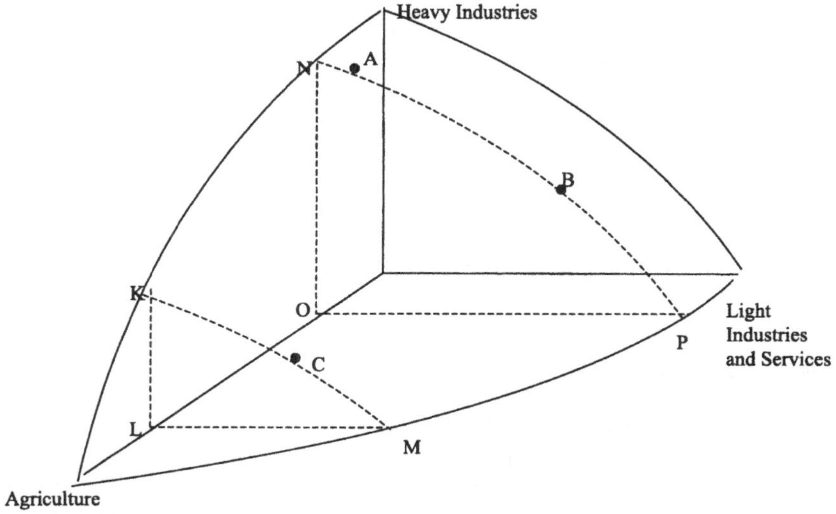

Figure 12.3 Production possibility frontier 1

marketization in 1992, and point C on plane KLM represents China in 1978. The difference between plane NOP and plane KLM is that the former represents economies that are more advanced in their industrialization and urbanization.

In Figure 12.4, we show in a heuristic picture that the movement from C to B is likely to be a less painful process than the movement from A to B. We project the KLM plane onto the NOP plane to produce the K'OM' plane, with C' being the projection of C. Within the context of the NOP plane, the movement from C' to B is Pareto-improving, while the movement from A to B involves the shrinking of the industrial sector. More generally, the movement from C to B is Pareto-improving because the marginal value product of labor (MVPL) is lowest in agriculture. Chow (1993) found the marginal value product of labor in China in 1978, measured in 1952 prices, to be 63 yuan in agriculture, 1027 yuan in industry, 452 yuan in construction, 739 yuan in transportation and 1809 yuan in commerce. This is the true source of the Pareto-improving outcome in China's economic reform, not the dual pricing system.

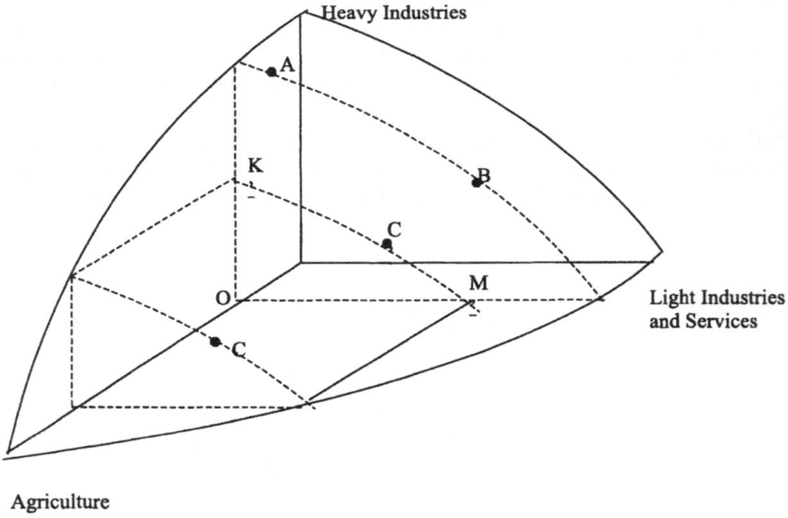

Figure 12.4 Production possibility frontier 2

An Important but Ignored Cost of the DTPS

One of the biggest claims of virtue for the DTPS is that by avoiding the creation of losers, it does not generate political opposition to economic reform (except, of course, from central planning ideologues). We find such a claim to be dubious because dual track pricing creates opportunities for corruption and serious corruption can undermine the political legitimacy of the government, if not also, the political stability of the country. In our understanding of the history of Chinese reforms, the DTPS was an unsustainable economic mechanism, not only from the management viewpoint of extreme difficulties in administration, but also from the political viewpoint of maintaining the cohesion of the ruling coalition.

To see this point it is important to first note that the DTPS was only one component of the serious attempt (beginning in 1984) to improve the rationality of the state-owned enterprise (SOE) system. The other component was the devolution of decision-making power to the SOEs. The political cost of the DTPS, as we will point out, came from its interaction with the operational autonomy of the SOEs in an unexpected way.

The plan track for inputs conferred instant profits upon the favored purchaser upon reselling quota inputs in the free market. Many children of top leaders were able to make purchases of inputs at plan prices and re-sell them at large profits. The general public was not happy with this widespread corrupt practice. The devolution of operational autonomy to SOEs in a soft budget situation caused demand for investment credit to soar. The accommodation by the state banks of this demand enabled inflation in 1985–89 to reach levels not seen since 1949.[11]

It was therefore natural that the general public linked the large illegal profits of the dual pricing system with the high inflation and perceived the inflation to be the result of price gouging by corrupt officials. This general perception brought public unhappiness with the corruption to new heights, which led to demonstrations against corruption and inflation in quite a number of large cities at the end of 1985 and 1986.

To address this social unrest, Hu Yaobang, then head of the Communist Party of China (CPC), started arresting corrupt officials and the sons of several top conservative leaders were apprehended. This crackdown was interpreted by some conservative leaders as an excuse by the liberal faction to depose them and this intensified the opposition to the continued leadership of Hu Yaobang on the grounds of administrative incompetence (for example, high inflation) and ideological revisionism (for example, his introduction of material incentives). By aggravating the infighting inside the ruling coalition, the plan track contributed to the dismissal of Hu Yaobang as general secretary of the CPC in January 1987.

It is worthwhile to quote two accounts of this matter at length. According to Richard Baum (1994, p.176–177):

> [In 1986] Hu Yaobang raised the ire of Hu Qiaomu [Politburo member] by proposing to formally charge the latter's son, Hu Shiying, with criminal corruption ... [The] incident provoked an immediate reaction among powerful party elders… a campaign to oust Hu Yaobang quickly took shape. At the same time, Hu Qiaomu reportedly threw himself at Deng Xiaoping's mercy, tearfully imploring the paramount leader to show mercy toward his errant offspring.
>
> The highest level *gaogan zidi* [offspring of a high-ranking cadre] to be judicially punished was the daughter of General Ye Fei, the former commander of the Chinese Navy...In 1982 the general had sharply criticized Hu Yaobang for failing to halt the spread of bourgeois liberalization.
>
> Other *gaogan zidi* who came under criminal investigation in this period included the prodigal offspring of conservative party elders Peng Zhen and Wang Zhen [both Politburo members]. Like Ye Fei and Hu Qiaomu, Peng and Wang had been vocal critics of bourgeois liberalization, and the raising of allegations of corruption against their children thus carried a strong hint of political retaliation.

According to Joseph Fewsmith (1994, p.177):

> In January 1986, Hu Yaobang presided over a huge rally of 8,000 cadres called to address the issue of corruption... A special committee headed by Hu Yaobang's associate Qiao Shi was established within the Central Committee to root out corruption. In February...three sons of high-level cadres were executed. There were soon reports that the children of a number of conservative party leaders, including Peng Zhen, Hu Qiaomu, and Ye Fei, were under investigation, suggesting that Hu Yaobang was targeting his critics. Moreover, the decision to set up a special committee within the Central Committee to tackle this issue appeared to be a challenge to the CDIC [Central Discipline Inspection Commission], headed by Chen Yun [leader of the conservative faction], as the agency of discipline within the party.

Deng Xiaoping's solution to the growing unrest within society and within the ruling coalition was not to arrest the profiteers but to end the dual-track price system that fostered such conflicts within the ruling coalition as a byproduct. This is why, in the middle of unprecedented (since 1949) inflation, in May 1988 Deng Xiaoping publicly urged that comprehensive price reform be finished within three to five years. The memorable slogan for this campaign was *zhuang jiage guan* (crash through the price obstacle).

The reality was that the working of the dual-track price system generated great social pressures to punish the profiteers but such acts threatened the viability of the ruling coalition. The choice facing the CPC elite was to either maintain the political coalition or maintain the dual track price system. For the Chinese politicians the choice was a no-brainer. This is why price liberalization was brought to virtual completion in the 1990–91 period even though this was the time that the pro-plan conservative faction had the upper hand in policymaking (in the aftermath of the June 1989 Tiananmen incident). Political reality is the reason why the plan track was reduced steadily even though this act was not Pareto improving and even though this contradicted the ideological position of the conservative faction.

China's SOE Reform: Succeeding Where Others Have Failed?

After the 1993 identification by the CPC that 'ambiguity in property rights' had been a major factor behind the inefficiency of the SOE sector, significant privatization of small and medium SOEs have occurred in a number of provinces. The notion that SOEs are generally un-reformable and hence need to be privatized has been and still is, an issue of great debate among China analysts.[12] This is exemplified by the exchange between Woo, Fan, Hai and Jin (WFHJ, 1994) and Jefferson, Rawski and Zheng (JRZ, 1994) over WFHJ's (1993) rejection of JRZ's (1992) finding of positive total factor productivity (TFP) growth in the SOE sector.

The WFHJ-JRZ debate started with the observation in WFHJ (1993) and Woo, Hai, Jin and Fan (WHJF, 1994) that the estimated deflators for value-added in JRZ (1992) and Groves, Hong, McMillan and Naughton (GHMN, 1994 and 1995), three studies that found large positive TFP growth in the 1980–89 period, declined secularly over their sample periods when the consumer price index (CPI) rose steadily. Such opposite trends between the CPI and the value-added deflators

(VADS) created by JRZ's and GHMN's deflation methods is troubling because such occurrences are internationally unprecedented.

WHJF pointed out that the condition for a secularly declining VAD is given by:
$[(P_t^G - P_0^G)/P_0^G] < [P_0^I M_t / P_0^G Q_t]*[(P_t^I - P_0^I)/P_0^I]$ where
M_t = intermediate inputs in period t in physical units;
Q_t = gross output in period t in physical units;
P_i^G = price of gross output in period t, (with t = 0 the base period); and
P_i^I = price of intermediate input in period t.[13]

Alternatively, the condition for a declining VAD can be rewritten as:
$[(P_t^G - P_0^G)/P_0^G] < [1-(GVA_0/GOV_0)]*[(P_t^I - P_0^I)/P_0^I]$ where
GVA_0 = gross value added in time t measured in base prices; and
GOV_0 = gross output value in time t measured in base prices.

WHJF suggested that the high TFP growth in JRZ (1992) and GHMN (1994, 1995) and the declining VAD were the joint results of under-deflating gross output and over-deflating intermediate inputs. This suggestion implicitly assumed that China's production structure (GVA_0/GOV_0) was similar to that in other economies in order to produce positive co-movements between VAD and CPI.

JRZ (1996) rejected WHJF's suggestion of incorrect deflation and attributed the declining VAD to China's industrial structure differing significantly from those in the advanced market economies. The alleged Chinese economic exceptionalism is that China's manufacturing sector had an usually low (GVA/GOV) ratio, which they computed to be 46 per cent for the United States, 40 per cent for Japan, 45 per cent for West Germany and 44 per cent for the United Kingdom compared to the (GVA/GOV) ratio for China, which was 33 per cent in 1980, 31 per cent in 1984, 29 per cent in 1988, and 25 per cent in 1992.

We identify two difficulties with JRZ's (1996) defense. The first difficulty is that the definition of the official Chinese value added data used by JRZ (1996) may be different from the definition of value added used in the advanced market economies. Specifically, there are two commonly used definitions of value added in China, one excludes some payments to intermediate factors and the other includes them. We will call them GVA-1 and GVA-2 respectively. GVA-2 matches the way that the US Census calculates GVA and the US (GVA/GOV) ratio cited by JRZ had the GVA calculated as GVA-2. Now if the official ratios for China reported in JRZ were constructed using GVA-1, then it is not surprising that (GVA/GOV) is so low in China compared to the U.S.A. But then this would be a comparison of apples and oranges.

The second difficulty with JRZ's finding of an unusual industrial structure for China, even if their value added data was constructed with the second Chinese definition, is that this is a very fragile finding, that is, not a definitive finding. JRZ's proposition, which is based on *Industrial Yearbook* data, does not hold when the 1987 Input-Output Table data are used instead. *Industrial Yearbook* data are based on the financial reports (similar to information given to the industrial census) filed by the enterprises, while the Input-Output Table data adjusted the industrial census data to be compatible with economy-wide input-output flows.

Table 12.3 Ratio of Gross Value Added to Gross Output Value, 1987 (GVA/GOV, %)

	Chinese ratios using different data sources and concepts			US
Source	Ind. Yearbook	Input-Output table		
Methodology	Not known	National account	US Census concept	US Census concept
Industry				
Food manufacturing	13.48	14.94	27.63	32.85
Beverages	25.02	33.55	45.62	44.61
Tobacco products	5.46	67.10	73.37	64.27
Textile mill products	19.21	25.63	35.51	38.84
Wearing apparel	26.51	29.40	38.81	48.65
Leather products and footwear	24.19	27.37	38.97	47.94
Wood products, furniture and fixtures	26.62	31.84	40.75	43.92
Paper products, printing and publishing	28.29	32.19	41.14	55.28
Chemicals products (incl. oil refining)	27.17	35.11	51.06	29.85
Rubber and plastic products	25.55	29.34	38.37	50.06
Non-metallic mineral products	40.37	40.98	49.06	52.40
Basic and fabricated metal products	27.05	32.36	39.86	42.94
Machinery and transport equipment	33.39	34.00	42.53	44.79
Electrical machinery and equipment	29.08	29.03	37.86	55.33
Other manufacturing industries	33.20	37.11	46.00	62.78
Total manufacturing industries	26.49	31.43	41.62	43.86
GVA/GOV from Jefferson, Rawski and Zheng (1996)				
	Total manufacturing industries			
	1980	1984	1988	1992
China	32.7	31.4	28.5	25.4
			1989	
United States			46.2	

Source: China data are from Industrial Census.

Table 12.3 reports the GVA/GOV ratio for different sectors calculated from different sources and according to different definitions of GVA. Column (i) reports the ratio as reported in the 1987 *Industrial Yearbook* (JRZ's data source). The ratios in column (ii) and (iii) are calculated from the Input-Output Table. Column (ii) is calculated using GVA-1 (that is using the Chinese national account method), and column (iii) is calculated using GVA-2 (that is using the US Census method).[14] The 1987 (GVA/GOV) ratio for the Chinese industrial sector was 26.5 per cent according to the Industrial Yearbook; 31.4 per cent according to the Chinese national account method; and 42 per cent according to the US Census method. The 1987 ratio for the US using the US Census method was 44 per cent.

Table 12.3 also shows that each of China's industrial sectoral (GVA/GOV) ratios calculated according to the US Census method was not only larger than the (GVA/GOV) ratios from the *Industrial Yearbook* but also closer to the US sectoral (GVA/GOV) ratios. When we know that the Chinese and US GVAs are calculated in the same way, there are no great differences between the industrial structures of the two countries.

JRZ's finding of a low and secularly declining (GVA/GOV) ratio for China suggests to us under-measurement of GVA caused by the growing appropriation of capital income by SOE personnel. Fan and Woo (1996) have shown that one unintended result of granting increasing operational autonomy to the SOE managers is that they have, over time, learned how to use various accounting subterfuges to overstate production costs in order to transfer enterprise income to themselves and the workers. This is why (GVA/GOV) calculated from the financial information supplied by the enterprises has been declining steadily in the reform period and why the adjustment of GVA, to be compatible with economy-wide flows, produced much higher (GVA/GOV). This also explains why China's SOEs have been running greater losses every year, even in years of high growth and in sectors where entry by non-state enterprises has been minimal.[15]

In our opinion, this steady stripping of state assets may subvert political legitimacy much more than a transparent method of privatization would. The increasing public outrage over the inequity of the informal privatization of the SOE sector is well captured in a recent book by He Qinglian who wrote that the SOE reform has amounted to:

> ... a process in which power-holders and their hangers-on plundered public wealth. The primary target of their plunder was state property that had been accumulated from forty years of the people's sweat, and their primary mean of plunder was political power.[16]

Just like their compatriots in EEFSU, Chinese SOE managers focus more on the looting of their firms than on improving their operations. In a study of SOEs in Chongqing, Chen (1998) reported:

> Municipal officials often find that factory directors appointed to money-losing firms do well and bring the firms out of the red in the first two years, and then start to take part in graft, embezzlement, bribery and, most frequently, pirating state assets.

For practical purposes, the TFP debate is over. There is now no doubt about which side of the debate the Chinese government has come down on. Premier Zhu

Rongji declared back in 1996, right after four years of double digit economic growth, that:

> The current problems of SOEs are excessive investments in fixed assets with very low return rates, resulting in the sinking of large amounts of capital; low sales-to-production ratio giving rise to mounting inventories. The end result is that the state has to inject an increasing amount of working capital through the banking sector into the state enterprises.[17]

The announcement at the 15th CPC Congress in September 1997 that there would be a determined effort to greatly diversify the ownership structure was the logical outcome of the above official verdict on the performance of the SOE sector and of official concern about the political repercussions of the accelerating process of spontaneous privatization.

Facing the Perils of Privatization, Chinese-Style

There are two analytical divides in describing the wide array of privatization practices. The first divide is between individual sales and mass privatization; and the second divide is between insider privatization and outsider privatization.[18] These two divides are not mutually exclusive. Management and employee buy-outs are insider privatizations and direct sales to third parties are outsider privatizations.

Voucher privatizations with generous concessions to employees of the SOEs are insider privatizations (for example Russia) and voucher privatizations conducted on a level playing field (for example the Czech Republic) are outsider privatizations. For some transition economies, mass privatization had appeared attractive because individual sales, in the absence of developed capital markets, would have taken too long and the perverse incentives facing the SOEs awaiting privatization would have generated management problems beyond the governments' ability to handle.

The experiences with mass privatization in Eastern European and the former Soviet Union (EEFSU) show that the task is an extremely difficult one and that the outcomes have consistently fallen below initial expectations. For example, in Russia, the 'loans-for-shares' privatization transferred the country's enormous mineral wealth to a group of oligarchs and the weak administrative and legal structures allowed many managers to take effective control of the privatized firms and loot them instead of improving their operations. In the judgment of Frydman and Rapaczynski (1998), despite the diverse privatization methods, the outcome in most cases in the majority of the countries (especially in the FSU) is that control of the firms went to some form of manager-labor coalition, producing what they aptly described as 'capitalism with a comrade face'. Privatization has certainly not unleashed massive productivity increases.

Furthermore, the EEFSU experiences warn that *mass* privatization is an exceedingly dangerous business politically, no matter how it is done, be it outsider privatization or insider privatization. This is because the mass privatization of SOEs generates so much rent that corruption is impossible to avoid and the resulting corruption inevitably delegitimizes the government. Corruption leading to political demise appears to be an inevitable byproduct of *mass* privatization, for example, Vaclav Klaus in the Czech Republic and Anatoli Chubais in Russia.

Most scholars of enterprise restructuring would now agree that privatization is a necessary, but not sufficient condition for improved enterprise performance. The emergence of a dynamic privately owned industrial sector from the old SOE sector requires the existence of hard budget constraints, competition, and legal (for example bankruptcy courts) and commercial (for example accounting standards) institutions that work properly. Since China, like most transition economies, has either inchoate or inexperienced administrative, legal, and economic institutions, does this mean that it should not have began privatization, least of all, to have accelerated the pace, as it has recently?

We see two reasons for why the non-stellar outcomes in EEFSU have not discouraged China from moving ahead with privatization. The first reason comes from John Nellis (1999) who points out that 'governments that botch privatization are equally likely to botch the management of state-owned firms'. The answer is not to avoid privatizations but to implement more careful privatizations. Governments in transition economies should 'push ahead, more slowly, with case-by-case and tender privatizations, in cooperation with the international assistance community, in hopes of producing some success stories that will lead by example'.

The second reason lies in that the delay of privatization can be costly to the government politically. Stealing by managers does occur during privatization and creates a social backlash against the government. But the maintenance of the status quo has become increasingly difficult because SOE managers in China know from the EEFSU experience that they are in an endgame situation. The widespread spontaneous privatization by SOE managers could create the same social unrest that would topple the regime.

China has so far avoided widespread organized public dissatisfaction with its partial privatization of the small and medium state enterprises. The central government has given itself an indirect role in the privatization process in order to avoid bearing the brunt of any negative fallout. It works by the central government passing to the local governments the financial responsibility for most of the state enterprises located in their areas. In the case of loss-making enterprises, the local government is forced to either come up with a subsidy or privatize them. The second option has been the common choice. The local party secretary who gets rid of the loss-makers without arousing local resentment is promoted. But if there is substantial public resentment over the privatization, then the party secretary is reprimanded or replaced for inept implementation of state policy.

The question is whether this strategy can continue to shelter the central government from the public backlash over 'inept' privatization, especially when the large state enterprises are privatized. The road to a prototype WTO market is a perilous one for China's policymakers, but it is an unavoidable journey if China is to continue moving up the value-added ladder and become a modern market economy.

Fiscal Contracting: The Newest Lesson from China to Russia?

A number of China scholars have observed that local governments in China have been a primary force for economic development. This phenomenon has been called 'developmental localism' by Zheng (1994), 'local corporatism' by Oi (1992) and 'market-preserving federalism' by Montinola, Qian and Weingast (1995). The pro-growth policies of China's local governments stand in sharp contrast with the 'status quo' policies of Russia's local governments. According to a comprehensive analysis of ten sectors of the Russian economy in 1999, the McKinsey Global Institute (1999) found that:

> In nine of the ten sectors, the direct cause of the low economic performance is market distortions that prevent equal competition. The distortions come from attempts to address social concerns, corrupt practices, and lack of information.
>
> In the manufacturing sectors, regional governments channel implicit federal subsidies to unproductive companies. Such subsidies take the form of lower energy payments and are allegedly intended to prevent companies from shutting down and laying off employees. This puts potentially productive companies at a cost disadvantage, blocking investments and growth on their part.
>
> In the service sectors, where employment should grow, investments by efficient companies are discouraged by the presence of well connected unproductive incumbents who benefit from favorable regulations, weak law enforcement, and privileged access to land or government procurements.
>
> Furthermore, these sector level market distortions are key contributors to macroeconomic instability, because they reduce government revenues and increase its expenditures. Macroeconomic instability itself is another important deterrent to investments.
>
> We found the other often mentioned reasons for Russia's economic problems to play a much smaller role (e.g. poor corporate governance and lack of a transport infrastructure).

The prevailing opinion among China scholars is that the enthusiasm of China's local government's for economic development came from post-1978 changes in the fiscal relationship between the central and local governments that allowed the latter to keep a greater proportion of the taxes that they collected for the central government. The extreme examples of fiscal decentralization were Guangdong and Fujian that, for long periods in the 1980s, paid fixed lump sum taxes and kept all tax revenue above the quota, that is a marginal retention rate (MRR) of 100 per cent.

Jin, Qian and Weingast (1999) found in cross-provincial regressions that MRR was positively linked with employment growth in non-state enterprises and with the degree of SOE restructuring during the 1982–92 period. They claimed that the absence of Chinese-style fiscal contracting (market-preserving federalism) in Russia is the reason for the 'status quo' policies of Russia's local governments. Is this the real lesson from China for Russia in the wake of earlier lessons that turned out to be inapplicable?[19]

In the judgment of Blanchard and Shleifer (2000), Chinese-style federalism cannot work in Russia because Russia is now a democratic state and no longer a Leninist state like China. To see their argument, suppose that the local government in a transition economy faces the following two policy choices:

- Policy X that requires the local government to prey on private businesses to pay for its expenditure and support the local SOEs that employ a significant proportion of the local work force; and
- Policy Y that requires the local government to reduce protection and subsidies to local SOEs (in order to force them to increase efficiency by laying off workers),

and to foster growth of new private enterprises by cutting taxes and fees (an action made affordable by the cuts in SOE subsidies).

Now assume the following consequences:

Policy X yields direct benefits to the local government worth b_x, and the probability p_x that the local government will stay in power.

Policy Y yields direct benefits worth b_y, which is a positive function of MRR, and the probability p_y that the local government will stay in power.

Obviously, policy Y will be enacted only if

$p_y b_y > p_x b_x$,

or $pb_y > b_x$ where $p= (p_y / p_x)$.

In a Leninist state, p is a policy variable because the central government appoints the local governor, which is the situation in China. So if the central government wishes policy Y to be chosen, it just sets $p_x = 0$ (as long as by is positive). Other things equal, an increase in MRR increases b_y, and hence the probability that policy Y will be chosen by the governor, but the level of the MRR is really just 'icing on the cake' for a local governor in a Leninist state. Whereas in a town in a democratic country where the local SOEs employ a large proportion of the workforce, p_y may well be sufficiently close to zero such that jacking up MRR tremendously by the central government will not be enough to induce the local government to choose policy Y.

It is interesting to note that in a country where the central government is committed to maximizing GDP growth, the relationship between MRR and the provincial growth rate may be one where causality runs both ways. The minimization of revenue losses from the use of MRR to promote the overall GDP growth rate would lead the central government to extend lower MRRs to provinces that have higher growth potential. The higher MRRs given to the southeastern coastal provinces of Guangdong and Fujian could well have been based on this consideration.

The key regressions in Jin, Qian and Weingast are essentially growth equations because the growth rates of provincial employment in the non-state non-agricultural sector are highly correlated with the growth rates of provincial GDP. However, the Jin, Qian and Weingast regressions do not contain any of the usual independent variables found in Barro-type growth equations. Chen (2000) added MRR and other proxies for fiscal decentralization into Barro-type provincial growth regressions and found all of them to have significant negative coefficients over the 1979–93 period. Chen also cited two studies by Justine Lin that found contradictory results about the impact of fiscal decentralization on economic growth. All of these suggest that the empirical case for the effectiveness of fiscal contracting in promoting provincial growth is a fragile one and that more research is needed.

A priori, the relationship between MRR and the growth rate in China could well be a Laffer-type curve. In some provinces the larger amount of retained revenue could have resulted in more 'white elephant' projects or larger subsidies to inefficient large SOEs that were deemed too big to fail. The negative coefficient for MRR in Chen's (2000) growth regressions is a warning that China might well have exceeded the optimal value of MRR by the end of the 1980s.

We are of course not denying either that the 1982–93 system of 'tax farming' was better than the pre-1979 tax system or that it stimulated the appetites of some local governments for economic development. Our point is just that China deserved a better tax system than the 1982–93 tax system of annual negotiations with individual provinces, which was a system that created extraordinary microeconomic distortions and a fiscal crisis for the central government to boot.[20] These flaws explain why China replaced fiscal contracting in January 1994 with a tax system that has value-added tax (VAT) as its centerpiece. The 1982–93 Chinese tax system extolled in Jin, Qian and Weingast was similar to the tax farming system of medieval Europe and the post-1993 Chinese tax system (at least on paper and in intentions) is similar to the tax systems of modern Europe. The right lesson for fiscal reform in Russia is the same lesson that China has learned over the last two decades, which is to allow its fiscal system to converge to those of the advanced WTO members.[21]

Gorbachev's Application of Chinese-Style Reforms: Two Lessons from Russia to China

It would be historically inaccurate to assume that market reforms in Russia started only in 1992 with the Boris Yeltsin government. The gross inefficiency of the Soviet economy and its slide into technological stagnation during the nomenklatura communism of Leonid Brezhnez in the 1970s had fermented much reformist thinking among Soviet economists. By the time Mikhail Gorbachev assumed political power in May 1985, there were already many established influential economists urging market-oriented reforms, for example, Boris Kurashvili argued for Hungarian-style market socialism, and Oleg Bogomolov for Chinese-style incremental liberalization.

However, Gorbachev was not a quick convert to market reforms. The first two years of his rule were spent trying to propel the economy out of its doldrums by accelerating the technological level of Soviet industries through large investments in the machine tool industry. The acceleration strategy failed, leading Gorbachev to seek 'radical reforms' of the economy. The influence of China's reform strategy is clearly seen in Gorbachev's arguments in August 1987 'in favor of family contract, family teams and... leasehold' to be introduced in Soviet agriculture.[22] Gorbachev's radical reform program was unveiled in June 1987 at the Soviet economic plenum, which passed the Law on State Enterprises and Basic Provisions for Fundamental Perestroika of Economic Management to devolve decision-making power from the ministries to the SOEs. Just as in China, Soviet SOEs were given more freedom in their output choices and freedom to enter into long-term contractual agreements for purchases and sales. They were also allowed to retain part of their profits to use at their discretion, for example, for technological upgrading and as incentive bonuses. In return, the SOEs were required to do 'full economic accounting', the euphemism for SOEs to be responsible for their losses. As in China, deliveries to the state would still be required (state orders), for which subsidized inputs would be made available to the SOEs, but state orders would be reduced over time to cover only 40–60 per cent of all production.[23]

The explosive growth China's non-state industrial sector had made a deep impression on the Russian reformers and inspired them to push for a double track on ownership as well. Academician Leonid Abalkin, a prominent leader in reform thinking, predicted in 1986 that the radical reforms of Gorbachev would, within a decade, enable cooperatives to account for ten per cent of GDP, and private enterprises for four per cent of GDP.[24] Various decrees had been issued earlier to stimulate the cooperative sector and they were greatly expanded with the adoption of the Law on Cooperatives in May 1988.

The Law on Cooperatives was categorical in making the formation of cooperatives an easy task: 'A cooperative is organized at the desire of citizens, exclusively on a voluntary basis. The creation of a cooperative is not conditional upon any special permission whatsoever by Soviet, economic or other bodies'.[25] There was no ceiling set on the number of members and there was no limit on the number of non-members that could be hired on contract. Furthermore, cooperatives could set their prices according to market conditions. In the words of Yevgenii Yasin, a senior member of the State Commission on Economic Reform:

> The 1987 reform was in many ways an attempt to implement the Chinese model in Russia. It envisioned enterprises, and joint ventures would constitute the free sector, existing alongside the state sector, with its mandatory state orders, fixed prices, and centralized allocation of inputs (Ellman and Kontorovich, 1998, pp.169).

The Soviet economy started disintegrating from 1989 onward, however, and, broadly speaking, there are two explanations about the causes: one, Gorbachev's Chinese-style reforms unraveled the Soviet economy and two, the reforms would have worked if Gorbachev had only tightened repression on his opponents instead of embracing glasnost.[26]

The claim that the reforms caused the collapse comes from two related views about the Soviet economy. The first view is that the existing heavy industrial sector was too large for a marketized Soviet economy, as depicted in Figure 12.3. This sector had to shrink because its value added at market prices was negative. Ericson's (1999b) careful examination of the changes in Russia's input-output table in 1991–1992 and Berg, Borensztein, Sahay and Zettelmeyer's (1999) thorough econometric investigation of EEFSU economies support this value-subtracting view of the Soviet-type industrial sector.

The second view is more general and is based on Kornai's (1992) argument that systemic stability is assured only when the regime in the political sphere is compatible with the regime in the economic sphere. A totalitarian Communist regime that is ideologically committed to the suppression of private ownership requires for its sustenance a centrally planned economy and vice-versa. If the nature of the regime changes in only one sphere, then the stability of the regime in the other sphere will be disturbed, culminating in systemic collapse. This means that unless partial marketization is matched by an appropriate modification in Communist ideology, either the economic reform will be reversed or the existing political regime will be toppled. Hence, in Kornai's framework, the 1987 Chinese-style reforms removed the last vestiges of coherence within the Soviet political-economy system and precipitated its collapse.

The counter-hypothesis to the views of Ericson and Kornai holds that the Chinese-style reforms would have effected a less costly economic transition for Russia if Gorbachev had only intensified the police state nature of Soviet society instead of lessening it as he did (Griffin and Khan 1993). The reasoning is that a systemic transformation necessarily creates losers, firm political control is therefore required to prevent the losers from creating social instability that would disrupt production. This viewpoint was echoed by Yevgenii Yasin:

> a gradual transition to a market economy [would have required]... a less radical and painful departure from socialist ideals. The secret police and censorship would perpetuate the old ideological cocoon, within which a new economic system would be developing like a butterfly... The last chance was lost in 1989, when Gorbachev's political reform removed the Communist Party from power. Afterwards, events unfolded spontaneously, no longer under the control of the government or the Party (Ellman and Kontorovich, 1998, pp.169).

The first serious problem with the view that political liberalization undermines economic liberalization is the limited validity of the assumption that only a totalitarian political regime can maintain adequate law and order in a society going through economic restructuring. The jackboot of military rule could not prevent Ceausescu of Romania and Soeharto of Indonesia from being deposed by their angry populace. Staying in power requires more than the liberal use of the stick. History clearly shows that carrots and compromise can sometimes be even more crucial.

The second serious problem with the necessity-for-brute-force hypotheses is that it ignores the fact that the bludgeoning cannot be confined just to laid-off state workers on strike, substantial amounts of it would also have to be directed at members of the Communist elite. This is because many Soviet officials who stood to lose their supervisory power over the SOEs had joined the Communist ideologues in sabotaging the implementation of the reforms.[27] Would the Communist Party of the Soviet Union have accepted Stalin-style purges by Gorbachev in his de-Stalinization of the economy? A positive answer is highly debatable because of the seemingly ironclad self-protective consensus of 'live and let live' among the post-Stalin Communist elite.

In trying to assess the relative merits of these two broad explanations for the disintegration of the Soviet economy, it is instructive to note how Gorbachev reacted to the failure of his Chinese-style reforms. He first replaced democratic centralism with open popular elections and then authorized Academician Stanislav Shatalin to draft a plan that would transform the planned economy to a market economy in 500 days.[28] These actions suggest that Gorbachev had concluded that the biggest obstacle to the development of a market economy was the Communist Party itself and that gradual reforms could not work in the Soviet Union.

Of the many interesting lessons for China from Gorbachev's unsuccessful Chinese-style reforms, we single out two that concern the viability of continued deepening of economic reform and opening. The first lesson derives from the fundamental message in Kornai's (1992) analysis that true systemic stability requires that the political regime be compatible with the economic regime. Sustained economic prosperity requires a market economy that is integrated into the international economy and a true market economy requires (constitutionally protected) private ownership to be its institutional norm. The lesson for China from

Russia is that the avoidance of economic disruptions from political upheavals lies in the willingness and ability of the ruling elite to make adroit changes to the nature of the political regime to accompany the changes in the economic regime. Seen in this light, China's aggressive push for WTO membership, the recent revision of China's constitution to give private property the same legal status as public property, and the reduction of the central bureaucracy by over a third since 1995 are signs of far-sightedness in the third-generation of Chinese leaders.

The second lesson for China from Gorbachev's reforms derives from the fact that the primary political opposition to marketization came from within the Party and that the primary resistance to implementation of reforms came from within the government. Because the policy dissent and implementation sabotage are of the in-house variety, purges could destroy the internal unity required for the political survival of the ruling elite and for maintaining stable center-provincial political arrangements. The second lesson is that the fourth generation of Chinese leaders will have to come up with creative mechanisms to offset the natural proclivity of loyal party incumbents to favor the status quo over additional institutional reforms.

Conclusion

The desirability of WTO membership for China depends on whether its economic successes to date are the result of its discovery of new institutional forms (for example, dual track pricing, SOE contracts, and fiscal contracts) that are optimal for China's particular economic circumstances or are the result of the convergence of its economic institutions to those of a typical advanced member of WTO. If the experimentalist interpretation is correct, then the institutional harmonization required by WTO may blunt future growth. If the convergence explanation is true, then WTO membership will help future growth.

Our dismissal of some recent claims of Chinese economic exceptionalism can be summarized as follows. The data do not support the general equilibrium effects of the DTPS as predicted by the 'gain without pain' analysis of Lau, Qian and Roland (2000). The serious flaw of the DTPS that has been downplayed in their paper was the widespread corruption that it spawned and the political disunity that the corruption created. It was because of the economic and political unsustainability of the DTPS that it was replaced by complete price liberalization in 1990–91, despite the fact that this was not a Pareto-improving change.

Jefferson, Rawski and Zheng (1996) defended their finding of a significant positive TFP growth rate from charges of implausibility by claiming that China's industrial structure was markedly different from those of the advanced capitalist economies. Their claim does not hold when the industrial structure is calculated from Input-Output data. In a way, the recent acceleration of privatization in China definitively settles the argument of whose estimation results are more plausible. Since the EEFSU experience shows that privatization can be politically dangerous for the government implementing it, this new direction in SOE reform will require unusually skillful political management by the Chinese leadership.

The fiscal decentralization that took the form of province-specific tax contracts rendered the revenue of the local governments more dependent on the local level of economic development and hence, induced many of them to promote local growth. The negative byproducts of the tax contracts were local protectionism, industrial duplication, and a great reduction in the ability of the central government to undertake pressing infrastructure investments and poverty alleviation projects. Finally, the empirical validity of the positive growth impact of fiscal decentralization, after the influences of other variables are controlled for, is still an open question.

The uniform tax system introduced in 1994, which is similar to the tax systems of the advanced members of the WTO, is a definite improvement over its predecessor. So if there is any lesson for Russia to learn from China's fiscal decentralization, as claimed by Jin, Qian and Weingast (1999), it should be based on the present tax system and not on the pre-1994 tax system. In any case, as pointed out by Blanchard and Shleifer (2000), it is unlikely that the kind of decentralized tax system designed for a politically centralized country will produce the same outcomes when applied to a politically decentralized country.

The failure of Gorbachev's 1987 reforms suggests, first, the limited applicability of China's double track transition strategy to EEFSU economies, and, second, that the greatest challenge to the deepening of economic reform and opening may come from the entrenched interests within the ruling structure. China's forthcoming WTO accession could be seen as an attempt by reformers to lock economic policies on to a course for further marketization and internationalization that is costly to reverse.

Notes

1 The earliest country in the industrial age to implement this operational principle successfully and hence attain first world status is Japan.

2 Kornai (2000, p. 25).

3 This part draws upon Woo (2000).

4 As will be documented later, in 1988 the Soviet Union produced 15 times more crude steel per dollar of GDP than the United States and eight times more than West Germany and Japan. The Soviet Union also produced five times more refined copper per dollar of GDP than the United States, West Germany and Japan.

5 The rise of the light industrial component of the industrial sector from 39 per cent of total industrial output in 1978 to 48 per cent in 1988 and 51 per cent in 1998 reflected, in part, its suppression under central planning.

6 State employment was 109.5 million in 1996 compared with 74.5 million in 1978.

7 This decline in agricultural employment is likely to be understated because it does not take illegal migration into account.

8 Woo (1998) estimated that the reallocation of Chinese agricultural labor into industries and services added 1.3 percentage points annually to the GDP growth rate over the 1985–93 period.

9 This point is very well seen in the production of the following metals expressed in thousands of metric tons per US billion dollars of GDP for the following countries in 1988 (from Lipton and Sachs, 1992):

	Soviet Union	United States	West Germany	Japan
Crude Steel	280.00	18.49	34.35	36.47
Refined Copper	1.71	0.38	0.36	0.33
Primary aluminum	4.28	0.80	0.62	0.01

10 Sachs and Woo (1994) pointed out that there had to be a big cut in welfare subsidies provided by the government through the state enterprises before workers could be induced to seek employment in the new non-subsidized private sector.
11 Fan and Woo (1996) discuss this systemic proclivity toward high inflation.
12 Recently, Nolan and Wang (1999) offered a positive assessment, while Chen (1998) offered a negative assessment.
13 The legacy of central planning is that at the beginning of industrial reform, prices of intermediate inputs to industry were artificially suppressed and prices of industrial goods artificially raised in order to concentrate revenue in the industrial sector to make revenue collection convenient for the state. So we expect $[P_0^{\,I} M_t/P_0^{\,G} Q_t]$ to be much smaller than unity.
14 Ren Ruoen (private communications) calculated column (ii) and (iii) of Table 11.3.
15 JRZ (1994, p. 240) criticized WFHJ (1993) for using a survey of urban residents to calculate the indirect income of SOE workers because the data included 'earning from second jobs, royalties, lecture fees, and transfer payments.' What WFHJ (1994) did not mention in their reply was that this criticism was invalid because JRZ thought that WFHJ (1993) were using Table 8 in Zhao (1992) when WFHJ were actually using Table 9, which was based on the bank records of SOE transactions, and hence did not contain information on the 'typical' worker's income from royalties and lecture fees.
16 He Qinglian, Zhongguo de Xianjing (China's Pitfall), Mingjing Chubanshe, Hong Kong. The translated quote is from Liu Binyan and Perry Link, 'China: The Great Backward?' *New York Review of Books*, 8 October 1998, p. 19.
17 'Guo you qiye sheng hua gaige ke burong huan,' (No time shall be lost in further reforming state owned enterprises), speech at the 4th meeting of the 8th People's Congress, *People's Daily*, Overseas Edition, 11 March 1996.
18 Mass privatization of course does not mean unloading all the SOEs at once, it means selling a large block of the SOE sector in each session.
19 See Woo (1994) for a discussion of some of the commonly claimed 'lessons from China' for Russia and Eastern Europe.
20 Tsai (2000) has suggested that 'market-thwarting federalism' might be a more accurate description of this system. See also Wong (1991) and Wong, Heady and Woo (1995).
21 Medieval-style tax farming is still inappropriate for the present Russian economic situation even if one agrees with the 'industrial feudalism' characterization of Ericson (1999a).
22 Aslund (1991, p. 103).
23 Ellman and Kontorovich (1998, p.103); but Aslund (1991, p. 127) reported the intended range to be 50–70 per cent.
24 Aslund (1991, p. 168).
25 Quoted in Aslund (1991, p. 169).
26 For contemporary accounts, see Central Intelligence Agency and Defense Intelligence Agency (1989 and 1990). Malia (1994) gives an excellent analysis of the politics of the period.
27 See accounts by Vladimir Mozhin and Vadim Medvedev in Ellman and Kontorovich (1988, pp. 151–4).
28 For details, see Yavlinsky et al (1990).

References

Aslund, Anders (1991), *Gorbachev's Struggle for Economic Reform*, updated and expanded edition, Pinter Publishers, London.

Baum, Richard (1994), *Burying Mao: Chinese Politics in the Age of Deng Xiaoping*, Princeton.

Berg, Andrew, Borensztein, Eduardo, Sahay, Ratna, and Zettelmeyer, Jeromin (1999), 'The Evolution of Output in Transition Economies: Explaining the Differences,' International Monetary Fund, WP/99/73.

Blanchard, Oliver and Kremer, Michael (1997), 'Disorganization', *Quarterly Journal of Economics*, Vol. 112 (4), pp. 1091–126.

Blanchard, Oliver and Shleifer, Andrei (2000), 'Federalism With and Without Political Centralization: China versus Russia', October, Massachusetts Institute of Technology, manuscript.

Central Intelligence Agency and the Defense Intelligence Agency (1989), *The Soviet Economy in 1988: Gorbachev Changes Course*, Report to the Subcommittee on National Security Economics, Joint Economic Committee, Congress of the United States.

Central Intelligence Agency and the Defense Intelligence Agency (1990), *The Soviet Economy Stumbles Badly in 1989*, Report to the Technology and National Security subcommittee, Joint Economic Committee, Congress of the United States.

Chen, Aimin (1998), 'Inertia in Reforming China's State-Owned Enterprises: The Case of Chongqing', *World Development*, Vol. 26 (3), March 1998, pp. 479–495.

Chen, Yu (2001), 'Decentralization, Local Provision of Public Goods and Economic Growth: The Case of China', in Ross Garnaut and Song, Ligang (eds.), *Sustainability of China's Economic Growth in the 21st Century*, Asia Pacific Press: Canberra, Australia.

Chow, Gregory (1993), 'Capital Formation and Capital Growth in China', *Quarterly Journal of Economics*, August.

Ellman, Michael and Kontorovich, Vlaclimor (1998), *The Destruction of the Soviet Economic System: An Insiders' History*, M. E. Sharpe, Armonk.

Ericson, Eric (1999a), 'The Post-Soviet Russian Economic System: An Industrial Feudalism', Columbia University, manuscript.

Ericson, Richard (1999b), 'The Structural Barrier to Transition: A Note on Input-Output Tables of Centrally Planned Economies', Columbia University, manuscript.

Fan, Gang and Woo, Wing Thye (1996), 'State Enterprise Reform as a Source of Macroeconomic Instability', *Asian Economic Journal*, November.

Fewsmith, Joseph (1994), *Dilemmas of Reform in China: Political Conflict and Economic Debate*, M.E. Sharpe, Armonk.

Frydman, Roman, Murphy, Kenneth, and Rapaczynski, Andrej (1998), *Capitalism with a Comrade's Face*, Central European University Press.

Griffin, Keith and Khan, Azizur Rahman (1993), 'The Transition to Market-Guided Economies: Lessons for Russia and Eastern Europe from the Chinese Experience', manuscript.

Groves, Theodore, Hong, Yongmiao, McMillan, John and Naughton, Barry (1994), 'Autonomy and Incentives in Chinese State Enterprises', *Quarterly Journal of Economics*, Vol. 109 (1), February, pp. 185–209.

Groves, Theodore, Hong, Yongmiao, McMillan, John and Naughton, Barry (1995), 'Productivity Growth in Chinese State-Run Industry', in Dong, Fureng, Lin, Cyril, and Naughton, Barry (eds.), *Reform of China's State-Owned Enterprises*, MacMillan, London.

Jefferson, Gary, Rawski, Thomas and Zheng, Yuxin (1992), 'Growth, Efficiency, and Convergence in China's State and Collective Industry', *Economic Development and Cultural Change*, Vol. 40 (2), January, pp. 239–66.

Jefferson, Gary, Rawski, Thomas and Zheng, Yuxin (1994), 'Productivity Change in Chinese Industry: A Comment', *China Economic Review*, Vol. 5 (2).

Jefferson, Gary, Rawski, Thomas, and Zheng, Yuxin Zheng (1996), 'Chinese Industrial Productivity: Trends, Measurement Issues, and Recent Developments', *Journal of Comparative Economics*, Vol. 23, pp. 146–80.

Jin, Hehui, Qian, Yingyi, and Weingast, Barry (1999), 'Regional Decentralization and Fiscal Incentives: Federalism, Chinese Style', August, manuscript.

Kornai, Janos (1992), *The Socialist System: The Political Economy of Communism*, Princeton.

Kornai, Janos (2000), 'Ten Years After "The Road to a Free Economy": The Author's Self-Evaluation', paper presented at The World Bank, Annual Bank Conference on Development Economics, April.

Lau, Lawrence J., Qian, Yingyi and Roland, Gerard (2000), 'Reform without Losers: An Interpretation of China's Dual-Track Approach to Transition', *Journal of Political Economy*, February.

Lipton, David and Sachs, Jeffrey D. (1992), 'Prospects for Russia's Economic Reforms', *Brookings Papers on Economic Activity*, Volume 2, pp. 213–65.

Malia, Martin (1994), *The Soviet Tragedy: A History of Socialism in Russia, 1917–1991*, Free Press, New York.

McKinsey Global Institute (1999), *Unlocking Economic Growth in Russia*, October.

Montinola, Gabriella, Qian, Yingyi and Weingast, Barry (1995), 'Federalism, Chinese Style: The Political Basis for Economic Success in China', *World Politics*, October.

Nellis, John (1999), 'Time to Rethink Privatization in Transition Economies?' International Finance Corporation Discussion Paper No. 38, World Bank.

Nolan, Peter and Wang, Xiaoqiang (1999), 'Beyond Privatization: Institutional Innovation and Growth in China's Large State-Owned Enterprises', *World Development*, Vol. 27 (1), January, pp. 169–200.

Oi, Jean (1992), 'Fiscal Reform and the Economic Foundations of Local State Corporation in China', *World Politics*, Vol. 45 (1), October, pp. 99–126.

Sachs, Jeffrey D. and Woo, Wing Thye (1994), 'Structural Factors in the Economic Reforms of China, Eastern Europe, and the Former Soviet Union', *Economic Policy*, April, Vol. 18, pp.101–45.

Sachs, Jeffrey D. and Woo, Wing Thye (2000), 'Understanding China's Economic Performance', *Journal of Policy Reform*, Vol. 4 (1), pp.1–50.

State Statistical Bureau of China (1999), *Comprehensive Statistical Data and Materials on 50 Years of New China*, China Statistical Press.

Tsai, Kellee (2000), 'Off Balance: Fiscal Federalism and the Rise of Extra-Budgetary and Informal Finance in China', paper presented at the 2000 Annual Meeting of the American Political Science Association, August, Johns Hopkins University, manuscript.

Wong, Christine P.W. (1991), 'Central-Local Relations in an Era of Fiscal Decline: The Paradox of Fiscal Decentralization in Post-Mao China', *China Quarterly*, December, pp. 691–715.

Wong, Christine P.W., Heady, Christopher and Woo, Wing Thye (1995), *Fiscal Management and Economic Reform in the People's Republic of China*, Oxford University Press.

Woo, Wing Thye (1994), 'The Art of Reforming Centrally-Planned Economies: Comparing China, Poland and Russia', *Journal of Comparative Economics*, Vol. 18 (3), June, pp. 276–308.

Woo, Wing Thye (1998), 'Chinese Economic Growth: Sources and Prospects', in Michel Fouquin and Lemoine, Francoise (eds.), *The Chinese Economy*, Economica, London (translated into Chinese as 'Zhongguo Quan Yaosu Shengchan Lu: Laizi Nongye Bumen Laodongli Zai Pei Zhi de Shouyao Zuoyong' in *Jingji Yanjiu*, Vol. 3, 1998).

Woo, Wing Thye (2000), 'Comments on 'Reform without Losers': An Interpretation of China's Dual-Track Approach to Transition by Lau, Qian and Roland', manuscript.

Woo, Wing Thye, Fan, Gang, Hai, Wen and Jin, Yibiao (1993), 'The Efficiency and Macroeconomic Consequences of Chinese Enterprise Reform', *China Economic Review*, Vol. 4 No. 2.

Woo, Wing Thye, Fan, Gang, Hai, Wen and Jin, Yibiao (1994), 'Productivity Change in Chinese Industry: Authors' Reply', *China Economic Review*, Vol. 5 No. 2.

Woo, Wing Thye, Hai, Wen, Jin, Yibiao and Fan, Gang (1994), 'How Successful Has Chinese Enterprise Reform Been? Pitfalls in Opposite Biases and Focus', *Journal of Comparative Economics*, June (translated into Chinese as 'Zhongguo qiye gaige jiujing huode le duo da chenggong,' in Jingji Yanjiu, 1994:6).

Yavlinsky, G., Fedorev, B., Shatalin, S., Petrakov, N., Aleksashenko, S., Vavilov, A., Grigoriev, L., Zadornov, M., Machits, V., Mikhailov, A. and Yasin, E. (1990), *500 Days: Transition to the Market*, St. Martin's Press, New York.

Zhao, Renwei (1992), 'Special Features of China's Income Distribution During the Transition Period', *Jingji Yanjiu*, Vol. 1, pp. 53–63.

Zheng, Yongnian (1994), *Quasi-Corporatism, Developmental Localism, and Behavioral Federalism*, PhD dissertation, Princeton University.

Appendix

Challenges and Implications of China Joining the WTO: What WTO Accession Means

Richard Eglin[1]

Introduction

The process of China becoming a Member of the WTO has been underway for 14 years. At times, it must have seemed to China that the process risked dying from exhaustion or going on forever, without any end in sight.

Developments over the past 12 months have confirmed beyond any doubt that the process of China's WTO accession is irreversible. Everyone now expects a conclusion to be reached soon. We have entered the final phase of the completion of China's accession. Everything is being done in Geneva to try to ensure that this final phase is an accelerated one. It must be recognized, however, that a substantial amount of work remains to be done.

At the *bilateral level*, negotiations still have to be completed with half-a-dozen or so WTO Members. Accession negotiations do not take place on the traditional GATT / WTO basis of reciprocity. What is on offer for China is rules-based, non-discriminatory market access at levels that apply currently between WTO Members. In exchange, WTO Members expect China to make market-access commitments of equivalent value. Some of the bilateral negotiations are likely to be difficult. Nevertheless, it is recognized that the Chinese Government is making every effort to conclude the remaining bilateral negotiations as soon as possible.

At the *multilateral level*, the conclusion of most of the bilateral negotiations between China and other WTO Members, in particular, those recently concluded with the United States and the European Union, has allowed the WTO Working Party on China's Accession to start the task of completing the accession Protocol and its Report. Three elements are involved. First, those parts of the 1997 draft Protocol that remain open must be finalized. Second, the results of China's bilateral negotiations with WTO Members must be tabled formally and discussed with a view to the Working Party agreeing on how they are to be incorporated into the multilateral system. Third, negotiations must be completed and agreement reached on the annexes to China's draft protocol.

An important amount of work of a technical nature remains to be completed in Geneva by the WTO Secretariat. The Secretariat is committed to devoting as much time and resources as necessary to ensure that the technical work is carried out efficiently and rapidly, so as not to hold back the process of China's accession.

Foremost here is the compilation of the draft schedules of commitments by China on goods and services, which result from China's bilateral negotiations with WTO Members. Such is the importance of China's accession that this will be by far the biggest exercise of its kind ever carried out by the WTO Secretariat. The Secretariat stands ready to begin this work as soon as the Chinese Government supplies it with the raw data necessary to undertake the exercise.

China's accession process is one of several which began under the GATT and which will be concluded under the WTO. The change from GATT to WTO was fundamental in many respects, not the least of which was a change to a more sophisticated approach towards development issues in the WTO, which emphasizes the unitary nature of the multilateral trading system for all its Members. The WTO system is designed to be inclusive of developing country interests.

A key aspect of accession to the WTO, whether the party acceding is least-developed, developing or developed, is that the acceding government's legislation and domestic enforcement mechanism must be brought into conformity with the WTO obligations. The terms of entry to the WTO are legally binding commitments. Those commitments give the process its credibility, and they are the benchmark against which each Member's participation in the multilateral trading system is constantly reviewed, including in the final analysis through the dispute settlement mechanism.

What WTO Accession Means for China

Twenty-five years ago, the Chinese Government took the decisive step of introducing the market-based economy, allowing private enterprise to begin developing and taking decisions on investment and production. China's international trade responded at once. By 1986, when China first applied to resume its membership in the GATT, exports had grown from five to ten per cent of China's GDP, and China was accounting for over one per cent of world exports. Trade had become a key factor in China's further economic growth and development.

The reform process was, nonetheless, still at a relatively early stage. China's import regime was still bound to the central planning system, still in large measure under the control of state trading monopolies and still heavily regulated by the centralized allocation of foreign exchange. Unless China had been able in 1986 to undertake a quite massive, and very rapid, further transformation of its trade regime, it seems doubtful that GATT membership at that time could have delivered its full economic benefits to China. A more profound and deeper phase of trade reform was needed to allow the rules-based multilateral trading system to play its key roles of guaranteeing China non-discriminatory market access abroad and access to cheaper imports at home.

Since 1986, the process of trade reform has matured considerably, and China's trade performance has reflected this. China's exports today account for over 20 per cent of its GDP and China has become a true giant in international trade, accounting for over three per cent of world exports. Imports have been liberalized considerably. Most important of all, the phase of moving from import planning to import licensing has given way to a new phase of moving from import licensing to import tariffs, bringing prices and the market mechanism into play as the key determinants of China's future trade relations with the rest of the world.

This truly impressive reform process had to come from within China; that is, it could not have been imposed from the outside. The GATT and WTO have no supranational power, but they can assist Member governments to maintain the process of trade reform once the political direction has been set.

That is the first and perhaps most important benefit that WTO accession will bring to China. Accession will involve a substantial process to consolidate the replacement of state and bureaucratic control of trade transactions by market mechanisms, and to consolidate China's legal and administrative framework that protects private property rights and private sector activity. It will 'lock-in', in other words, the accumulated trade reform process that the Chinese government has undertaken to date and provide a platform from which China can sustain its reform process into the future. Nothing can substitute for the courage and determination of the Chinese Government itself in carrying forward China's reform program, but WTO membership can help support that process. By placing China's reforms within the broader conext of trade liberalization by all WTO Members, it can increase the returns to trade reform in China through reciprocal market access abroad, and help the Chinese Government to resist pressure domestically to reverse the process of reform.

Accession will also mean that China can replace the bilateral relationships it has had to use until now to shape its trade with its major trading partners, by a single, multilateral trade relationship with the rest of the world. Bilateral relationships can be fickle and uncertain, increasing the risk for producers and investors, and demanding a huge investment of time and effort by government officials to negotiate and administer them.

The multilateral trade relationship provided by the WTO is far less costly and more permanent. It is defined by the WTO rules and the WTO's dispute settlement system for enforcing those rules. The rules are legally binding upon each Member, and they require from each Member a solemn commitment to respect and to implement the rule of law.

The WTO rules will protect China's rights, and the expectations of its exporters, against damaging protectionist policies in overseas markets. China's vulnerability to discriminatory, *ad hoc* protectionism in its major export markets has grown, along with China's success in increasing its exports over the past 20 years. Were this to continue, and perhaps escalate in the future if world economic growth were to suffer a serious decline, it could prove a major setback to China's economic growth and development and even to China's economic reform process. Once WTO accession is complete, China's exporters will more confidently be able to make long-term business decisions on the expansion of their activities. The more open the Chinese economy becomes, the more China will benefit from the legal security of the rules-based trading system.

The WTO is not an ideological charter for free trade, but one of its main purposes is to assist its Member governments to achieve the progressive liberalization of trade. Successive rounds of trade liberalization in the past fifty years have made the world economy more open, more integrated and more competitive. The benefits, in terms of economic growth, are well known.

WTO Members began new multilateral trade negotiations to further liberalize trade in agriculture and trade in services on 1 January 2000, and many of them favor the eventual launch of more comprehensive trade negotiations. China's membership in the WTO will give it a very important voice in helping shape new WTO negotiations, to meet not only China's own needs for its future economic growth and development, but also the needs of the rest of Asia, Africa, Latin America and the OECD countries too. Naturally, each WTO Member pursues its own export interests as vigorously as possible in a trade negotiation, but the glue which holds the multilateral trading system together, and which ensures that each new WTO Round can produce a more liberal outcome than its predecessor, is the realization of each participant that its export markets can only grow if producers abroad can increase their exports too. The sub-plot to the mercantilist bargain of a WTO Round, in other words, is the need to open one's own market to higher imports if anything is ever to be gained. The reforming zeal that we expect the Chinese Government to bring to the next WTO negotiation will make it a very important partner indeed in helping move the liberal trading system further forward.

The remainder of this chapter presents an overview of the WTO and its rules. In the end, they provide the real key to the question of what China's accession to the WTO will mean for China as well as for all other WTO Members.

The World Trade Organization

The Agreement Establishing the World Trade Organization

The World Trade Organization is the institutional and legal foundation for the multilateral trading system that came into being on 1 January 1995. The WTO Agreement defines the functions of the organization, its structure, and the qualifications for membership, decision-making procedures and requirements.

Functions of the WTO The principal objectives of the WTO, as of the GATT, include raising standards of living, ensuring full employment, expanding production and trade and allowing optimal use of the world's resources. In addition, the WTO refers to production of and trade in services (the GATT spoke only of goods), it states the objective of sustainable development, 'seeking both to protect and preserve the environment'; and it recognizes the need for positive efforts to ensure that developing countries, and especially the least-developed countries, 'secure a share in international trade commensurate with the needs of their economic development'.

The means of achieving these objectives is the same as that laid down in the GATT, namely, 'reciprocal and mutually advantageous arrangements directed to the substantial reduction of tariffs and other barriers to trade and to the elimination of discriminatory treatment in international trade relations'.

The WTO has five functions. The first, and broadest, is to 'facilitate the implementation, administration and operation, and further the objectives, of this Agreement and of the Multilateral Trade Agreements', and also to 'provide the framework for the implementation, administration and operation of the Plurilateral Trade Agreements'. The wording reflects the difference between the multilateral agreements, to which all Members are committed, and the plurilateral agreements, which are under the WTO umbrella, but do not attract the same degree of support.

The second is to be a negotiating forum.

The third and fourth functions of the WTO are to administer the arrangements for the settlement of disputes that may arise between Members and for the review of trade policies.

Finally, the WTO is to co-operate, as appropriate, with the International Monetary Fund and the World Bank 'with a view to achieving greater coherence in global economic policymaking'.

Structure of the WTO The WTO is headed by a Ministerial Conference, composed of all WTO Members, which is to meet at least once every two years. The Conference has full powers under the Agreement. It is to 'carry out the functions of the WTO and take actions necessary to this effect', and has 'the authority to take decisions on all matters under any of the Multilateral Trade agreements'.

Between sessions of the Ministerial Conference, its functions are exercised by the General Council, also made up of the full membership of the WTO. The General Council is responsible for the regular management of the organization, and it supervises all aspects of the WTO's work. It meets regularly, and most of the national representatives at these meetings are the permanent heads of their countries' delegations in Geneva.

The General Council also convenes as the Dispute Settlement Body and as the Trade Policy Review Body.

The Council for Trade in Goods, the Council for Trade in Services, and the Council for Trade-Related Aspects of Intellectual Property Rights (TRIPS Council) operate under the guidance of the General Council and carry out the functions assigned to them by the goods, services or TRIPS agreements and by the General Council. Each of the Councils is open to all WTO Members who wish to attend. The Councils meet as necessary and can set up subsidiary bodies. The Goods Council has a large number of such bodies, many established under the terms of specific Uruguay Round agreements such as those on agriculture or subsidies, and the Committee on Market Access, which handles work on both tariff and non-tariff matters. The Council for Trade in Services has also set up a number of subsidiary bodies. Most have the task of carrying forward one or another aspect of the program of negotiations on services issues called for by the GATS or by related Ministerial Decisions taken at Marrakesh.

Membership The WTO Agreement provides for two ways of becoming a Member of the organization. The first, 'original membership', covers the situation of governments which were Contracting Parties to the old GATT. The possibility of joining by this route was available only for a limited period.

The second approach to membership is 'accession', by negotiating the terms of membership with the governments that are already Members. The conditions for accession are not specified. Accession is simply to be 'on terms to be agreed between it and the WTO'.

Once membership has been achieved, original Members and Members by accession are all on the same footing, subject to any special terms of accession.

Membership requires, *inter alia*, that governments ensure the conformity of their laws, regulations and administrative procedures with their obligations under the WTO agreements.

For political or other reasons, certain Members may not wish to have WTO rules apply between them. This is possible, provided either of the Members concerned makes its position clear at the time of accession. 'Non-application' may not be invoked thereafter.

Decision-making The WTO Agreement states that, except as otherwise provided, the WTO is to be 'guided by the decisions, procedures and customary practices' followed under the old GATT. This is spelled out further in the wording that 'the WTO shall continue the practice of decision-making by consensus followed under GATT 1947'.

Formal voting is provided for, where consensus cannot be reached, but only in the General Council or the Ministerial Conference. Each WTO Member has one vote. The rules on voting are precise and complex, varying according to the nature of the decision that is to be taken. Decisions on the accession of new Members, for example, require approval by two-thirds of the membership.

These voting requirements, tougher than those set by the old GATT, make it likely that formal votes will be even less frequent in the WTO than they were under the GATT. Reaching decisions by consensus is viewed universally as the far preferable route to take.

Settlement of Disputes

The effectiveness of any rules depends on whether they are obeyed and also on whether there is agreement on what they require and imply. Each WTO Member takes on a very wide range of obligations and in return, expects to enjoy the rights created for it by the assumption of similar obligations by the other Members. The task of ensuring that all Members live up to their commitments and that there is a common understanding of the nature of these commitments, is a central part of the work of the WTO. It falls into two parts. One part can be described largely under the heading of 'multilateral review and transparency', and is discussed below. The other is handled by the dispute settlement process, which is concerned with specific situations in which one or more Members seek a remedy for damage to their trade interests caused by the actions (or failures to act) of another Member or Members.

Basic principles The Uruguay Round Understanding on the Rules and Procedures Governing the Settlement of Disputes states that 'The dispute settlement system of the WTO is a central element in providing security and predictability to the multilateral trading system'. The system serves to preserve rights and obligations under the Agreements it covers and to clarify, but not alter, those rights and obligations. Among other principles set out in the understanding are many based on GATT experience. These include the importance of prompt settlement of disputes to effective functioning of the WTO and a proper balance of rights and obligations; the objective of achieving a satisfactory settlement of disputes in accordance with those rights and obligations and the understanding that requests to consult and use the dispute settlement procedures should not be considered contentious acts. Members are to use their judgement as to whether action under the procedures would be fruitful and are reminded that the aim of the dispute settlement mechanism is to

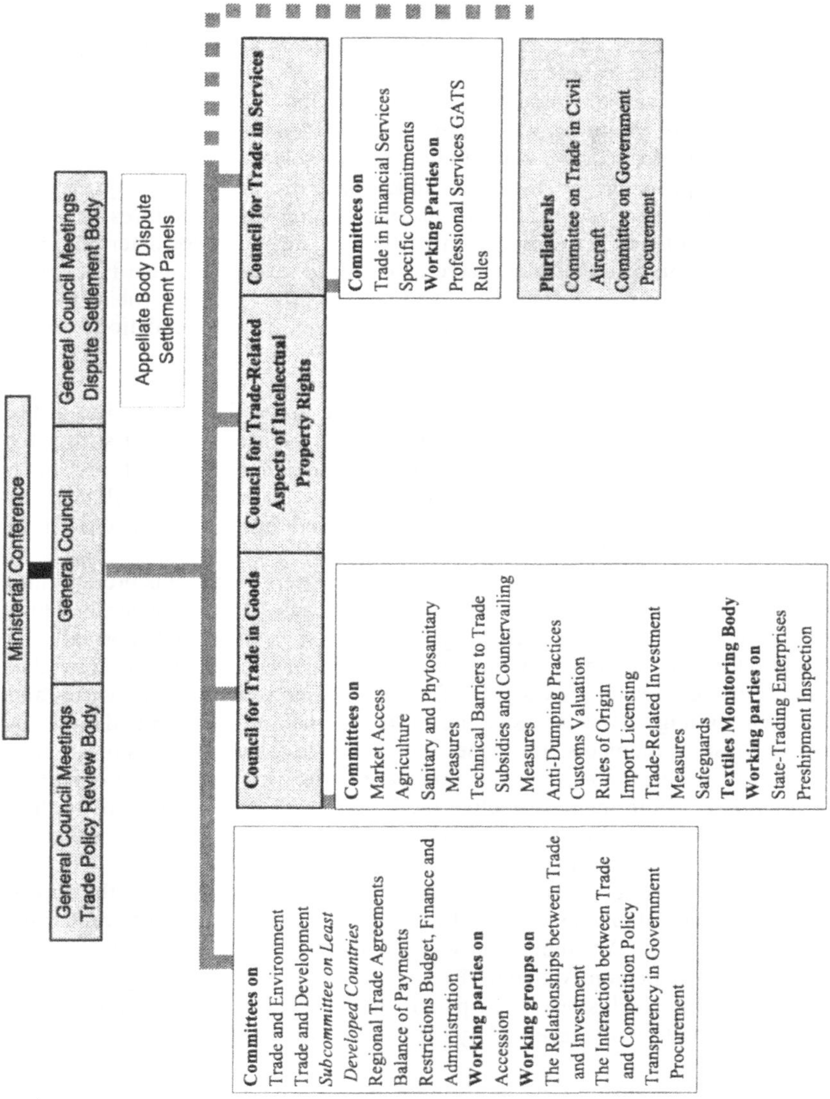

Figure A.1 Organization and responsibilities

secure a positive, and if possible mutually acceptable, solution to a dispute. The preferred solution to a dispute is usually withdrawal of measures found inconsistent with Agreements under the WTO. Failing withdrawal, provision of compensation is a less satisfactory substitute. The least desirable outcome is retaliation, in which the injured Member may, after authorization, suspend trade concessions or obligations towards the other Member concerned.

A very important set of principles set out in the Understanding is titled 'Strengthening of the Multilateral System'. This effectively prohibits unilateral actions by Members to redress what they see as violations of obligations, or nullification or impairment of benefits, under any of the WTO Agreements. Members are required to use the WTO dispute settlement procedures to settle grievances related to these Agreements. In particular, they may not determine that violations, nullification or impairment have taken place, except in accordance with approved panel or appellate findings, and must follow other rules in the Understanding that give a reasonable time for panel recommendations to be followed and govern resort to retaliation.

Institutions The dispute settlement arrangements are under the supervision of the Dispute Settlement Body (DSB), which is the WTO's General Council sitting for this purpose under a different name. The DSB has the sole authority 'to establish panels, adopt panel and Appellate Body reports, maintain surveillance of implementation of rulings and recommendations, and authorize suspension of concessions and obligations'.

Individual panels are set up to examine particular matters. A panel is brought into existence by the DSB to carry out a specific task and ceases to exist when that task has been completed. Unless the parties agree otherwise, a panel will normally be given standard terms of reference, which require it to examine the matter referred to it 'in the light of the relevant provisions' of the Agreements cited by the parties and 'to make such findings as will assist the DSB' in making recommendations or rulings under those Agreements. The panel is expected to assess the facts of the case and the extent to which the Agreements concerned apply and have been complied with. An important requirement, reflecting the traditional GATT priority of settling the trade problem at issue, is that panels should give parties to the dispute 'adequate opportunity to develop a mutually satisfactory solution'.

Parties to a dispute are given the right to appeal against a panel report, the appeal being limited to issues of law covered in the panel report and to legal interpretations developed by the panel. An appeal on a particular case will be heard by three members of the seven-person Appellate Body. They can uphold, modify or reverse the legal findings and conclusions of the panel, and their report, once adopted by the DSB, is to be unconditionally accepted by the parties to the dispute.

Decision-making The most important difference between the GATT and the WTO dispute settlement rules is in their decision-making procedures. Under the GATT, key decisions depended on consensus agreement to move ahead. This meant that if a party to a dispute was unwilling to have a panel established, or objected to its membership or terms of reference, or did not accept the panel's conclusions, it could refuse its support and thereby block the achievement of consensus and progress.

Crucially, the consensus requirement has been turned around under the WTO's rules and progress on each of those points cannot be blocked unless there is consensus to do so. Thus if a panel has been requested, the DSB must establish it 'unless the DSB decides by consensus not to establish a panel'. Such consensus is improbable, since the requesting country is unlikely to change its view unless the dispute has been settled. A panel report shall be approved by the DSB unless appealed or the DSB decides by consensus not to adopt it. In the case of an appeal, the Appellate Body's report must again be adopted by the DSB unless there is consensus agreement in the DSB not to do so. These provisions effectively remove the opportunities that existed under the GATT procedures for blocking the multilateral dispute settlement process.

Retaliation The first objective in dispute settlement is to reach a mutually agreed settlement or failing that, to secure the withdrawal of measures found inconsistent with a WTO Agreement. The next best solution is to have the offending member provide appropriate compensation for whatever injury has been caused. In practice, settlement, withdrawal or compensation were the normal outcome of all GATT disputes, except to the extent that the dispute settlement process was for some reason blocked. However, there remains a fourth alternative: retaliation, or in formal terms 'the possibility of suspending the application of concessions or other obligations under the covered agreements on a discriminatory basis *vis-à-vis* the other Member'. For a government found at fault in a dispute, the possibility of this ultimate sanction of retaliation is undoubtedly a strong inducement to settle the matter by withdrawing the offending measure or by giving compensation.

A Member found at fault by an adopted panel or Appellate Body report is required to inform the DSB of the action it will take to comply with the report's recommendations and rulings. It is given a 'reasonable period of time' for compliance. In the absence of agreement in the DSB or between the parties to the dispute, this period may be determined by arbitration and will not normally be more than 15 months. If the Member found at fault fails to implement the recommendations and rulings, it may voluntarily grant compensation to the injured party to the dispute. If, however, no agreement on compensation is reached, the injured party may request the right to retaliate, and once again the rule that consensus is needed to block progress applies. The request will be granted unless there is consensus to reject it. Elaborate rules govern the form which retaliation may take, their purpose being, on the one hand, to restrict action as far as possible to the same area of trade as that in which injury has been caused and on the other, to permit the injured party to find adequate compensation that is 'equivalent to the level of the nullification or impairment'. The general principle is that the complaining party should first seek to retaliate in the sector in which its rights have been found to be nullified or impaired. But if the injured party considers this not to be 'practicable or effective', retaliation may be sought in another sector or even, when circumstances are 'serious enough', under another WTO Agreement altogether. If the Member affected objects that the action proposed is excessive, it can appeal to arbitration by the members of the original panel, or by an independent arbitrator, whose decision is final.

Arbitration, good offices, conciliation and mediation Arbitration can also be used in circumstances other than a disagreement over the amount of compensation. When clearly defined disputes arise, and the parties agree, it is open to them to resort to arbitration, provided they also agree to accept the arbitration award. Another means of stepping outside the panel and appeal procedures is by asking a third party to offer good offices, conciliation or mediation. Although this can be requested at any time, the provisions place most emphasis on efforts to settle a dispute before it reaches the formal stage of a panel. The Director-General may offer good offices, conciliation and mediation *ex officio* and, along with the chairman of the DSB, is required to give such help if so requested by a least-developed country involved in a dispute.

Non-violation complaints Most complaints under the GATT concerned situations in which one Member claimed that another had caused injury to its trade interests by taking a measure inconsistent with the GATT rules. Such 'violation complaints' will also account for the great majority of disputes under the WTO. However, a complaint may also be brought, and may be found justified, even if no actual violation has occurred. This may happen if the government complained against has taken a measure that nullifies or impairs a benefit which the complainant can show it had reason to expect to receive under the provisions of a WTO agreement. In such cases, the normal dispute settlement rules apply, except that the Member complained against cannot be forced to withdraw the measure. Mutually satisfactory adjustment, possibly including compensation, is regarded as a normal means of settling the matter.

Multilateral Review and Transparency

A government's assent to an international agreement should be enough to ensure that it will apply the agreement's provisions, changing its national laws, policies and procedures to whatever extent may be required. In practice, this may not happen. At worst, governments may deliberately choose to disregard international obligations they have assumed. More likely, however, an obligation may be overlooked, or interpreted in a way different from the understanding that other signatories have of it. The rules of the WTO exist primarily to create a predictable and liberal economic, as well as legal, environment for international trade. To plan and invest for the future, both business and governments need confirmation that their trading partners are applying the rules and that they are doing so, moreover, in the same way. The means by which the WTO achieves this end is its arrangements for multilateral review and transparency.

Trade Policy Review Mechanism (TPRM) TPRM reviews are intended to enable 'the regular collective appreciation and evaluation of the full range of individual Members' trade policies and practices and their impact on the functioning of the multilateral trading system'. Their purpose is to help improve 'adherence by all Members to rules, disciplines and commitments made' under the WTO Agreements. However, this collective scrutiny is carefully distinguished from the operation of other WTO bodies, which look at each Member's performance in relation to particular agreements. It is also distinct from dispute settlement procedures. The TPRB is not an enforcement body, nor can it impose new policy commitments on Members. Although the focus of the reviews is on the trade policies of the Member under examination, they also take account of wider national economic and development needs, policies and objectives, and of the external environment.

All WTO Members are subject to review. The frequency of review depends on the impact of the Member on the multilateral trading system. Thus Members with the largest share in world trade are reviewed most frequently. The four largest, currently the European Union (which is counted as one), the United States, Japan and Canada are reviewed every two years and the next 16, every four years. Remaining Members are subject to review every six years, although least-developed countries may be reviewed at longer intervals. These review cycles imply that, with a membership of well over 100, the TPRB is called on to review the trade policies of 20 or more countries every year.

Notification Although GATT Article X contains a general obligation to publish trade-related laws and regulations, it does not require that this information be transmitted to other Members. As obligations regulating non-tariff measures affecting trade became more comprehensive and elaborate, specialized committees were established to ensure that national measures were consistent with these obligations. As the basis for this work, each Member was usually required to notify regularly any changes in its relevant laws and regulations and to give details of how these were being applied. Virtually all the Uruguay Round Agreements establish notification requirements of this kind, and set up committees or other bodies which are required to oversee the operation of the agreement concerned, largely on the basis of the notifications made. Some agreements also provide for 'reverse' notifications in which a Member draws attention to the measures of another.

A Ministerial Decision taken as part of the final Uruguay Round package establishes a general obligation to notify, backed up by central arrangements in the WTO. The obligation, although stated in terms of the WTO Agreements as a whole, focuses on measures affecting trade in goods. As a guide to measures that should be notified, whether or not such notification is specifically required under a particular WTO agreement, the decision provides an annexed indicative list of some twenty types of measures, rules or arrangements. The decision sets up a central registry in the WTO Secretariat to track all notifications received, remind Members of their notification obligations and provide Members with information on the content of notifications.

The Panel Process

The various stages a dispute can go through in the WTO. At all stages, countries in dispute are encouraged to consult each other in order to settle 'out of court'. At all stages the WTO Director-General is available to offer his good offices, to mediate or to help achieve a conciliation.

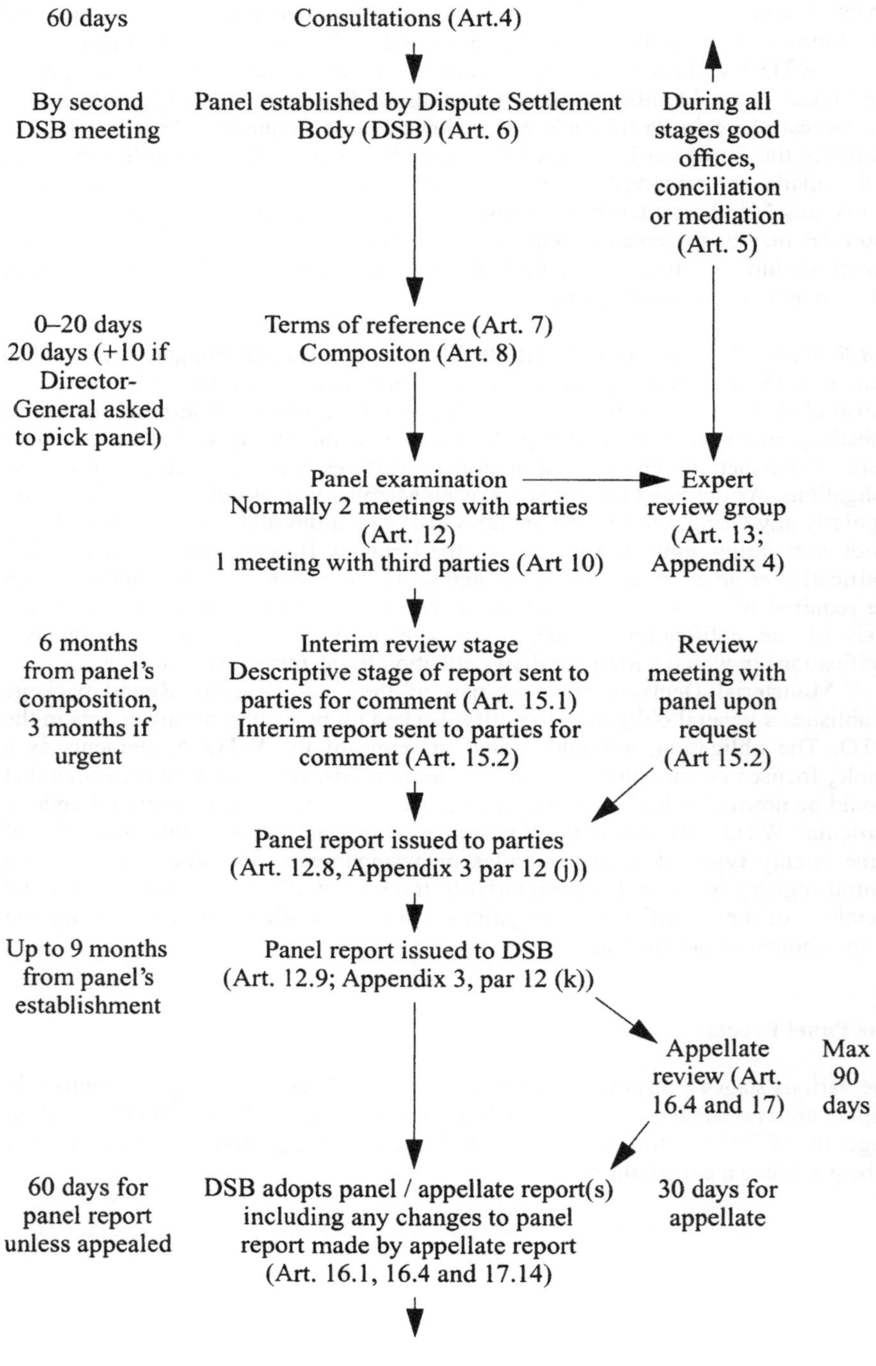
60 days
Consultations (Art.4)
By second DSB meeting
Panel established by Dispute Settlement Body (DSB) (Art. 6)
During all stages good offices, conciliation or mediation (Art. 5)
0–20 days
20 days (+10 if Director-General asked to pick panel)
Terms of reference (Art. 7)
Compositon (Art. 8)
Panel examination
Normally 2 meetings with parties (Art. 12)
1 meeting with third parties (Art 10)
Expert review group (Art. 13; Appendix 4)
6 months from panel's composition, 3 months if urgent
Interim review stage
Descriptive stage of report sent to parties for comment (Art. 15.1)
Interim report sent to parties for comment (Art. 15.2)
Review meeting with panel upon request (Art 15.2)
Panel report issued to parties (Art. 12.8, Appendix 3 par 12 (j))
Up to 9 months from panel's establishment
Panel report issued to DSB (Art. 12.9; Appendix 3, par 12 (k))
Appellate review (Art. 16.4 and 17)
Max 90 days
60 days for panel report unless appealed
DSB adopts panel / appellate report(s) including any changes to panel report made by appellate report (Art. 16.1, 16.4 and 17.14)
30 days for appellate

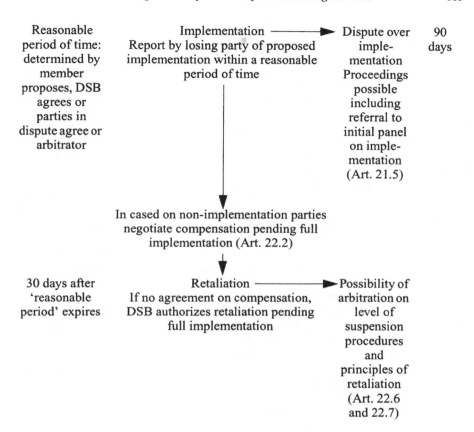

Reasonable period of time: determined by member proposes, DSB agrees or parties in dispute agree or arbitrator	Implementation → Report by losing party of proposed implementation within a reasonable period of time	Dispute over imple-mentation Proceedings possible including referral to initial panel on imple-mentation (Art. 21.5)	90 days
	↓ In cased on non-implementation parties negotiate compensation pending full implementation (Art. 22.2)		
30 days after 'reasonable period' expires	↓ Retaliation → If no agreement on compensation, DSB authorizes retaliation pending full implementation	Possibility of arbitration on level of suspension procedures and principles of retaliation (Art. 22.6 and 22.7)	

Note: Some specified times are maximums, some are minimums; some binding, some not.

Figure A.2 The panel process

Trade in Goods

The Agreements The WTO agreements on trade in goods fall into four groups. First is the 'GATT 1994', a modified version of the original, 1947 version of the GATT, together with certain agreements, which interpret or bring up to date particular GATT provisions, and a legal text (the Marrakesh Protocol) that brings under the multilateral GATT umbrella the individual tariff and non-tariff commitments made by WTO Members in the Uruguay Round. A second group consists of two major agreements that aim to bring trade in agricultural products and in textiles and clothing within the normal trading rules from which they have until now largely escaped. A third group is made up of five agreements, which go well beyond the original GATT rules in prescribing how particular aspects of policies affecting trade should be applied. And finally, a further group of six agreements deals with different aspects of the traditional GATT concern to regulate and ease the necessary formalities of customs and trade administration.

The General Agreement on Tariffs and Trade 1994 The core principles of the GATT are fundamental to the conduct of trade relations between WTO Members. They are the most-favored-nation (MFN) rule (Article I), the principle of reduction and binding of national tariffs (Article II), the rule of national treatment (Article III), transparency (Article X) and the prohibition, subject to defined exceptions, of protective measures other than tariffs (Article XI).

The MFN rule is basic to the whole edifice of the GATT. It requires that if one WTO Member grants to another 'more favorable treatment' (such as a reduction in the customs duty payable on imports of a particular product), it must immediately and unconditionally give the same treatment to imports from all other Members. The MFN, or non-discrimination, obligation applies to customs duties and charges of any kind connected with importing and exporting, as well as to internal taxes and charges, and to all the rules by which such duties, taxes and charges are applied. The major, and continuing, exceptions to the MFN rule are Article XXIV, which allows members of customs unions and free trade areas to give more favorable treatment to imports from one another, and a 1979 understanding which permits preferences for and among developing countries.

The second core principle is that the Members undertake commitments in which they state the maximum level of import duty or other charge or restriction that they will apply to imports of specified types of goods. These commitments, or 'bindings', may result initially from bilateral negotiations, in which, for instance, the government concerned has agreed to another Member's request that it reduce the import duty on certain products. However, the commitments are then recorded in national schedules which, through the provisions of Article II, become part of each Member's obligations under the GATT and because of the operation of the MFN rule, apply to imports from any Member. The provisions of Article II, combined with technical rules in Article XXVIII, provide the basis for further WTO negotiations to reduce barriers to trade in goods.

The rule of national treatment, in Article III of the GATT, is also of fundamental importance. It complements the MFN rule. Whereas Article I, by requiring MFN treatment, puts the products of all of a Member's trading partners on equal terms with one another, the national treatment principle puts those products on equal terms also with the products of the importing country itself. It says that, once imports have passed the national frontier and in so doing, have paid whatever import duty is imposed, they must be treated no worse than domestic products. Internal taxes or other charges on the imports must be no higher than on domestic products and laws and regulations affecting their sale, purchase, transportation, distribution or use must be no less favorable than for goods of national origin. The national treatment principle means that protection of the domestic supplier of a product should be given only through action at the border.

The fourth core GATT principle aims to restrict border protection, as far as possible, to the single instrument of import duties. Quantitative restrictions on imports and exports are in general banned by Article XI, although a number of provisions in this and other articles state exceptions to this general rule. Alternative forms of protection permitted if domestic industries are threatened by imports that are subsidized or dumped are also elaborately regulated by further Uruguay Round agreements. However, the basic aim of making import duties the sole form of trade restriction has been retained under the GATT 1994. Indeed, it has been greatly reinforced in the very important sector of trade in agricultural products.

Finally, transparency is a major element in the WTO. It appears in the general requirements imposed by GATT Article X for trade policies and regulations affecting trade in goods and in more specific requirements built into many other Uruguay Round agreements.

Scope of GATT 1994 The GATT 1994 consists of four elements:

(a) The provisions of the old GATT of 1947, 'as rectified, amended or modified' at the time of the entry into force of the WTO.
(b) Legal instruments setting out pre-WTO tariff agreements, the terms of agreements on accession to the old GATT, decisions on waivers granted under Article XXV of the GATT 1947 and still in force, and other decisions taken by the GATT contracting parties.
(c) and (d) The third and fourth elements of the GATT 1994 are agreements reached in the Uruguay Round. These are, respectively, six Understandings, which interpret particular points in a number of the GATT articles and the Marrakesh Protocol, which incorporates the market access commitments of each WTO member. Three of the most significant of those Understandings relate to GATT provisions on regional trading arrangements, balance-of-payments restrictions and state trading enterprises.

Regional trading arrangements One of the most striking developments in trade relations in recent years has been the proliferation of regional agreements under which groups of Members have agreed to reduce trade barriers among themselves. Such arrangements inherently favor imports from members of the grouping and discriminate against imports from other countries. This departure from the MFN principle is permitted by Article XXIV of the GATT. Although the text of Article XXIV remains unchanged in GATT 1994, a Uruguay Round understanding clarified certain points in the Article.

The rules of Article XXIV are designed to ensure that countries, which form regional agreements, move to genuinely free trade among them, and provide adequate compensation for any damage done to the trade interests of other WTO Members. The rules distinguish between two technically different forms of arrangement, the customs union and the free trade area. Both involve the removal of trade barriers among their members. However, the member countries of customs unions all charge the same rates of import duty on imports from non-members, while members of free trade areas retain their own national tariffs. Article XXIV requires that customs unions set their common import duties and other regulations affecting imports into the union at a level not higher or more restrictive on the whole than the overall level ('general incidence') of those of the countries involved before the union was formed. Compensation must be provided for any increases. Free trade areas are unlikely by their nature to raise duties against outsiders, but they use rules of origin to identify products that qualify for the duty-free treatment. These rules must not be allowed to become a trade obstacle in themselves. To qualify as either a customs union or free trade area, members must remove duties and other restrictions affecting 'substantially all' the trade between them.

The Uruguay Round understanding on Article XXIV clarifies some of these points. It provides a methodology for measuring whether the 'general incidence' of a customs union's common duties and trade regulations are higher than those existing before it was formed, based importantly by comparing *applied*, not bound, tariff rates and duties collected. It also clarifies how compensation is to be offered if formation of the customs union results in a member raising a bound duty. Second, an interim agreement leading to the formation of a customs union or free trade area shall normally not exceed ten years. Third, it strengthens the requirement that 'substantially all' trade be included in the elimination of barriers between members, by 'recognizing' that the arrangement's contribution to the expansion of world trade will be increased if the removal of duties and other restrictions extends to all trade, and diminished 'if any major sector of trade is excluded'.

Balance-of-payments provisions The GATT allows Members in balance-of-payments difficulty to introduce trade restrictions as one of the major exceptions to the basic principles of tariff bindings and 'tariffs only'. GATT Articles XII and XVIII:B set out the conditions that are to be met, by developed and developing country Members respectively. The most significant change brought in by the Uruguay Round Understanding on this subject is that Members are now required to favor price-based measures when they resort to using balance-of-payments restrictions and to seek to avoid using quantitative restrictions for this purpose. Price-based measures can include tariffs set above the Member's bound rates, as well as measures such as import surcharges or import deposit requirements, which in economic terms have a far greater validity than quantitative restrictions in the context of a balance-of-payments adjustment program. In addition, they have a less disruptive effect on the trade of other Members. Other changes introduced through the Understanding include an obligation to announce publicly time schedules for phasing out restrictive import measures, or to provide justification where this is not possible, and the tightening up of the procedures for regular consultation with other Members as long as the restrictions are maintained.

State trading enterprises The understanding on GATT Article XVII concerns the definition of state-trading enterprises and transparency of their activities. The main aim of Article XVII is to ensure that government-owned enterprises, or enterprises that have special privileges granted by the government, are not permitted by this privileged situation to escape the GATT rules of non-discrimination (the MFN and national treatment rules). The article does not cover purchases by governments for their own use. This is beyond its scope. The point is that enterprises which, due to their relationship with the government, are able to influence imports or exports, should not distort trade by favoring particular suppliers, restricting quantities imported or exported, subsidizing exports or fixing high prices. The understanding establishes, as a working definition for the purpose of the Article XVII, that 'state trading enterprises' are governmental and non-governmental enterprises, including marketing boards, which through the exercise of exclusive or special rights or privileges granted to them can influence through their purchases or sales the level or direction of imports or exports. Such enterprises must be notified to the WTO.

(a) The Marrakesh Protocol The Marrakesh Protocol is the legal instrument by which each WTO Member's commitments in the Uruguay Round to eliminate or reduce tariff rates and non-tariff measures applicable to trade in goods became an integral part of the GATT 1994. All of the thousands of pages of national schedules, representing the detailed results of the market access negotiations, including specific commitments under the agricultural agreements, were attached to the Protocol.

The schedules are divided into four parts:

Part I
- *Section I–A* – Agricultural products: Tariff concessions on an MFN basis
- *Section I–B* – Agricultural products: Tariff quotas
- *Section II* – Tariff concessions on an MFN basis on other products

Part II – Preferential tariff (if applicable)

Part III – Concessions on non-tariff measures (generally on non-agricultural products)

Part IV – Agricultural products: Commitments limiting subsidization
- *Section I* – Domestic support: Total AMS commitments
- *Section II* – Export subsidies: Budgetary outlay and quantity reduction commitments
- *Section III* – Commitments limiting the scope of export subsidies

In the past, GATT schedules consisted almost entirely of tariff bindings affecting imports on an MFN basis. These corresponded to the concessions listed in Part I, Section I-A (although, for many Members, the number of bindings affecting agricultural products was low) and Section II. Bindings of preferential tariffs (Part II) were rare. The tariff concessions on non-agricultural products in Part I, Section II are impressive both in their total quantity and in the number of Members which have made them. However, the real innovations in the commitments attached to the Marrakesh Protocol are those on agricultural products and policies in Part I, Section I and Part IV.

Agriculture Agriculture has been one of the great problem areas of international trade. While most sectors of trade were increasingly liberalized over the years following the establishment of the GATT, trade in agricultural products remained beset by restrictions and distortions. The GATT rules, as well as accession conditions and waivers permitted GATT members to maintain greater protection against agricultural imports and to provide wider-ranging subsidies for agricultural exports than was allowed for industrial goods. Few market-opening commitments were made, so that the degree of binding achieved was far less than for industrial products and quantitative restrictions were widely applied. Disagreements over the precise implications of the rules affecting agricultural trade led to frequent disputes. Helped by the worldwide proliferation of market restrictions and subsidies, uncompetitive agricultural production flourished at the expense of efficient producers and surpluses grew. The Uruguay Round agreements on agriculture represent a major break with the past. They commit all WTO Members to long-term reform, with the aim of making agricultural trade more market-oriented.

This pledge of reform is embodied in the combined force of the Agreement on Agriculture and the individual commitments on agriculture included in national schedules attached to the Marrakesh Protocol. The main elements of the Agreement itself are its provisions on three areas of policy: market access, domestic support and export subsidies. These are reinforced by an undertaking to continue the reform process through further negotiations.

The Agreement on Agriculture's Preamble makes many of these points, and also sets out several guiding principles. Developed countries have agreed that their market access commitments will take fully into account the need to improve opportunities for agricultural products of particular interest to developing countries, including tropical products and crops grown in order to diversify away from illicit narcotic crops. Commitments under the reform program should be shared equitably among members, and should take into account non-trade concerns such as food security and the need to protect the environment, the integral principle of special and differential treatment for developing countries and the possible negative effects that the reform program might have on least-developed and net food-importing developing countries.

Agricultural market access The key elements of the market access commitments for agricultural products are the establishment of a tariff-only regime ('tariffication'), tariff reduction and the binding of all agricultural tariffs. The Agreement on Agriculture itself says little about any of these elements. The tariffication process was based on application of negotiating 'modalities' that are not included in the published Uruguay Round texts, and the tariff reductions are set out in the national schedules of commitments that are attached to the Marrakesh Protocol and governed by the Protocol itself.

The tariffication process has brought about a radical change in the structure of worldwide protective barriers against imports of agricultural products. It carried to a logical conclusion the GATT principle that protection should as far as possible be given only by import duties. All of the quantitative restrictions, variable levies, import bans or other non-tariff measures that have been widespread elements in agricultural protection at national frontiers have been replaced, for each product by an import duty set at a level calculated to be substantially the same in effect to the total protection (tariff and non-tariff barriers combined) previously given. This requirement applied even if the country maintaining a border measure had previously been specifically authorized to do so, for instance under the terms of its original accession to the GATT. The tariff resulting from this calculation could be expressed in percentage terms (*ad valorem*) or as a fixed sum per unit or amount (a *specific duty*).

Some of the non-tariff measures previously in force were very restrictive. The tariffication process inevitably resulted in very high tariff equivalents for these products. For this reason, the tariffication package also required Members to maintain current access opportunities at least equivalent to those 'existing'. In addition, if that current access were equivalent to less than five per cent of domestic consumption of the product concerned during the base period, they were required to open tariff quotas on an MFN basis, that is, available to all suppliers, at a low or minimal rate of duty, so as to offer 'minimum access opportunities'. Taken together, the current and minimum access commitments were to provide access opportunities equivalent, in the first year of the implementation period to three per cent of domestic consumption in the base period and these opportunities were to be increased to five per cent of that consumption by the year 2000, for developed countries, or 2004, for developing countries. The final element of the package was that countries which tariffied had the right to resort to a special agricultural safeguard mechanism provided they claimed this right in their schedules.

Under the *tariff reduction* provisions, all Members were required to reduce and bind all their customs duties on agricultural products, including the duties resulting from the tariffication process. Developed countries were required to reduce their duties by a simple average of 36 per cent, with a minimum reduction on individual products of 15 per cent, and to make these reductions in equal annual installments over six years from 1995. Developing countries were allowed to make reductions only two-thirds as great, that is, an average of 24 per cent and a minimum of ten per cent, and could apply the reductions over a ten-year period. Least-developed countries were not required to make reductions. The starting point (the base rate) for the reduction process depended on the circumstances of each case. If the product concerned had been subject only to tariffs before the Round began, the base rate would be either the rate bound in the GATT schedule of the Member concerned or, if no binding existed, the rate actually applied to imports in September 1986. Developing countries had the option, if a duty had not been bound as a result of past negotiations, to set new maximum tariffs ('ceiling bindings') on these products, generally fixing them immediately at a level which would not be further reduced. If imports of the product had been subject to non-tariff measures, a new base rate had first to be established. Again, as in the case of unbound items, developing countries could offer ceiling bindings instead, with the further obligation to remove the non-tariff measures.

Although the provisions just stated are of interest in explaining the commitments which Members made in their market access schedules for agricultural products, they no longer have force, except to the extent that they may also have been reproduced in the Agreement on Agriculture. The obligations that count, and that could give rise to dispute settlement procedures if individual WTO Members fail to live up to them, are the detailed commitments in each national schedule or in the market access provisions of the Agreement on Agriculture. A particularly important such provision is the agreement's Article 4.2, which makes the tariffication process irreversible by requiring that, with two exceptions, balance-of-payments restrictions and GATT Article XX restrictions, Members shall not maintain, or revert to, any of the types of non-tariff measures that were covered by the tariffication requirements.

The exceptions are the possibility of taking *special safeguard action*, and provisions, which allow 'special treatment' for certain products. These exceptions are stated in the Agreement on Agriculture, but are hedged with strict conditions.

The provisions on special safeguards apply only to products subject to tariffication. In other words, they cannot be invoked for products for which protection already took the form only of tariffs. They allow additional duties to be applied in case of a surge in imports or in case of shipments at prices below a certain reference level. The rules are complex. In brief, in the case of import surges, the trigger level that will permit safeguard action depends on the proportion of the domestic market already taken by imports: the higher the proportion, the less the surge required to trigger the safeguard action. Action based on prices may be triggered if the c.i.f. price of imports of a tariffied product falls below a reference price based on average import prices in the period 1986 to 1988.

Special treatment This takes two forms, of which one is open only to developing countries. These options could only be exercised in the course of drawing up schedules of commitments and therefore, now govern access opportunities solely for the few products and markets concerned. The first set of provisions, available to all countries, allowed 'special treatment' of any primary agricultural product and the processed products based on it, that met a series of stringent conditions. Imports of the product had to account for less than three per cent of domestic consumption; the product could not be one for which the Member concerned gave export subsidies; and domestic production of the primary product had to be under effective restriction. In these circumstances, the product could be listed in the national schedule as subject to 'special treatment reflecting factors of non-trade concerns, such as food security and environmental protection'. For a product covered by these provisions, non-tariff measures may be retained during the implementation period, subject to the offer of enlarged minimum opportunities of access to the domestic market. These opportunities, greater than those required under the general liberalization rules that have already been described, are to be an immediate four per cent of domestic consumption of the product concerned in the base period and eight per cent by the end of the implementation period. The second alternative was available only for 'a primary agricultural product, which is the predominant staple in the traditional diet of a developing country member'. In this case, retention of non-tariff restrictions is subject to similar conditions, but with minimum access set initially at only one per cent of domestic consumption, rising gradually to four per cent over ten years, and with the further condition that 'appropriate market access opportunities' shall have been provided for other agricultural products. In both cases, any continuation of the right to maintain non-tariff restrictions beyond the implementation period applicable would depend on the successful completion, by the end of that period, of negotiations in which 'additional and acceptable concessions' will be demanded. Four WTO Members used the special treatment option. Under both sets of rules, the main product for which special treatment has been obtained is rice.

Domestic agricultural support The thrust of the domestic support provisions is to encourage a further shift, over time, towards measures and policies that distort production and trade as little as possible. The basic consideration underlying this concept is that there are two types of domestic support, one preferable to the other.

The first type, provided through what are sometimes called 'Green Box' measures, has little or no distorting effect on trade. To be regarded as Green Box, support measures must meet strict criteria. A broad requirement is that any exempt measure shall be part of a publicly funded government program, not involving transfers from consumers, and shall not provide price support to producers. In summary, measures qualifying as 'Green Box' include: general services, not involving direct payments to producers or processors, such as research, pest and disease control, extension and marketing services and infrastructure; stockholding for food security; domestic food aid for the needy; direct payments to producers that are decoupled from production; income insurance and safety-net programs; disaster relief; structural adjustment programs; and environmental and regional assistance programs. Such measures remain exempt from reduction commitments during the implementation period only if they continue to conform to the criteria. Within the limits set by these criteria, however, a WTO Member may modify existing Green Box measures, including giving increased support through them, or may at any time introduce new Green Box measures. Governments thus retain a high degree of flexibility for achieving the aims of their agricultural policies.

The other type, Amber Box measures, does distort trade. All domestic support measures in favor of agricultural producers that cannot be shown to meet the Green Box criteria are considered to be trade-distorting measures. The Agreement commits each WTO Member that provides support to agriculture through Amber Box measures to make reductions in the aggregate monetary value of such measures. Those reduction commitments are stated in Part IV, Section I of the each Member's schedule, attached to the Marrakesh Protocol.

As far as those measures subject to reduction commitments are concerned, their combined annual value is calculated as the Total Aggregate Measure of Support (AMS). The Total AMS figure is arrived at by adding support for individual products to support, which is not product-specific. 'Support' includes both budgetary outlays and revenue foregone, and even the effects of price support measures where no budgetary outlays are involved. Where calculation of the AMS is not practicable, provision is made for an alternative Equivalent Measure of Support (EMS). The initial AMS or EMS calculations for each Member formed the starting point for their reduction commitments included in schedules attached to the Marrakesh Protocol. The commitments themselves were expressed in terms of annual and final bound commitment levels, setting out the maximum AMS that could be provided during the implementation period and thereafter. The initial AMS or EMS calculations were based on the support given in the years 1986 to 1988. Developed countries were required to reduce their AMS by 20 per cent over the six years from 1995. For developing countries, the reduction was 13.3 per cent, over ten years. Least-developed countries were not required to make any reduction.

The three types of Amber Box measures exempted from reduction are so-called *de minimis* support; certain measures to encourage agricultural and rural development in developing countries, including generally available investment subsidies, subsidies to low-income producers, support to diversification away from growing illegal narcotic crops and certain direct payments under production-limiting programs (sometimes dubbed 'Blue Box'). The *de minimis* levels at which support is regarded as having minimal effect are defined, for developed countries, as support not exceeding five per cent of the value of production of individual products or in the case of non-product-specific support, of the value of total agricultural production. For developing countries, the *de minimis* maximum is ten per cent.

Agricultural export subsidies The Agreement on Agriculture establishes new basic rules to govern export subsidies for agricultural products. The original GATT rules explicitly permitted such subsidies, although an effort was made to limit the trade distortion they could cause. The Agreement bans their use unless they qualify under one of four exceptions. The exceptions are export subsidies subject to reduction commitments as specified in Part IV, Section II of a Member's schedule of commitments attached to the Marrakesh Protocol; export subsidies by developing countries consistent with the agreement's provision for special and differential treatment in their favor; spending on export subsidies, or quantities of subsidized exports, that exceed those limits specified in a member's schedule, provided the excess is covered by the agreement's 'downstream flexibility' provisions; and export subsidies not covered by reduction commitments, provided they conform to the agreement's anti-circumvention disciplines.

In outline, the export subsidies subject to reduction commitments are direct subsidies contingent on export performance; government export sales or stock disposals at prices below domestic market prices; other payments on the export of an agricultural product that are financed by virtue of government action, including levies; subsidies on agricultural products contingent on their incorporation in exported products; and subsidies affecting marketing and transport costs of exports. Subject to some conditions, developing countries were not required to make reduction commitments during the agreement's implementation period on this group of subsidies.

For developed countries, the reduction commitments are based on requirements that, for each product group, for example, coarse grains or cheese, the subsidies concerned be reduced by 36 per cent in value, normally by comparison with outlays in 1986 to 1990, over a six-year implementation period. Over the same period, the quantity of products benefiting from such subsidies (except for subsidies for products incorporated into exported products) had to be reduced by 21 per cent. Developing countries are subject to lower reduction requirements (cuts of 24 per cent in value and 14 per cent in quantity) and have the benefit of a ten-year implementation period. Least-developed countries are not required to make reduction commitments. Developing countries are not, in general, required to reduce subsidies affecting the marketing and transport costs of exports.

The 'downstream flexibility' provision allows some fluctuation between years in fulfilling reduction commitments. A Member's budgetary outlays and quantities of subsidized exports in a particular year may exceed the annual limits shown in its schedule by small margins, provided it meets its commitments over the implementation period as a whole.

The Agreement on Agriculture includes a prohibition on the use of any of the listed export subsidies on any agricultural product that is not subject to specific reduction commitments, or subject to the special and differential treatment available to developing countries. The effect is that WTO Members are not allowed to introduce new export subsidies in the future.

As far as other export subsidies are concerned, the agreement contains anti-circumvention provisions intended to prevent them from taking the place of those subsidies brought under restraint by the main reduction commitments. These provisions include criteria to ensure that food aid genuinely deserves to be classified as such and a pledge by WTO members to work towards inter-national agreement on rules for export credits and export credit guarantee and insurance programs. If subsidies are paid on processed agricultural products, they must not be more than proportionate to the subsidy that would be paid for the primary products that have been included in the final processed product.

Export restrictions are also covered by the Agreement on Agriculture. Developed countries introducing an export prohibition or restriction on foodstuffs in accordance with GATT Article XI:2(a), which deals with critical shortages, shall give due regard to the food security of importing Members, shall provide advance notice and shall be ready to consult about it. Developing countries are not covered by the rule, unless they are net exporters of the foodstuff concerned.

Peace clause For three years beyond the developed-country implementation period, that is, for nine years from 1995, a 'peace clause' will be in effect which restricts the right to take action that might otherwise be possible against domestic support measures and export subsidies, which conform to the requirements of the agreement. Among its points are provisions that no countervailing action may be taken against Green Box measures, and that countervailing action against domestic subsidies, subject to reduction commitments, or against export subsidies which conform with the agreement's provisions, may be taken only if they are determined to be causing or threatening injury. Moreover, 'due restraint' shall be shown in initiating countervailing duty investigations. The 'peace clause' is in effect a time-limited exception to some of the rules of the Agreement on Subsidies and Countervailing Measures.

Further negotiations An important element of the Agreement on Agriculture is the 'Continuation of the Reform Process'. This provided that WTO Members shall initiate further negotiations towards the long-term objective of substantial progressive reductions in agricultural support and protection. Those negotiations began formally on 1 January 2000. The negotiations are to be based on the experience gained by then from implementing the reduction commitments and on the effects these reductions have had on trade. They are to take into account non-trade concerns, special and differential treatment for developing countries, the objective of establishing a fair and market-oriented agricultural trading system, the other concerns and objectives included in the agreement's preamble and what further commitments are necessary to achieve the long-term objective.

Agreement on the Application of Sanitary and Phytosanitary Measures The Agreement on the Application of Sanitary and Phytosanitary Measures (SPS) is closely linked with the Agreement on Agriculture. The right of governments to restrict trade when necessary to protect human, animal or plant life or health has always been recognized under the GATT (in Article XX (b)), provided that the measures are not applied in a manner which unjustifiably discriminates between countries with the same conditions or are not applied as a disguised restriction on trade. Many countries feared, however, that with non-tariff barriers to agricultural imports banned as a result of tariffication, greater and unjustified use might be made of sanitary and phytosanitary restrictions on trade. The new SPS Agreement, designed to head off this threat, was largely modeled on the Agreement on Technical Barriers to Trade.

The aim of the SPS Agreement is to ensure that the effects on trade of government actions to ensure the safety of food and the protection of animal and plant health are kept to a minimum. The agreement covers all measures which are taken to protect animal and plant health from pests and diseases, and to protect human and animal health from risks in food or feedstuffs (such as toxins or pesticide residues) as well as to protect humans from animal-carried diseases (such as rabies). The agreement recognizes the right of governments to take measures necessary to these purposes. Such measures should however be applied only to the extent necessary to protect life or health, they must be based on scientific principles, and should not be maintained if scientific evidence is lacking. This means that SPS measures can be put in place only on the basis of careful laboratory testing and analysis, and if genuine concerns about food safety or serious threats to animal or plant health have been identified. However, governments may impose provisional precautionary restrictions when sufficient scientific information is not yet available. The measures should not arbitrarily or unjustifiably discriminate between members where identical or similar conditions prevail, or constitute a disguised restriction on trade.

The SPS Agreement gives governments two alternatives in meeting these obligations. The first is that they base their measures on standards, guidelines and recommendations developed by the relevant international technical bodies, where these exist (for example, Codex Alimentarius). These measures are presumed to be consistent with the SPS Agreement. Alternatively, the measures can be set at a higher level of protection if there is a scientific justification for this, or a risk, assessed in the light of criteria set out in the Agreement, that is considered to make such protection appropriate. This 'appropriate level of sanitary or phytosanitary protection' is often referred to as the 'acceptable risk level', and the consequence is that where no relevant international standard exists, the measure must be based on a risk assessment.

Textiles and clothing The Agreement on Textiles and Clothing will lead to the elimination of quantitative restrictions which have affected a large proportion of international trade in this important sector for more than 30 years. The Agreement provides explicitly for its own termination. The Agreement and all restrictions covered by it 'shall stand terminated' on 1 January 2005, 'on which date the textiles and clothing sector shall be fully integrated into GATT 1994'. It concludes, 'There shall be no extension of this agreement'.

Since 1974 in particular, an extensive and complex network of bilateral agreements has been developed that permits quantitative limits to be placed on exports of specific textile and clothing products from particular countries. This was done mainly under the provisions of the Arrangement Regarding International Trade in Textiles (known as the Multifibre Arrangement or MFA), although other forms of restriction, not always consistent with GATT rules, were also applied. The restrictions have been applied mainly against developing countries, by developed countries. Because the textiles sector is one in which many developing countries have comparative advantage in a number of areas, this Agreement is one of the most important for them in the whole WTO.

The Agreement on Textiles and Clothing (ATC) is intended to permit a smooth and progressive transition from an initial situation of extensive trade restrictions to one in which the normal GATT rules will apply. The main elements in the agreement are the list of products to which it applies, together with a program for the integration of all these textiles and clothing products into the GATT over a ten-year period; a process for the gradual enlargement of all quantitative restrictions; special safeguard arrangements to operate during the transitional period; and arrangements for continuous supervision of the whole process by a body with conciliation and quasi-judicial functions.

Product coverage The product coverage of the ATC is given in its annex, which lists each product at the six-digit level of the Harmonized System. This includes all textile and clothing products that were subject to MFA or MFA-type restraints in at least one importing country when the agreement was negotiated.

The transition process is to proceed simultaneously on two tracks: the removal of products from the Agreement, so that they are covered by ('integrated into') the normal GATT rules and the enlargement of quotas for products still restricted. Both processes are to take place in three successive stages lasting three, four and three years. Separate provisions cover each phase. Since 31 December 1994, no new restrictions can be introduced, except as provided for under the Agreement or under GATT provisions such as the balance-of-payments rules.

Integration into GATT rules All WTO Members must apply the integration program, even if they did not apply restrictions under the MFA, unless they specifically renounce the right to use the agreement's special safeguard mechanism. On 1 January 1995, importing WTO Members were required to integrate not less than 16 per cent of the products covered by the Agreement, as measured by their 1990 volume of imports. Their trade in these products would thereafter be covered by the general rules of GATT. For Canada, the European Community, Norway and the United States, which carried over restrictions imposed under the earlier MFA, integration means that any restrictions on these integrated products had to be removed. No new restrictions could be imposed except as permitted by the GATT rules. Safeguard action against these integrated products would be possible only under Article XIX of the GATT. An additional 17 per cent of the covered products was integrated on 1 January 1998. A further minimum of 18 per cent is due on 1 January 2002. The final 49 per cent will come under the GATT rules on 1 January 2005. The choice of products to be integrated at each phase is left to the Member concerned. The only conditions are that products must be included from each of the four main product areas, that is, tops and yarns, fabrics, made-up textile products and clothing, and that at least 12 months notice be given of the products to be integrated. Faster integration is possible, provided only that it takes effect for the products concerned at the beginning of the year and prior notice is given.

Liberalization While the integration process goes forward, opportunities for exporters to sell products still under restriction will also be progressively enlarged through increases in quota growth rates under the provisions for liberalization. Each remaining restriction carried over from the MFA is to be eased progressively. The required quota increase is related to the growth rate that was originally notified. During the first stage of the transition period (from 1995 to 1997), the notified growth rate was increased by a factor of at least 16 per cent. In the second stage (from 1998 to 2001) and the third stage (from 2002 to 2004) the rates of growth are to be raised by at least a further 25 per cent and 27 per cent, respectively. These rates imply, for a product originally allowed a six per cent growth rate under the MFA, that permitted annual growth in the three stages of the transition period would have to be about seven per cent, nine per cent and 11 per cent respectively. Faster growth rates for the first and second stages apply for certain small suppliers. The growth is automatic unless the WTO's Council for Trade in Goods or Dispute Settlement Body suspends growth factors for the second or third stages for imports from Members found not to be complying with their obligations under the agreement. The liberalization rules for any non-MFA restrictions, which are not justified under the GATT, are somewhat more flexible, but all such restrictions must also be eliminated by the end of the transition period.

As was the case under the MFA, the administration of restrictions, which in practice mainly means the allocation and distribution of licenses among suppliers, is in the hands of the exporting members. Changes relating to the administration of restrictions, for instance, changes in origin rules are subject to consultation requirements.

WTO Members undertake to have laws or administrative procedures to counter efforts to circumvent it by actions such as transshipment, re-routing and false declaration of documents. They agree to cooperate and consult against such acts and to take appropriate measures to prevent them. The measures taken may include denial of entry to the goods concerned, adjustment of charges to restraint levels to reflect the true country or place of origin, introduction of restraints on imports from Members through whose territories goods have been transshipped and measures against exporters or importers who have made false declarations about the merchandise itself.

Transitional safeguards During the transitional period, a specific safeguard mechanism is available if surges in imports of a product (a) not currently under restraint and (b) not yet integrated into GATT 1994, cause or actually threaten serious damage to domestic producers. This transitional safeguard, which the agreement states 'should be applied as sparingly as possible', permits measures to be taken against injurious imports of particular products from particular sources. The right to use transitional safeguards is tied to the obligation to apply integration programs.

The rules governing transitional safeguard measures are more stringent than those, which governed restrictions under the MFA. In outline they call first, for the importing member to determine formally that the domestic industry is seriously damaged or threatened by serious damage; that total imports of the product concerned are increasing and that the damage is in fact caused by the increased imports and not by other factors such as changes in technology or consumer tastes. Transitional safeguard measures are to be applied 'on a Member-to-Member basis', that is, against a particular supplying Member. Imports of the product from that

Member must have increased, or be about to increase, sharply and substantially, both in absolute terms and relative to other imports. Except in 'highly unusual and critical circumstances, where delay would cause damage which would be difficult to repair', consultations must then normally follow before action is taken. Whether a restraint is agreed bilaterally or is imposed unilaterally, no restriction applied may be lower than the actual level of imports from that source during a recent 12–month period and the action taken may not remain in place for more than three years. If the measure is in place for more than one year, permitted growth shall normally be no less than six per cent. When the transitional safeguard clause is used, more favorable treatment shall be given to least-developed countries, small suppliers, new entrants and re-imports from 'outward processing'.

Technical barriers to trade The TBT Agreement is a response to two broad policy considerations. First, technical regulations and standards, including packaging, marketing and labeling requirements, as well as procedures for testing and certifying compliance with these regulations and standards, should not create unnecessary barriers to international trade. Secondly, WTO Members must nevertheless be able to protect national security, prevent deceptive practices and protect human health or safety, animal or plant life or health and the environment. To these ends, the Agreement requires that standards and regulations are not drawn up with the aim of restricting trade and that, in their application to imports, the basic GATT principles of most-favored-nation and national treatment are applied. It encourages members to use international standards, where these exist, in drawing up their own regulations and standards and requires them to keep one another informed about their standards-related activities. It calls for national testing and certifying bodies to avoid discrimination against imports and, as far as possible, to recognize the equivalence of each other's tests and certificates. To make sure that these rules work in practice, it provides elaborate procedures for notification and consultation. The reach of the Agreement extends to the activities of local and non-governmental bodies, and to the formulation and application of voluntary standards. The disciplines of the TBT agreement apply to both industrial and agricultural products, but because of the existence of the SPS Agreement they do not cover sanitary and phytosanitary measures.

Trade-related investment measures The TRIMs Agreement reasserts that no Member shall apply any TRIM that is inconsistent with Article III or Article XI of the GATT. An 'illustrative list' of TRIMS that are inconsistent with Article III:4 or Article XI:1 of GATT 1994 is given in an annex to the Agreement. They all belong essentially to two broad categories. They either demand that there be certain local content in the products of the enterprise concerned or require some degree of balancing of trade between exports and imports.

The Agreement requires that all TRIMS that are inconsistent with its provisions be eliminated over a set period. Developed countries had the benefit of a two-year transition period, up to 1 January 1997, developing countries had three years longer, until 1 January 2000, to eliminate notified TRIMS. Least-developed countries have until 1 January 2002. Provisions exist for these transition periods to be extended on a case-by-case basis by the Council for Trade in Goods.

Anti-dumping The WTO Agreement represents an effort to balance potentially conflicting interests: the interest of importing countries in imposing anti-dumping measures to prevent injury to domestic industries and the interest of exporters that anti-dumping measures and procedures should not themselves become obstacles to fair trade. Its key provisions deal with how to establish whether imported goods are being dumped; how to establish whether the dumped imports are causing or threatening to cause injury to the domestic industry; and procedures to be followed in initiating and conducting investigations, collecting information and making determinations, imposing anti-dumping duties, reviewing determinations and terminating anti-dumping duties.

(a) Are goods being dumped? The Agreement states that a product is to be considered dumped, that is, 'introduced into the commerce of another country at less than its normal value', 'if the export price of the product exported from one country to another is less than the comparable price, in the ordinary course of trade, for the like product when destined for consumption in the exporting country'.

The process of price-to-price comparison is seldom straightforward, and may well be impossible or inappropriate. The 'like product' may not be sold on the home market of the exporting country at all. Or it may be sold on terms that do not reflect its costs or in such small quantities that fair comparison is impossible. If so, two alternative approaches are possible. One compares the export price of the goods allegedly being dumped with the price at which the product is sold when exported to another Member's market. The other uses for comparison a constructed normal value, calculated by adding together the exporter's production cost for the product and a reasonable figure for administrative, sales and other costs and for profit. The Agreement sets out detailed rules for when actual home market prices can be disregarded and governing the calculation of constructed normal values. For example, a judgement on whether sales of the product in the exporter's own market were or were not 'in the ordinary course of trade' could be crucial in deciding whether such sales may be disregarded in establishing the normal value. The Agreement says that below-cost sales, in order to be treated as not being 'in the ordinary course of trade', and therefore disregarded in establishing the home market selling price, must be below per-unit fixed and variable costs, plus administrative, selling and general costs. They must also be carried on over an 'extended period of time', normally one year, and in substantial quantities and must not allow recovery of costs within a reasonable period of time. Moreover, the Agreement sets strict requirements on the sources of information to be used. Costs, for instance, must normally be calculated on the basis of the records of the exporter or producer under investigation and must take into account all available evidence on how fixed costs, such as depreciation charges and development costs, should be spread over production. Figures for administrative and selling costs and profits should be reasonable and based on actual data for the home market for the like product, or failing that, for similar products or for sales by other producers in that market.

A similar level of detail applies in the other rules designed to ensure that governments in importing countries can arrive at a fair basis for price comparison, while not leaving out evidence that would tend to disprove charges of dumping. For example, there may be doubts over the genuineness of a selling price that has been set between an exporter and an importer that are both part of the same firm. In this case the export price used for comparison may be 'constructed' either on the basis of the price at which the goods are first sold to an independent buyer, or on some other reasonable basis. Price comparisons have to make allowances for differences in conditions of sale, taxation, levels of trade and other factors affecting price comparability. When comparisons require currency conversions, fluctuations in exchange rates are to be ignored and exporters are allowed at least 60 days to adjust their export prices to sustained changes in rates.

A special problem with determining the home market price may arise if the exporter is a non-market economy. A provision in the Agreement states that 'in the case of imports from a country which has a complete or substantially complete monopoly of its trade and where all domestic prices are fixed by the State – a strict comparison with domestic prices – may not always be appropriate'. Countries applying anti-dumping measures have invoked this provision as a basis for using special methodologies to determine the normal value of imports from non-market economies.

(b) Is the domestic industry being injured? Article VI of the GATT establishes that even if imports are being dumped, an anti-dumping duty may not be imposed against them unless their effect is to cause or threaten material injury to an established domestic industry or to 'retard materially' the establishment of a domestic industry. The WTO Anti-Dumping Agreement goes into considerable detail about how the government of the importing country is to decide whether injury has occurred or is threatened. Among the main points covered are the definition of 'domestic industry', whether the industry is being injured or threatened by injury and whether the dumped imports are responsible for this injury.

The definition of 'domestic industry' is important, not least because dumping investigations may not normally be launched except in response to an application by or on behalf of the industry. The agreement's basic definition is 'the domestic producers as a whole of the like products or those of them whose collective output of the products constitutes a major proportion of the total domestic production of those products'. However, domestic producers related to exporters or importers of the dumped products can be left out of the assessment. In exceptional circumstances, if producers in a single regional market in the importing country are in effect largely isolated from the rest of the domestic producers, they may be dealt with separately, but any anti-dumping action taken should also be confined as far as possible to that region. Applying the same logic in the opposite direction, the agreement requires that when two or more Members in a regional trading arrangement covered by GATT Article XXIV have reached the stage of being a single unified market, the industry of the entire area of integration shall be the 'domestic industry' for the purpose of any anti-dumping investigation.

The agreement prescribes that a determination of injury must be based on 'positive evidence', and involve an examination of both (a) the volume of the dumped imports and their effect on prices in the domestic market and (b) the impact of these imports on domestic producers of the like product. Once again, detailed guidance is provided on these points.

As far as the volume of dumped imports is concerned, government investigators are to look at whether there has been a significant increase either in absolute terms or relative to production or consumption in the importing country. Price effects may have to be studied from several angles, looking at whether the dumped imports are undercutting local prices, or are depressing price levels significantly, or are preventing increases that would otherwise have occurred. A new feature of the WTO agreement is that consideration of the combined impact of dumped imports coming from several supplying countries is explicitly authorized. This 'cumulation' is only allowed if the margin of dumping on imports from each country included has been shown to be more than *de minimis*, and the volume of imports from each country is not negligible. Dumping is *de minimis* if it amounts to less than two per cent of the export price. Imports are normally considered negligible if the supplying country accounts for less than three per cent of total imports of the product. But if several countries with less than three per cent apiece together account for more than seven per cent of total imports their shares need not be regarded as negligible.

The question of the impact of the dumped imports on the domestic industry demands a careful look at the state of the domestic industry. The Agreement provides a long, but non-exhaustive, list of factors to be considered. They include actual and potential decline in sales, profits, output, market share, return on investment, capacity utilization, cash flow, inventories, employment, wages, growth and ability to raise capital or investments, as well as how large the margin of dumping is. Even if the investigation shows the industry to be in difficulty, the authorities must look too at other factors that may be causing injury, including non-dumped imports, falling demand, changing patterns of consumption, and technological developments and must not attribute to imports the injury caused by such other factors.

In the case of allegations of *threat* of material injury, the agreement warns that a determination by the government must 'be based on facts and not merely on allegation, conjecture or remote possibility'. 'The change in circumstances which would create a situation in which the dumping would cause injury must be clearly foreseen and imminent'. Among the factors that an investigating authority should consider in examining threat is whether there has been a significant rate of increase of dumped imports, the capacity of the exporter to increase supplies and the price of the imports. 'Special care' is required in considering and deciding on the use of anti-dumping measures when injury is only threatened.

Procedures Detailed procedural requirements are laid down with the aim of ensuring that the principles just described are applied in practice. They divide the handling of anti-dumping cases into successive stages, namely, the initiation of a case; the investigative process, which may include provisional measures or may be brought to a halt if price undertakings are given; imposition of an anti-dumping duty; possible judicial review and the final termination of the duty.

Subsidies and countervailing duties The thinking behind the rules on subsidies and countervailing measures in the WTO is similar to that on anti-dumping duties. The aim is again to balance potentially conflicting concerns: that domestic industries should not be put at an unfair disadvantage by competition from goods that benefit from government subsidies and that countervailing measures to offset those subsidies should not themselves be obstacles to fair trade. Because subsidies result from the decisions of governments, as opposed to the pricing decisions of individual exporters, the rules not only regulate the unilateral action, countervailing duties, that may be taken against subsidized imports, but also establish multilateral disciplines to control the use of subsidies themselves. The WTO Agreement on Subsidies and Countervailing Measures (SCM) represents a radical change of approach from that of GATT Article XVI, which imposed effective disciplines only with respect to export subsidies. Under the SCM Agreement, binding disciplines are imposed for the first time on the provision of subsidies related to production and other non-trade factors. Moreover, these subsidies can, in certain circumstances, be challenged without a requirement that they be proved to have adverse effects on trade.

The new agreement adopts a '*traffic light*' approach. It defines certain kinds of subsidy as unlikely to cause harm to trade ('green'), and some as clearly harmful and therefore not to be used ('red'). The effect is to leave a residual ('amber') range of subsidies, which are open to challenge only if they are believed to cause adverse effects such as 'serious prejudice', 'injury' or 'nullification and impairment' of benefits. Within this amber category, certain types of subsidies give rise to a *presumption* of serious prejudice. On countervailing duties, the rules laid down in the Agreement are close to those, which now govern application of anti-dumping duties.

Coverage and definitions The SCM Agreement defines 'subsidy' and makes its operative provisions applicable only to those subsidies that are 'specific'.

A subsidy exists only if (a) a financial contribution is provided *and* (b) the contribution is made by a government or a public body within the territory of a WTO member *and* (c) that contribution confers a benefit. 'Financial contribution' is defined by an exhaustive list of measures, including direct transfers of funds, for example, grants, loans or equity infusions, potential direct transfers, such as loan guarantees, revenue foregone or not collected, for instance, through tax credits, the provision of goods and services other than general infrastructure and the purchase of goods.

Only subsidies that are 'specific', ie. given to particular enterprises or industries, are subject to disciplines. The argument for this distinction is that rules are needed only to regulate subsidies that distort the allocation of resources within an economy. Non-specific subsidies, widely available, are presumed not to create such distortions. The agreement recognizes four types of specificity: enterprise-specificity, in which a government picks out a particular company or companies to be subsidized; industry-specificity, in which a government targets a particular sector or sectors for subsidization; regional specificity, in which a government subsidizes producers in specified parts of its territory and prohibited subsidies, in which a subsidy is linked to export performance or the use of domestic inputs.

Prohibited subsidies Prohibited subsidies are most clearly designed to affect trade and are thus most likely to have adverse effects on the interests of other WTO Members. They fall into two categories. The first consists of 'export subsidies', those that are contingent, in law or in fact, and whether wholly or as one condition among several, on export performance. The second are 'import substitution subsidies', subsidies contingent wholly, or as one condition among several, on the use of domestic over imported goods. An annex to the Agreement sets out an illustrative list of export subsidies, including not only direct subsidies contingent on exports, but a variety of practices that have a similar effect, such as export-linked exemptions from taxes and social welfare charges and export credit guarantees provided at premium rates insufficient to cover long-term costs. Important, but largely time-limited, exceptions to the rules on prohibited subsidies apply to developing countries and countries in transition to a market economy.

Actionable subsidies Actionable subsidies are neither prohibited nor exempt from challenge and are therefore potentially open to complaint, or to countervailing action, provided the necessary conditions are met. The general principle is that no Member should cause, through the use of a specific subsidy, adverse effects to the interests of other Members. Three types of adverse effects are identified. These are injury to the domestic industry of another member; nullification or impairment of benefits accruing under GATT 1994 and 'serious prejudice' to the interests of another Member.

Injury which one government's subsidies cause to the domestic industry of another WTO member, is closely parallel to injury to the domestic industry caused by dumping. As in the case of dumping, a Member may impose a countervailing duty if it determines that subsidized imports are causing injury to a domestic industry or challenge an injurious subsidy through dispute settlement.

Nullification or impairment of benefits is most typically likely to arise when a Member finds that the improved market access, it might have expected to gain as the result of another Member's tariff binding, has been undercut by the effects of a subsidy given by that member.

Serious prejudice is a wider concept, which focuses on situations where a Member's export interests are affected by another Member's subsidization. Serious prejudice may arise where the subsidy has one of several effects such as where exports from another Member into the market of the subsidizing Member, or into the market of a third country, are displaced or impeded or significant price undercutting, price suppression or price depression are caused, as compared with sales of a like product of another Member in the same market or the subsidized product causes significant loss of sales in the same market or the subsidy leads to an increase in the subsidizing country's share in the world market for a primary product.

Non-actionable subsidies There are three categories of non-actionable subsidies, in addition to the general exclusion of non-specific subsidies. In outline, these 'green' subsidies are assistance for basic research, up to a maximum of 75 per cent of the cost, or for 'pre-competitive development', up to a maximum of 50 per cent; assistance to disadvantaged regions, provided that the aid is not limited to specific enterprises or industries within a region, is given as part of a general scheme of regional development and the region can be shown to be disadvantaged, in terms of such measures as GNP and unemployment rates, by comparison with the member country as a whole; or assistance to adapt existing facilities to new environmental requirements, provided the help is given on a one-time basis, is limited to 20 per cent of total costs and is generally available.

The Agreement provides for the possibility that even a subsidy program that qualifies as non-actionable may have serious adverse effects on the domestic industry of another Member. If the committee which oversees the agreement so finds and the subsidizing member does not modify the subsidy program concerned so as to remove these effects, the committee must authorize 'appropriate countermeasures'.

This 'green' or protected category of subsidies, like the rules, which assume serious prejudice for some forms of actionable subsidies, was recognized only on a provisional basis, for five years.

Countervailing duty and investigation The rules on the use of countervailing duties are very similar to those in the Anti-Dumping Agreement. A countervailing duty is 'a special duty levied for the purpose of offsetting any subsidy bestowed directly or indirectly upon the manufacture, production or export of any merchandise'. Obviously, the questions to be asked in establishing the existence of an actionable subsidy differ from those aimed at establishing dumping. The issues which arise in the investigation of injury, or the threat of injury, to the domestic industry are on the other hand virtually the same, and the rules that govern this side of anti-dumping and countervailing action, as well as how and how long measures may be applied differ little. Similarly, a Member's failure to respect the substantive or procedural requirements in taking countervailing action can be challenged through WTO dispute settlement and may lead to invalidation of its action. In outline, the rules require that there be both subsidized imports and injury or threatened injury and a causal link between the two.

Transition period and developing countries Developed countries were allowed three years, that is, to the end of 1997, to phase out prohibited subsidy programs already established before the Member concerned signed the WTO Agreement. Developing countries benefit not only from longer time frames to adapt to the agreement's rules but also from some more lasting special treatment, reflecting the agreement's recognition that 'subsidies may play an important role in [their] economic development programs'. Of the three categories of developing countries recognized in the agreement, the least-developed countries receive the widest concessions. A further group of 20 Members, listed in an annex to the agreement, share the right to use export subsidies until their GNP per capita reaches $1,000 a year. The third group consists of all other developing countries.

Special treatment for developing countries is most far-reaching as regards the use of prohibited subsidies. Least-developed countries, and the 20 countries with per capita incomes below $1,000 per annum, may maintain export subsidies indefinitely. The sole exception to this right arises if a country reaches 'export competitiveness' in a particular product, defined as a situation in which its exports of the product reach a share of at least 3.25 per cent of world trade in that product for two consecutive years. In this case, it will be required to phase out any export subsidy to the product over eight years. All other developing countries may maintain export subsidies for a period of eight years, that is, until the end of the year 2002. There is provision for the Subsidies Committee to extend this period in particular cases. However, this general right to go on using export subsidies for eight years is subject to some conditions. A developing country Member must not increase the level of its export subsidies, and must remove them in less than eight years if they are 'inconsistent with its development needs'. For these wealthier developing countries, the same rule on export competitiveness applies to subsidies to products which gain more than 3.25 per cent of world trade in the product but in this case, the subsidy must be removed within two years.

The least-developed countries may go on using import-substituting subsidies for eight years, but other developing countries were required to remove these subsidies within five years, that is, by the end of 1999.

For as long as a developing country has the right to use an export subsidy, it will be treated, for the purpose of any multilateral action taken against it, under the agreement's rules for actionable, rather than prohibited, subsidies.

Developing countries also benefit from some special and differential treatment regarding countervailing measures taken under Part V of the agreement. Countervailing action against a developing-country product must be halted if the subsidy is found to represent two per cent or less of the product's value. For least-developed countries, the under-$1,000 group and, up to 2003, those developing countries which have removed their export subsidies in less than the eight years allowed to them, the *de minimis* figure is three per cent, rather than two per cent. Countervailing action must also be halted if the subsidized product accounts for less than four per cent of the importing Member's market, except that it may continue if developing countries who have below four per cent shares together account for more than nine per cent of the market.

Transition economy Members are allowed to apply programs and measures necessary to the transformation. They may maintain prohibited export and import-substituting subsidies until the end of 2001 and are immune from dispute settlement action against these subsidies. During this period, to help privatization and restructuring, they may forgive government-held debt and make grants to cover debt repayment without being subject to action under the 'serious prejudice' rules. The *presumption* of serious prejudice does not apply to subsidies provided by these Members that would otherwise be deemed to cause serious prejudice. Serious prejudice must be *demonstrated* in such cases. No action may be taken against their other actionable subsidies unless these cause nullification and impairment of benefits that displaces or blocks imports into their own markets, or cause injury to a domestic industry in an importing member's market. 'In exceptional circumstances' departures from this time frame may be authorized.

Safeguards There are five main elements in the Agreement on Safeguards. The first three, which parallel the provisions of GATT Article XIX, set out the requirements that must be fulfilled before a safeguard measure may be applied, the rules that govern application of safeguard measures and the compensation or offsetting action to which such measures may give rise. Balancing these elements, which are together intended to establish a workable and usable safeguards mechanism, is the fourth, that is the rules which will remove pre-existing gray area measures and ban their use in future. The fifth element provides the machinery to ensure that the agreement functions effectively.

(a) When a safeguard measure can be applied The essential requirements for application of a safeguard measure are a determination by the Member that increased quantities of imports are causing or threatening to cause serious injury to the domestic industry producing like or directly competitive products. All these elements are similar to the requirements for anti-dumping or countervailing measure, except, of course, that there is no need to show that the imports are either dumped or subsidized.

(b) How a safeguard measure may be applied Application of safeguard measures is governed by the general requirement that they may be used only to the extent needed to prevent or remedy serious injury and to help adjustment. If quotas are used, they must not reduce imports of the product being restricted below the average level of the last three years, unless clear justification is given that a lower level is needed to prevent or remedy the injury. The general principle is that quotas are to be applied regardless of the source of supply and that if they are allocated among supplying members, the allocation should reflect the past market share of each supplier. However, a different approach ('quota modulation') may be used, if certain strict conditions are met, to target certain suppliers harder than others. Quota modulation is possible only in cases of actual injury, *not* threat of injury.

The Agreement provides incentives to keep measures short-lived and discourages their renewal. A safeguard measure should be applied only for as long as necessary to prevent or remedy serious injury and to help adjustment. The standard limit on duration is four years, which may be extended, in no more restrictive form than at the end of the initial period, to a maximum of eight years, if it has been determined under the Agreement's procedures that continuation is necessary *and* that the industry is adjusting. If the measure is applied for more than one year, it must be progressively liberalized throughout the period of application. If its duration is more than three years, there must be a mid-term review, which shall, if appropriate, lead to its withdrawal or more rapid liberalization. Once a measure terminates or is removed, no new safeguard measure can be applied to the same product until after an interval at least as long as the duration of the original measure.

Compensation The rules on compensation or offsetting action call for the Member imposing the measure to consult with those Members who have a principal supplying interest in the product and to try to maintain 'a substantially equivalent level of concessions'. Members may agree on any adequate means of trade compensation. Failing agreement, the affected exporting member can suspend equivalent concessions or other obligations on 30 days' notice; that is, it can retaliate, provided the Council for Trade in Goods does not disapprove. However, this right to retaliate is not unlimited. In particular, it may not be exercised during the first three years that a safeguard is in effect, provided the action has been taken because of an absolute, rather than relative, increase in imports and provided that the rules of the Agreement on Safeguards have been followed.

Grey-area Measures There is an absolute ban on any voluntary export restraints, orderly marketing arrangements or any other similar measures, unilateral, bilateral or plurilateral, on the export or the import side.

(a) Customs and trade administration The remaining four Uruguay Round agreements on trade in goods share the characteristic of being concerned with the 'machinery' of foreign trade, that is, the means by which customs and other trade administration officials check imports and decide what trade regulations apply to them. These are customs valuation, pre-shipment inspection, rules of origin, and import licensing.

(b) Customs valuation The access to a market promised by a low tariff rate can be denied if the duty payable is inflated because the imported goods are overvalued by the customs authorities. GATT Article VII, on 'Valuation for Customs Purposes', for many years provided the only agreed guidance on how customs officials should value imported goods, and thus arrive at a price to which they could apply the appropriate rates of customs duty and taxes. The central principles are that the value for customs purposes should be based on the actual value of the imported merchandise, not on that of goods of national origin or 'arbitrary or fictitious values', and that 'actual value' should be the price at which the product or 'like merchandise' is sold in the ordinary course of trade under fully competitive conditions. These rules nonetheless still left room for considerable differences in customs valuation practices and for occasionally arbitrary and protectionist procedures. This meant that traders were often unable to be certain in advance what customs duty their goods would actually have to pay.

In the Tokyo Round negotiations a new set of rules was negotiated, with the aim of establishing a predictable system of customs valuation that would follow commercial realities as closely as possible. Accepted by most developed countries, but by less than a dozen developing countries, it became one of the group of limited-membership 'codes' governing non-tariff trade measures. It was widely considered a success. During the Uruguay Round, the code was re-examined, principally to see whether some adaptation, without changing its basic principles, might make it more attractive to developing countries. The outcome was a minimally revised new agreement, supplemented by two Ministerial Decisions designed to ease developing-country fears that the rules would not fully meet their needs. The biggest difference between the old and new versions lies not in their respective provisions but in the fact that, as an integral part of the Uruguay Round package, the rules of the new agreement bind all WTO member countries.

The Agreement sets up a sequence of six alternative methods of valuing goods for customs purposes. They are to be applied in a strict hierarchy. Only if customs value cannot be determined under the first method may the authorities use the second method and only if this second method is inapplicable, may they move to the third and so on. The starting point for valuation – the priority method – bases customs value on the 'transaction value', the price actually paid for the goods when sold for export to the country of importation. The successive alternatives establish the valuation instead by the transaction values of identical or similar goods, by looking at sale prices or production costs, or finally by a fallback method, which gives greater flexibility but excludes several possible approaches to valuation.

(c) Preshipment inspection Increasingly, developing countries have made presentation of a 'clean report of findings' from a designated preshipment inspection

firm a condition for clearing imports through customs or for releasing foreign exchange to pay for imports. The purpose is primarily to check that the real value of the goods matches their declared value. Some Members have made preshipment inspection a condition for a large proportion of imports, while others require it only for specified imports, such as those for government use. From the point of view of the developing countries concerned, the aim is to prevent fraud and to reinforce their own customs administrations, ensuring that value is not under or over-declared. Under-declaration, unless detected, will result in lower duties being imposed and thus, in loss of revenue. Over-declaration, now rarer, provides an opportunity for disguised export of capital. Exporters have been concerned that preshipment inspection may hamper trade by increasing their costs and causing delays and that imposed changes in valuation amount to interference in the contractual relationship between buyer and seller. A sensitive point for governments is that the preshipment inspection takes place in the exporting countries on behalf of the importing countries. The aim of the Agreement on Preshipment Inspection is to establish a framework of rights and obligations, based on non-discrimination and transparency, that provides guidelines for the use of inspection firms, 'entities' in the agreement, by governments and for the work of these firms in verifying prices. It also sets up procedures to resolve disputes that may arise between traders and inspectors.

(d) Rules of origin Many products moving in international trade today include materials or components from more than one country and may also have undergone processing in several countries. From the point of view of the importing country, this mixture of origins can raise difficulties. A particular product from one country may be subject to anti-dumping or countervailing duties or to safeguard measures. Its origin may need to be known because of marking requirements, because import quotas for the product have been filled for some supplying countries but not for others or for statistical reasons. Finally, a product may be entitled to preferential or duty-free treatment if it comes from a developing country or a partner country in a regional agreement. Most customs administrations apply rules that decide the origin of goods according to where the product underwent its last substantial transformation. Several alternative means are used to decide whether a particular country qualifies on this basis as the place of origin. The most widely applied criterion attributes origin to a country if the product was sufficiently changed there to move its customs classification from one heading to another. The 'percentage criterion', which exists in several variants, measures how much value was added to the product in that country. Origin can also depend on specific technical tests – positive, if prescribed processes have been carried out in the country concerned or negative, if certain processes are not considered sufficient to confer origin.

No origin rules are yet recognized world-wide, although agreed rules are applied, for instance, among members of particular regional agreements. Uncertainty about whether products will meet origin requirements can in itself be a serious obstacle to trade. Moreover, the possibility that rules may be altered or manipulated means that they can themselves be used as a protective instrument, in addition to their role as a mechanism for applying protection such as safeguard restrictions. The Agreement on Rules of Origin reached in the Uruguay Round is intended to change this situation by leading to harmonization on the basis of some agreed broad principles of rules of origin applied by all WTO members. The only exception to this harmonization will be rules used for preferential arrangements. Even in this case members have declared that they will observe many of the same agreed principles. The core of the agreement is the work program to establish the new harmonized rules. Now well advanced, the work program is being carried out jointly by the WTO and the specialized organization expert in this field, the World Customs Organization. It is based on some clear guiding principles, among them, that rules of origin should not be used as instruments of trade policy; that the rules should be objective, predictable, coherent and based on positive standards and that the originating status of a particular good should be either the country where it has been wholly obtained or, when more than one country has been concerned in its production, the country where the last substantial transformation was carried out.

(e) Import licensing Governments generally use import licensing for one of two purposes: to administer quantitative or other import restrictions, or as a means only of keeping track of imports, usually for statistical purposes. Licenses for the first purpose are classified as *non-automatic*, because they will only be issued if an applicant is allocated a part of whatever import quota is available. Issuance of the second category of licenses is normally *automatic*. The Agreement contains general provisions that apply to both kinds of import licensing, as well as provisions that apply specifically to non-automatic or automatic licensing. The general provisions seek to reduce the scope for discrimination or administrative discretion in the application of both kinds of licensing. Rules are to be neutral in application and administered fairly and equitably.

Automatic licensing escapes the tighter rules governing non-automatic licensing only if it meets qualifying conditions. These are (a) anyone legally qualified to import the products concerned must be able to apply for, and receive, a license; (b) applications must be acceptable on any working day before the goods are cleared through customs and (c) applications in due form must be approved either immediately or within ten working days.

Licensing that does not meet these conditions is regarded as non-automatic. The central requirement under the agreement is that such licensing shall not restrict or distort trade any further than the measures it applies. Enough information must be published for traders to know the basis on which licenses will be given and governments with a trade interest have the right to ask for detailed information about how licenses have been distributed and about trade in the products concerned. If the licenses are administering import quotas, information must be published about the size or value of the quotas and the dates to which they apply. If the quotas are allocated among supplying countries, all interested supplying members must be informed and the requirement of publication also applies. Any importer that fulfils the legal and administrative requirements must be eligible to apply and to be considered for a license. In addition any potential importer refused a license can ask why and shall have a right of appeal or review. If the quotas are allocated on a first-come, first-served basis, applications must considered within 30 days. If considered simultaneously, the maximum period is 60 days. Other rules call for licenses to be valid for long enough to permit imports even from distant sources to be sufficiently large to cover economic quantities, and for allocation to take account of whether the applicant has made full use of licenses allocated in the past. Opportunities should be given to new importers, and especially to those who import the products concerned from developing countries.

Trade in Services

In broad outline, the Uruguay Round services package resembles the package for goods. First, there is a central set of rules, the General Agreement on Trade in Services (GATS), which to a great extent was directly modeled on the GATT and relies on many of the same principles. These rules are supplemented by further agreements, some in the form of with specific sectoral and other issues. Finally, there are the national annexes to the GATS, others embodied in Ministerial Decisions, which deal schedules, one for each WTO Member (except that customs unions may share a single schedule). The schedules set out precise commitments not to impose greater restrictions than are specified on the supply of particular services by other Members.

However, some of the similarities with the GATT are misleading. The principle of 'national treatment', for instance, is fundamental to the GATS, as it is to the GATT, but is applied very differently. Whereas GATT obligations can to a great extent be understood by reference only to the general rules set out in its articles, the GATS obligations of each Member depend significantly on what it has specifically undertaken, in its own schedule, for each service or service sector.

The GATS: The Basic Agreement

The preamble states three considerations that shaped its negotiation. First, the establishment of a multilateral framework of principles and rules, aimed at progressively opening up trade in services, should help this trade to expand and to contribute to economic development worldwide. Second, WTO members, particularly developing countries, will still need to regulate the supply of services to meet national policy objectives. Third, developing countries should be helped to take a fuller part in world trade in services, particularly through strengthening the capacity, efficiency and competitiveness of their own domestic services.

Scope and coverage The GATS applies to 'measures by WTO members which affect trade in services'. The reach of this definition goes beyond central governments to include measures taken by regional and local governments and includes those of non-governmental bodies exercising powers delegated to them by governments. As under the GATT, member governments are required to do their best to ensure that these sub-national governments observe GATS obligations and commitments. All services are covered, except those 'supplied in the exercise of governmental authority', these being defined as services, such as central banking and social security, which are neither supplied on a commercial basis nor in competition with other service suppliers.

Modes of supply Trade in services is defined in terms of four different modes of supply, namely, cross-border, consumption abroad, commercial presence in the consuming country and temporary movement of natural persons. This definition helps in understanding the special problems and regulatory issues that arise in trade in services and that have shaped the principles and rules embodied in the GATS, as well as the specific commitments that WTO members have undertaken in their schedules.

Cross-border supply of services corresponds with the normal form of trade in goods. It is in many ways the most straightforward form of trade in services, because it resembles the familiar subject matter of the GATT, not least in maintaining a clear geographical separation between seller and buyer. Only the service itself crosses national frontiers.

Consumption abroad is the supply of a service 'in the territory of one Member to the service consumer of another Member'. Typically, this will involve the consumer travelling to the supplying country, perhaps for tourism or to attend an educational establishment. Another example would be the repair of a ship or aircraft outside its home country. Like cross-border supply, this is a straightforward form of trade, which raises few problems, since it does not require the service supplier to be admitted to the consuming country.

Examples of *commercial presence* of the foreign supplier in the territory of another WTO Member would be the establishment of branch offices or agencies to deliver such services as banking, legal advice or communications. This is probably the most important mode of supply of services, at least in terms of future development. It also raises the most difficult issues for host governments and for GATS negotiations. A large proportion of service transactions require that the provider and the consumer be in the same place. But rules governing commercial presence are very different from the tariffs and other border measures that principally affect trade in goods. The GATS has been forced to grapple with internal policy issues such as rights of establishment that are inherent in the commercial presence of foreign interests. In doing so and establishing multilateral rules that guarantee the opportunities for firms and individuals to establish themselves in a foreign market, the GATS has broken new ground.

Commercial presence does not necessarily require the presence of foreigners, since the foreign supplier's office may be staffed entirely by local personnel. However, the supplier may well feel a need to employ some foreign managers or specialists. When this is the case, the *presence of natural persons* may be coupled with commercial presence, or it may be found alone. The visiting persons involved may be employees of a foreign service supplier or may be providing services as independent individuals. An annex to the GATS makes it clear that the agreement has nothing to do with individuals looking for employment in another country, or with citizenship, residence or employment requirements. Even if Members undertake commitments to allow natural persons to provide services in their territories, they may still regulate the entry and stay of the persons concerned as long as they do not prevent the commitments from being fulfilled.

Commitments covering roughly 150 different forms of service activity are embodied in the schedules resulting from the Uruguay Round negotiations. Some of these services can be supplied in several of the four ways, while many others by their nature, cannot. For instance, the services of a professional adviser may possibly be supplied through any of the four modes, that is, by a visit to him by his foreign client, by mail, through an office maintained in the client's country or by a personal visit to that country. On the other hand, a tourist can only enjoy a foreign country's beaches by going there and road-building services obviously must be provided on the spot. Unlike market access for a shipment of goods going from one country to another, which is principally a matter of customs duties and other formalities at the border, the ability to provide a service to another country depends on government regulations that may be quite different for one of the four modes of supply than for another.

General obligations and disciplines The GATS sets out basic rules that apply to all Members and, for the most part, to all services. It is not true, as is sometimes suggested, that because a Member has left out of its schedule any access commitments for a service sector, it has no obligations affecting that sector.

GATS *most-favored-nation treatment* directly parallels the GATT, but it is qualified. A Member is permitted to maintain a measure inconsistent with the general MFN requirement if it has established an exception for this inconsistency. During the Uruguay Round, it became clear that unqualified liberalization in some service sectors could not be achieved and that liberalization subject to some temporary MFN exceptions would be preferable to no liberalization at all. The result was that more than 70 WTO members made their scheduled services commitments subject to a further list of exemptions from Article II.

These exemption lists are governed by conditions set out in a separate annex to the GATS. The annex makes it clear that no new exemptions can be granted at least by this route. Any future requests to give non-MFN treatment can only be met through the WTO waiver procedures. Some listed exemptions are subject to a stated time limit. For those that are not, the annex provides that in principle they should not last longer than ten years, that is, not beyond 2004, and that in any case, they are subject to negotiation in future trade-liberalizing rounds.

Apart from services specified in individual MFN exemption lists, the only permitted departure from MFN treatment under the GATS is among countries that are members of regional trading arrangements. The GATS rules on 'Economic Integration' are modeled on those of the GATT, although the absence of services equivalent to import duties means that there is no distinction comparable to that between customs unions and free trade areas. Any WTO Member is permitted to enter into an agreement to further liberalize trade in services only with other Members that are parties to the agreement, provided the agreement has 'substantial sectoral coverage', eliminates measures that discriminate against service suppliers of other members in the group and prohibits new or more discriminatory measures.

A second basic principle carried over from the GATT is *transparency*. Traders will be badly handicapped in doing business in a foreign country unless they know what laws and regulations they face. This problem is particularly serious for trade in services, because so many of the relevant government rules are domestic regulations. The GATS requires each Member to publish promptly 'all relevant measures of general application', that is, measures other than those which involve only individual service suppliers, that affect operation of the agreement. Members must also notify the Council for Trade in Services of new or changed laws, regulations or administrative guidelines that affect trade in services covered by their specific commitments under the agreement. Each Member was required to have established, by the end of 1996, an enquiry point to respond to requests from other Members for information on these matters.

Other rules are intended to ensure that GATS benefits are not blocked by domestic regulations. Generally applied measures that affect trade in service sectors for which a member has made commitments must be applied reasonably, objectively and impartially. Applications to supply services under such commitments must receive a decision within a reasonable period of time. There must also be tribunals or other procedures to which service suppliers can apply for a review of administrative decisions affecting their trade. The Council for Trade in Services is developing rules to prevent requirements on qualifications for service suppliers, technical standards or licensing from being unnecessary barriers to trade. Until multilateral rules are ready, governments are to follow the same principles in applying their own requirements and standards, so that these do not nullify or impair specific commitments they have made. The GATS also urges Members to recognize the educational or other qualifications of service suppliers of other countries. It allows governments to negotiate agreements among themselves for mutual recognition of such qualifications, provided other Members with comparable standards are given a chance to join. Qualification requirements are not to be applied in a way that discriminates between Members or constitutes a disguised restriction on trade in services and they should be based wherever appropriate on internationally agreed standards.

GATS Article VIII is close to GATT's Article XVII on state trading. A monopoly supplier of a service must not to be allowed to act inconsistently with a member's MFN obligations or its specific commitments or to abuse its monopoly position. If a country that has made specific commitments to allow supply of a service later grants monopoly rights for that supply, and thus negates or impairs the commitments, it will have to negotiate compensation. Article XII on restrictions to safeguard the balance of payments sets out provisions similar to those in the GATT. Governments are exempt from the basic GATS obligations in purchasing services for their own use, but negotiations on government procurement in services have begun and are expected to lead to commitments to open up some government purchases to foreign service suppliers.

Two other provisions in the GATS represent unfinished business. These deal with safeguards and with subsidies, for which negotiations on rules are underway.

Rules for scheduled sectors The two main rules, which have shaped each WTO Member's individual commitments to admit foreign suppliers of services to its market, deal with market access and national treatment. These apply *only to scheduled sectors*, that is, service sectors in which a member has made commitments.

Each member is to give no less favorable treatment to the services and service suppliers of other members than is provided in its schedule of commitments. This provision makes it clear that service commitments resemble those in a GATT schedule at least in one very important respect. They are *bindings*, which set out the minimum, or worst permissible treatment of the foreign service or its supplier and in no way prevent better treatment from being given in practice.

Six types of measure affecting market access *may not be applied to the foreign service or its supplier, unless their use is clearly provided for in the schedule.* The six cover all the aspects of limitation of market access that may be specified in national schedules. They are limitations on the number of service suppliers; limitations on the total value of services transactions or assets; limitations on the total number of service operations or the total quantity of service output; limitations on the number of persons that may be employed in a particular sector or by a particular supplier; measures that restrict or require supply of the service through specific types of legal entity or joint venture; and percentage limitations on the participation of foreign capital or limitations on the total value of foreign investment.

With regard to *national treatment*, each Member, *in the sectors covered by its schedule, and subject to any conditions and qualifications set out in the schedule*, shall give treatment to foreign services and service suppliers treatment, in measures affecting supply of services, no less favorable than it gives to its own services and suppliers. The basic obligation is stated in terms very similar to those of the GATT national treatment rule but, of course, is limited in the case of the GATS to services sectors for which commitments have been given in the schedule of the Member concerned. As in the case of market access, the requirement that any limitations on national treatment be specified in the schedule gives these limitations the same character as a GATT-bound tariff. The stated conditions or qualifications represent the worst treatment that may be given, and nothing prevents better treatment being given in practice.

The reason why the right to national treatment is restricted under the GATS to services for which commitments have been undertaken lies in the nature of trade in services. National treatment for goods is possible without creating free trade, because the entry of foreign goods into a national market can still be controlled by import duties, quantitative restrictions and other border measures. By contrast, a foreign supplier of most services, particularly if those services are supplied by commercial or personal presence in the importing country's market, will in practice enjoy virtually free access to that market if given national treatment, since this, by definition, will remove any regulatory advantage enjoyed by the domestic service supplier.

Preparing, modifying and withdrawing commitments The elements covered in each Member's schedule form 'an integral part' of the GATS. This underlines the point that the detailed commitments in each schedule are international obligations on the same level as the GATS and indeed, as the WTO package as a whole. Circumstances may arise in which a government may wish to take back something it has given in past negotiations. It can do so, but only at a price and after due notice. As far as notice is concerned, no commitment can be modified or withdrawn until at least three years after it entered into force. At least three months notice must be given of the proposed change. The price to be paid will be a readjustment of the balance of advantage in commitments with any WTO member affected by the change. This will normally be settled by negotiation, to be undertaken at the request of the affected member as soon as notice has been given of the proposed change. If all goes well, agreement will be reached on new commitments to offset those being withdrawn so that the general level of commitments between the countries concerned is no less favorable to trade than before. These compensatory adjustments are to be applied on an MFN basis.

Further negotiations The GATS provides that, starting not later than January 2000, WTO members shall enter into 'successive rounds of negotiations ... with a view to achieving a progressively higher level of liberalization' of trade in services. These negotiations began on 1 January 2000.

GATS annexes and Ministerial Decisions The eight annexes attached to the GATS are integral parts of the package of agreements on trade in services reached in the Uruguay Round. Four of them contain special provisions that relate to the specific sectors of air transport, financial services, telecommunications and maritime transport.

Protection of Intellectual Property

The basic objective of the Agreement on Trade-Related Aspects of Intellectual Property Rights (TRIPS) is to give adequate and effective protection to intellectual property rights so that the owners of these rights receive the benefits of their creativity and inventiveness and are thereby also encouraged to continue their efforts to create and invent. The TRIPS Agreement covers all seven of the main areas of intellectual property, namely, copyright, trademarks, geographical indications, industrial designs, patents, layout designs of integrated circuits and undisclosed in-formation, including trade secrets. In each area, it sets minimum standards of protection, requires governments to provide procedures and remedies so that these standards can be enforced and provides effective means of settling disputes between member governments.

Structure The TRIPS Agreement is largely concerned with applying basic principles to each area of intellectual property protection. One section of the Agreement establishes minimum substantive standards for the availability, scope and use of intellectual property rights. For each of the seven categories of rights, it sets out the minimum protection that must be given for these rights in the national law of each WTO Member. The section on enforcement lays down procedures and remedies to be provided by each country for the enforcement of intellectual property rights with the twin aims of ensuring effective action against any infringement of rights and yet not hampering legitimate trade. Dispute settlement is provided through the integrated procedures of the WTO. Other important elements of the Agreement are the principles of national and most-favored-nation (MFN) treatment. There are also general rules to ensure that procedural difficulties in acquiring or maintaining intellectual property rights are not allowed to negate the protection that is due.

General provisions and basic principles Members must provide the intellectual property protection specified in the Agreement, making it available to the nationals of all other WTO members. They are free to give greater protection, as long as this does not contravene the agreement. How they choose to give protection, in terms of their national legal systems and practices, is up to them, provided they comply with the agreement.

The Agreement requires all Members to comply with the main provisions of the Paris Convention and the Berne Convention and adds to their copyright protection obligations and, more substantially, to their obligations to protect industrial property.

Members are required to give both national treatment and MFN treatment in intellectual property protection, subject to certain exceptions mainly consisting of those already provided for under existing intellectual property agreements.

An issue in intellectual property protection is the question of exhaustion of rights. It is generally accepted that the holder of intellectual property rights in a product loses ('exhausts') those rights over the further distribution in a particular market once he has sold the product: he has no control over whether the buyer re-sells the product in that market. There is less agreement over the issue of 'parallel imports'. In this case, the question concerns the extent to which a right-holder in one jurisdiction can use his intellectual property right to prevent the import into, or sale in, that country of products that he has authorized for sale in another country. The TRIPS Agreement states that whatever a Member does in this respect cannot be challenged under WTO dispute settlement, provided that the TRIPS national treatment and MFN obligations have been complied with.

Standards The TRIPS agreement takes up the minimum standards, which WTO members are to accord in respect of the availability, scope and use of intellectual property rights in each of seven basic areas.

Copyright and related rights The principal copyright standards under the TRIPS Agreement are those set by the Berne Convention. The main additions or clarifications are requirements to:

> protect computer programs as literary works under the Berne Convention, and also protect databases or other compilations whose arrangement or selection make them intellectual creations, even when the individual elements are not protected by copyright;
>
> give authors of computer programs and films the right to authorize or prohibit commercial rental of their copyright works. (For films, the right needs to be made available only if rental has led to widespread copying), and
>
> limit limitations or exceptions to exclusive rights to special cases that do not conflict with normal exploitation of the works concerned or unreasonably prejudice the right-holder's legitimate rights.

'Related rights', known in some countries as 'neighboring rights' are the rights of performers, producers of sound recordings ('phonograms') and broadcasters, when not covered by copyright. Although these rights were largely covered by the Rome Convention, that Agreement had comparatively few signatories, particularly among the countries with a common law tradition. The TRIPS agreement thus provided the first truly multilateral recognition that performers, as well as authors, should benefit from protection, although it leaves substantial differences between countries in the amount of protection they give. Performers are required to have the possibility of preventing unauthorized sound recording or broadcasting of their performances and of copying of such recordings. Producers of sound recordings must have exclusive rights over reproduction of these recordings, as well as exclusive rental rights for them. Broadcasters must have the right to prohibit unauthorized recording, copying of recordings, and rebroadcasting of their broadcasts or, where this is not done, authors must have such rights over the subject matter of broadcasts. The rights of performers and producers must be protected for at least 50 years and those of broadcasters for at least 20 years.

Trademarks The basic rule on establishing whether subject matter is protectable by trademarks is that any sign, or any combination of signs, capable of distinguishing the goods or services of one undertaking from those of other undertakings must be eligible for registration as a trademark, provided that it is visually perceptible. Service marks must be protected in the same way as marks distinguishing goods.

The Agreement defines the minimum rights that must be conferred by a trademark. In respect of additional protection which the Paris Convention requires for well-known marks, account must be taken of knowledge in the relevant sector of the public acquired not only as a result of the use of the mark, but also as a result of its promotion. Subject to certain conditions, the protection of registered well-known marks must extend to goods or services, which are not similar to those in respect of which the trademark was registered. Cancellation of a mark on the grounds of non-use cannot take place before three years of uninterrupted non-use has elapsed and even then, not if valid reasons based on the existence of obstacles to such use are shown by the trademark owner. Circumstances arising independently of the will of the owner, such as import restrictions or other government restrictions, shall be recognized as valid reasons for non-use. Registration must be for a minimum of seven years, renewable indefinitely for further periods of at least seven years. Use of the trademark in the course of trade must not be unjustifiably encumbered by special requirements, such as use with another trademark, in special form or in a manner detrimental to its capability to distinguish the goods or services.

Geographical indications Geographical indications 'identify a good as originating in the territory of a Member, or a region or locality in that territory, where a given quality, reputation or other characteristic of the good is essentially attributable to its geographical origin'. It was not easy to find a balance between preventing fraudulent indications that a product comes from a place that it does not and recognition that some geographical names attached to products have lost their link to the original place of origin. The generic use of a geographical indication as no more than an indication that a product is of a certain type. 'Cheddar' cheese, for example, is particularly widespread for food and drink. It is especially controversial when the indication is associated with high-quality wines and spirits, whose distinct reputation their producers are anxious to defend.

The basic obligation is that all WTO Members must provide means for interested parties to prevent use, which might mislead the public about the geographical origin of goods or, which would constitute unfair competition. This includes prevention of use of a geographical indication which although literally true, 'falsely represents' that the product comes from somewhere else. Even stronger protection is to be given to geographical indications, which identify wines and spirits. These may not be used for other wines or spirits, even if they are neither misleading nor represent unfair competition. There are exceptions, notably to deal with the situation where a geographical indication has already become a generic term in the local language, or where there are other forms of established usage. In these cases, however, a WTO Member must be ready to enter into bilateral or multilateral negotiations aimed at increasing the protection of individual indications for wines and spirits. The Council for TRIPS is to negotiate further on the subject with the aim of establishing a multilateral system, under which participating countries could notify and register geographical names of wines eligible for protection.

Industrial designs The Agreement provides that at least ten years' protection must be given to independently created industrial designs that are new or original. Textile designs, which typically have a short life cycle, exist in large numbers and are very subject to copying, are given special attention: requirements set for obtaining protection, especially cost, examination and publication requirements, should not stand unreasonably in the way of gaining that protection. The owner of a protected design must be able to stop unauthorized third parties from making, selling or importing, for commercial purposes, products, which copy the design.

Patents The Paris Convention leaves it to each country to define which inventions must be patentable, what rights must flow from ownership of a patent, what exceptions to those rights are permissible or how long the protection should last. On all these important issues in patent protection, as in the other areas of intellectual property covered, the TRIPS Agreement sets out binding standards.

On patentability, the agreement lays down that patents shall be available in principle for any inventions, whether they concern products or processes, in all fields of technology. The invention must be new, involve an inventive step, in other terms, be 'non-obvious', and be capable of industrial application ('useful'). This requirement is subject to two kinds of exception. The first permits some types of inventions to be excluded from patentability. Members need not give patents for products the prevention of whose commercial exploitation is necessary to protect public order or morality, including protecting human, animal or plant life or the environment. Nor need Members give patents for plants and animals other than microorganisms or, for essentially biological processes, for their production, other than microbiological processes. However, new plant varieties must be effectively protected by other means if patenting is not allowed.

The Agreement sets out the basic rights of a patent-holder. These include the usual right, when the patent covers a product, to prevent unauthorized persons from making, using, selling or importing it. They also include protection, if the patent covers a process, not only against unauthorized use of the process but against unauthorized use, sale or importation of products directly obtained by that process. Compulsory licensing and government use of a patent without the authorization of its owner are allowed, but only subject to a list of conditions aimed at protecting the legitimate interests of the right-holder. These include an obligation, in general, not to grant such licenses unless attempts to acquire a voluntary license on reasonable terms have been unsuccessful and a requirement to pay adequate remuneration to the right-holder. The legal validity of a decision to authorize such use of a patent, and the amount of remuneration to be provided, must be subject to judicial or other review by a distinct higher authority. Compulsory licensing must also not discriminate on the basis of technology or between imports and local products. Some of these conditions may be relaxed if it has been established that compulsory licensing is required to correct a practice that a judicial or administrative process has decided is anti-competitive.

Patent protection is to last at least twenty years from the date that the application for the patent is filed. The agreement does not explicitly deal with one well-known difference between national patent systems, namely, the adoption by some countries, notably including the United States, of the date of invention rather than the filing date as the date for determining priority between two claims for the same invention. But Article 27.1 lays down that Members may not discriminate according to place of invention in the patent protection they give.

Integrated circuits The TRIPS Agreement requires WTO Members to protect the layout designs ('topographies') of integrated circuits in accordance with the provisions of the IPIC Treaty of 1989, together with four additional provisions. These relate to the term of protection, the treatment of innocent infringers, and the applicability of the protection to articles containing infringing integrated circuits and to compulsory licensing.

Members are to consider unlawful, if not authorized by the right-holder of the design, the importation, sale or other commercial distribution of a protected layout design, of integrated circuits incorporating such a design, or of articles which contain such integrated circuits. This protection is to last for a minimum of ten years. Innocent infringers, who import, sell or distribute integrated circuits that use unlawfully-copied layout designs must not be held to have acted unlawfully, but if they sell remaining stocks after being told of the infringement, must be liable to pay a reasonable royalty to the right-holder.

Undisclosed information Trade secrets or know-how are also protected by the TRIPS Agreement. Protection must be given to information that is secret that has commercial value because it has been kept secret and that has been subject to reasonable steps to keep it secret. The Agreement does not require undisclosed information to be treated as a form of property, but it does require that a person lawfully in control of such information must have the possibility of preventing it from being disclosed to, acquired by, or used by others without his consent 'in a manner contrary to honest commercial practice'. The latter is defined as practices such as breach of contract or confidence and includes acquisition of undisclosed information by third parties that knew, or were grossly negligent in failing to know, that these practices were involved. Confidential data submitted to governments in order to obtain marketing approval for pharmaceuticals or agricultural chemicals are also protected against unfair commercial use.

Anti-competitive practices The Agreement recognizes that practices in the licensing of rights can have adverse effects on trade and may hamper the transfer and spread of technology, and that WTO members may adopt, consistently with the other provisions of the agreement, measures to prevent or control practices or conditions that may constitute abuse of rights and hamper competition. Examples given include exclusive grantback conditions and coercive package licensing. The Agreement provides a mechanism whereby a Member that wants to take action against practices involving companies of another WTO Member can consult with that member to seek relevant information.

Enforcement of intellectual property rights The TRIPS Agreement sets out in some detail the legal procedures and remedies that each WTO Member should make available to holders of intellectual property rights so that they can enforce these rights effectively. It not only prescribes the procedures and remedies that must be provided by each Member, expressed largely in terms of the authority to be available to the Member's judges and courts, but also sets requirements for the effectiveness of these procedures and remedies in practice. The five sections of the agreement dealing with enforcement cover general obligations, civil and administrative procedures and remedies, provisional measures, border measures, and criminal procedures.

Dispute settlement Disputes about matters under the TRIPS Agreement are subject to the integrated dispute settlement procedures of the WTO. However, as in the case of disputes involving trade in goods or services, it is only when a dispute reaches the stage of formal consultations, at which a subsequent request for a panel is clearly likely, that it moves beyond the area of responsibility of the specialized Council concerned, in this case, the Council for TRIPS. The basic task of maintaining transparency about each country's laws and other measures affecting intellectual property and of monitoring compliance with the TRIPS Agreement is in the hands of the Council for TRIPS, as is the discussion of problems that may arise.

Transitional arrangements All WTO Members were given some extra time, beyond the date of entry into force of the WTO itself, to adapt to the new disciplines of the TRIPS Agreement. For developed countries, this grace period lasted only one year, so that for them the TRIPS rules have been in full effect since 1 January 1996. All Members have been required, since the same date, to apply towards other members the national treatment and MFN provisions of the agreement's Articles 3, 4 and 5. Developing countries were given a further four years, to 1 January 2000, before most other provisions of the TRIPS Agreement apply to them.

Developing countries which will be required by the Agreement to extend product patent protection into areas of technology that they do not at present treat as patentable will be given a further 5 years, up to 1 January 2005, to come into line with the rules on patents. The effects of this additional postponement of patent protection will be felt mainly by producers of pharmaceuticals and agricultural chemicals, which typically take long periods to develop, test and be approved for public sale. Taking account of this situation, the Agreement requires that Members delaying patent protection for pharmaceutical and agricultural chemical products shall meanwhile allow patent applications to be filed for these products so that not only new inventions, but also inventions made during the 1995–2005 transition period, will be able to gain patent protection from January 2005. Countries in transition from a centrally-planned economy into an economy that is based on market, free-enterprise principles were given the same extra four years of exemption, to January 2000, from the TRIPS Agreement's requirements if they are still engaged in structural reform of their intellectual property system and facing special difficulties in doing so.

Note

1 This chapter contains the views of the author and does not necessarily reflect the position of the WTO Secretariat or of WTO Members. The bulk of the chapter is based on a publication by the WTO Secretariat (1999), *Guide to the Uruguay Round Agreements*, Kluwer Law International, London, which should be consulted for further details about the WTO Agreements.

Index

For Product Safety Concerns and Information please contact our EU representative GPSR@taylorandfrancis.com Taylor & Francis Verlag GmbH, Kaufingerstraße 24, 80331 München, Germany

Printed and bound by CPI Group (UK) Ltd, Croydon, CR0 4YY
01/05/2025
01858348-0001